COMPUTER ESSENTIALS IN EDUCATION

COMPUTER ESSENTIALS IN EDUCATION

THE TEACHING TOOLS

FRITZ J. ERICKSON
Millersville University of Pennsylvania

JOHN A. VONK
University of Northern Colorado

McGRAW-HILL
New York St. Louis San Francisco Auckland Bogotá
Caracas Lisbon London Madrid Mexico Milan Montreal
New Delhi Paris San Juan Singapore Sydney Tokyo Toronto

McGRAW-HILL

Computer Essentials in Education

2 3 4 5 6 7 8 9 0 SEM SEM 9 0 9 8 7 6 5 4

ISBN 0-07-021241-4

Sponsoring Editor: Dean Barton
Production supervisor: Richard DeVitto
Project manager: Graphics West
Interior designer: Graphics West
Cover designer: Tom Trujillo
Printer and binder: Semline, Inc.

Library of Congress Card Catalog No. 93-79634

Brief Contents

Detailed Contents

CHAPTER 6 ESSENTIALS OF SPREADSHEETS 109

CHAPTER 7 ESSENTIALS OF GRAPHICS 125

Preface

It is crucial in today's world to be able to use and understand microcomputers. Most schools, from the elementary through high school level, acknowledge that one of their responsibilities is to teach students about computers.

Computer Essentials in Education: The Teaching Tools is designed to help meet this challenge, especially for those students who wish to become teachers. First, this text provides a framework for prospective teachers to learn about the most widely-used computers. Second, the text focuses on what people should learn about current microcomputer applications. These applications include word processing, spreadsheets, databases, desktop publishing, telecommunications, and multimedia. Third, we suggest strategies for teachers to use software applications in the classroom as tools to enhance teaching. We also suggest ways that teachers and administrators may use these applications for classroom management.

The best way to learn about computers is to first develop a conceptual understanding of computer applications, then apply that understanding to using appropriate microcomputer applications. For this reason, we have designed this text to accompany our *ClarisWorks for Macintosh* or *ClarisWorks for Windows* tutorials. This book is also designed to accompany any of McGraw-Hill's First Look series of software application tutorials.

Acknowledgments

We were very fortunate to have capable, professional people provide reviews and make helpful comments at numerous stages in the development of this text. We thank our reviewers J. Steven Soulier from Utah State University, James H. Wiebe at the California State University at Los Angeles, and Christine Swarm with Northeastern Illinois University. We are also indebted to our many colleagues and students for their insight and inspiration. Most notably we would like to thank Troy Isaak for his thoughtful suggestions and for acting as a sounding board. Finally, we are also most grateful to our friends at McGraw-Hill.

Welcome home John Andres.

To Dean Barton: You've made it all worthwhile.

1

COMPUTERS AND EDUCATION

LEARNING OBJECTIVES

Learning the material in this chapter will enable you to:

- identify the differences among the various types of computers used in education and their uses
- describe three major families of microcomputers used in education
- formulate a working definition of a computer
- describe the two basic features that make up any computer system
- list several members of each major family of microcomputers
- describe the importance of software in a microcomputer family
- describe typical tasks performed by different types of computers

CHAPTER OVERVIEW

Introducing microcomputers to the classroom began a fundamental change in the teaching and learning processes. Not all at once—nor is the change complete. At first, only computer hobbyists or enthusiasts brought computers into the classroom. Computers, a novelty, were limited to technical teaching, but over time teachers began to see the possibilities inherent in these remarkable machines. Today, computers in schools are commonplace. Teachers in almost every discipline can and do use computers to enhance instruction.

The shift from the computer as a machine to the computer as teaching and learning tool changed perception of the computer from a novelty to an integrated instructional device. The emphasis changed from the equipment to the curriculum. Not so long ago, learning about computers in education meant learning about only the technical operation of a computer. Today, learning about computers in education is far more complex. Teachers must be not only technically proficient, but must also know how the machine, the software, and the curriculum work together to enhance instruction.

Learning only about the idiosyncrasies of the different pieces of equipment commonly found with educational microcomputer systems is only part of learning how computers help teachers. Many people can operate a computer with technical precision, but technical knowledge of computers is not enough. The same holds true for software. You must know how to use a word processor before you try to teach students to use a word processor. However, using a word processor skillfully does not mean you can use a word processor to help students better their writing skills.

Throughout this text, the machine, the software, *and* the curriculum are the focus of learning. However, you cannot learn about software and curricular issues without first understanding the various types of equipment found in schools. Predictably, the first step is to gain the technical competence to use computers and related technologies in an educational setting.

In this chapter, we will focus on simply and meaningfully defining a computer. This begins with learning to see a computer as a piece of equipment, learning to control that equipment, and learning to use it for educational purposes. We will then introduce the major types of computers commonly found in schools.

A COMPUTER IS A MACHINE

Show kindergarten students a picture of a machine that has a keyboard and a monitor, and they will readily identify it as a computer. Computers, after all, are as familiar to today's children as television sets were to children in the 1950s. Ask those same students what makes the machine a computer and they, like many adults, will have a difficult time answering. Although most people know a computer when they see one, many cannot answer the basic question, What is a computer?

The word *computer* comes from the word *compute,* meaning "to count." In fact, a computer is nothing more than a very sophisticated counting machine; however, defining a computer as a counting machine is insufficient, because so many other machines count. Any good definition of a computer must take into account what the machine does. The definition must also cover what the computer's uses are and what makes it unique. The beginnings of a much more complete definition identifies a computer as a *programmable machine that receives, stores, and processes data, and outputs information.* Let's examine that definition.

Programmable

Programmable means that the machine can receive and act on a set of instructions called a *program.* The program, written in a language that a computer understands, tells the computer exactly what to do and when to do it. A program begins by telling the computer what type of data it will receive. The program then tells the computer how it should act on this data. Finally, the program determines what the computer does with the information.

FIGURE 1-1
Computers need data to process. These devices provide a way to enter data.

Teaching Tool

Global Classrooms

No longer are teachers limited to the four walls of their classrooms, or even the school library, for teaching and information resources. With a modem, simple software, and a desire to reach out, teachers can now bring the world into their classrooms. More than any other teaching tool, modems and telecommunication can change a teacher's approach to teaching. Instead of teachers acting as sole disseminators of knowledge, teachers truly become facilitators of knowledge. For example, if students are studying about Japan, what better way to learn than to contact students in Japan to share ideas and experiences? If students want to communicate in French or German, why not communicate with students in France or Germany?

There are many projects and ways for teachers to become involved in a global classroom. AT&T's Learning Network links teachers and students in several countries. Computer Pals Across the World, Inc. was developed by Australian teachers and links over a dozen countries. The Global Common Classroom at the University of California is another link for sharing ideas and experiences with others around the world.

Receives Data

For a machine to be a computer, it must be able to receive data from outside sources. (*Data* refers to the raw elements that the computer processes to create information.) We send data to computers through different devices; keyboards are common, but many computers can receive data through other mechanisms such as disk drives, scanners, modems, and many others. No matter what the device, the ability to communicate with the computer by having the computer receive data is critical. The reason is simple. A computer must have a way to get data to produce information.

Stores Data

Many machines receive, but cannot store, data. A television receives data but cannot store data. Storing data is important to a computer, because it allows the computer to act on data long after receiving it. Computers can store a wide range of both programs and data. In fact, what makes a computer programmable is its ability to store an assortment of programs.

A computer's storage capability is its memory. Computer memory is flexible, and altering the contents of memory is a routine task for any computer. Thus, even a computer programmed to perform a single task can quickly be reprogrammed to do different tasks by changing the contents of memory. For example, a robotic arm is an extension of a computer and performs the same task over and over, but reprogramming the computer allows most robotic arms to perform different tasks.

Processes Data

For a machine to be a computer it must also process data. *Processing* is how a computer changes data into information. Processing sometimes alters existing data and sometimes creates new information.

For example, most supermarket check-out lanes have built-in bar code scanners connected to computers. A computer receives data by scanning the bar codes on packages. The computer then processes the data and displays the product name and price. Processing goes even further—the computer manipulates the data and produces the total price for all items. In addition, the computer processes data on quantities sold and creates important information for supermarket inventory. The computer may also analyze sales, determine buying trends, generate charts and graphs, and process a wealth of information for the supermarket.

Outputs Information

The final part of the definition of computer concerns **output**. *Output* is the result of the computer's processing of data. After the computer receives data, stores it in memory, and processes data into information, it must display the information. A computer produces output as a result of changing data into information. The output may be playing a song, moving a robotic arm, or printing a list of students in a class. If a computer could not output information, it would not be of any use.

A COMPUTER IS A SYSTEM

Defining a computer as a programmable machine that receives, stores, and processes data and outputs information is a sufficient definition of a computing machine, but one must think further when considering *educational* computers. When considering computers in education, one must consider how computers approach problems and perform tasks.

The phrase *computer system* signifies an approach for effectively using computers. Because the physical devices (keyboard, monitor, and so on) have no value without the commands to control them, and the commands or programs that control computers are of little value without the physical devices, both are equal partners. Therefore, a definition of a computer must also include the two components that make up the computer system—hardware and software.

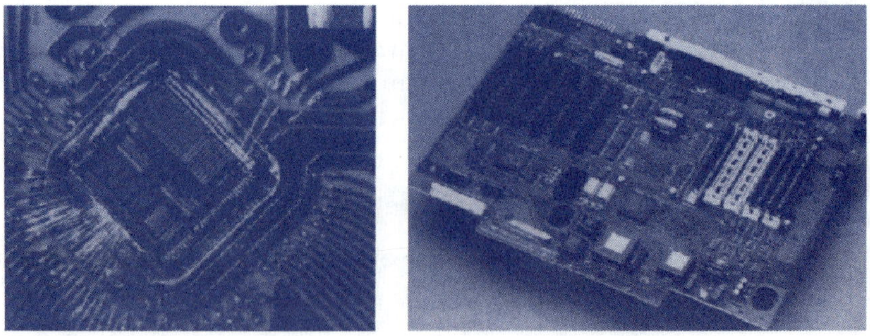

FIGURE 1-2
Inside every microcomputer is an electronic processing unit called a microprocessor. This device performs processing tasks such as calculation and other data manipulation.

FIGURE 1-3
A variety of educational software packages.

Hardware

Hardware refers to the physical devices we can see or touch. Hardware is the equipment of the computer system, made up of a keyboard, monitor, printer, disk drive, and tape drive, as well as highly specialized devices, for example a light pen, scanner, digitizer, or sound device.

A computer system's hardware depends on the purpose of the computer system. A computer system in an office may use a printer, while a computer system in a factory may use a robotic arm. A grocery store computer system may include a bar code reader at the check-out counter. A bank's computer system may include a magnetic ink reader to process checks. An educational system may include a scanner for reading test scores.

Software

Software is the set of instructions that directs the hardware to perform specific tasks. Software, also called a *computer program,* causes the computer to work with words and numbers, play games, and do the many tasks that we need computers to do. The software usually has more of an impact on what tasks a computer system can perform, and how these tasks are performed, than does hardware.

There are many ways to classify software. The broadest classification divides programs into two types: **operating system** software and **applications** software. *Operating system* software consists of commands that control the flow of data to and from the computer. For the Apple II series computer, ProDOS (Professional Disk Operating System) is one common operating system. For the IBM and IBM compatible world, MS-DOS (Microsoft Disk Operating System), PC-DOS (Personal Computer Disk Operating System), and OS/2 are common operating systems. Macintosh computers use an operating system called System. Whatever the type of computer used, computers require operating system software for the machine to work at all.

FIGURE 1-4
The opening screen of MS-DOS, the most popular operating system for IBM and IBM compatible computers.

The second broad group of software is applications software. This group's programs make computer hardware perform specific tasks. Word processors, chess games, math tutorial programs, and numerical calculation programs are just a few examples of applications software. The software available on a system determines how that system can be used.

By including the notion of *system* in the definition of a computer, our concept of a computer expands from a programmable machine to a system made up of both hardware and software designed to solve problems and perform tasks. However, when considering a computer that is easy to use in education, one must think further still.

AN EDUCATIONAL COMPUTER IS THE CURRICULUM

The concept of an educational computer must include users and uses. After all, a computer is a computer regardless of its uses, but a computer used as a teaching and learning tool is much more than a machine. "A programmable machine" defines a specific piece of equipment, and "computer systems" defines computers as both hardware and software. How teachers, parents, administrators, and students put a computer to effective use is of ultimate importance to teachers, administrators, and most of all, to students.

Teachers

Of course, computers can help teachers teach. However, they may be a far better teaching tool than you might think; consider curriculum-based software, software designed to teach concepts and ideas normally taught in the classroom, which provides students with instruction in a wide variety of areas. (Much of this type of software is discussed in later chapters.) However, computers also help teachers manage student data and generate necessary reports. Computers can reduce the time teachers must spend in the noninstructional tasks.

Teaching Tool

Who Graduates?

For administrators, school counselors, and teachers, determining who gets to graduate is not as easy as it might at first appear. Making sure a student has the required number of credits, required courses, and passing grades in the required classes is a paperwork nightmare. Computer software makes this process much easier. The computer can determine when a student has enough of the correct type of credits to graduate and can even produce a report of students who are on questionable ground. This is one of many administrative computer advantages.

Administrators

Administrators rely on computers to help store information about students, maintain transcripts, control student registration, and keep track of student accounts. In elementary and high schools, computers maintain cumulative records, generate course schedules, assign students to classes, check tests, and perform many other activities.

Students

For students, computers are much more than game machines. Computers can be very valuable instructional supplements and tools for reinforcement. Just think of a student who is out sick for a week. Instead of trying to learn from someone's limited notes, computer software can be a valuable tool for independent learning. Students also use computers as tools for completing a variety of instructional assignments. For example, students who become proficient with a word processor often find it much easier to write reports, edit essays, and collaborate on writing assignments. Teachers can even copy assignments to disk for student homework. Students may then use computers both at home and school as an important instructional tool.

The examples cited here for teachers, administrators, and students are only simple and elementary illustrations of how computers can be used as tools to further the curriculum. Throughout this text, we will discuss many of the issues raised about using computers in education.

FIGURE 1-5
How can these students best use their computers?

TYPES OF COMPUTERS

To understand the use of computers in education, it is important to understand that all computers share the same basic characteristics. However, computers also differ. The computer systems that NASA uses to model spacecraft trips have capabilities far beyond those of the personal computers in a school library. The computers used to register students at a university also have different capabilities. While all computers perform basically the same types of tasks, the speed at which they complete these tasks, the number of users that can use a computer at the same time, and the amount of data manipulated differs among computers.

One common way to classify computers is based on how fast they complete a single task, the amount of data that can be handled by the computer, and the number of users the computer can accommodate at one time. The most common classifications based on these differences are supercomputers, mainframe computers, minicomputers, and microcomputers.

One of the major distinctions in computer classifications is speed. Speed is determined by the number of instructions performed in one second. This is usually in millions of instructions per second (MIPS), or, for some computers, billions of instructions per second. It is not an issue of how many instructions can be performed at once. All computers process instructions one at a time, but the interval between instructions can differ dramatically.

Supercomputers

Supercomputers are the most powerful computers—they can process exceptionally complex data with extreme speed. A supercomputer such as Cray Y-MP performs as many as 4 billion instructions per second. Compare this with the original IBM XT, which only performed about 290,000 instructions per second. Because of their extreme speed, supercomputers can execute very complex calculations and perform intricate analyses on exceptionally complicated data. For this reason, they are used to solve such complex problems as plotting the course of intercontinental ballistic missiles, weather forecasting, space navigation, and other problems requiring analysis of an excessively large amount of information.

This speed also allows for several hundred users to use a single supercomputer at one time. This is done by connecting, or *networking,* several computers and terminals to a single computer. While the Cray can only process one instruction at a time, the interval between each instruction is so small that, for all practical purposes, it appears to be doing multiple tasks.

Mainframe

Mainframe computers are not nearly as fast as supercomputers. A typical mainframe operates between 40 and 100 MIPS. But compare this with the original Apple II or the IBM XT and they are amazingly fast computers. The advantage of mainframes is that they are more affordable than supercomputers (a few hundred thousand to a few million dollars), yet mainframes offer many of the same advantages. Most important is the high speed and the ability to support several users. As with supercomputers, the speed of a mainframe can support hundreds of users at the same time.

Minicomputer

Minicomputers provide small businesses and school districts an affordable computer that several users can access. Minicomputers do not have the speed of mainframes, nor can they support the same number of users. A typical mini may operate at 4 to 8 MIPS and allow 32 to 64 users. Prices of minicomputers range from $10,000 to more than $300,000. But considering price and speed, they offer a fine alternative to a mainframe. Minicomputers are often found in the administrative offices of schools, in small businesses, and in some governmental agencies.

One of the issues facing the computer industry is the diminishing difference between micro- and minicomputers. As you will see in the next section on micros, microcomputers are advancing at such a rapid pace that they are replacing minicomputers. However, minicomputers are still the computer of choice if the need for storing and recalling large amounts of information is greater than a microcomputer can handle.

Microcomputers

Microcomputers are personal tools. In fact, microcomputers are commonly known as *personal computers* because they were designed for a single user. As with the primary difference between the other types of computers, the major characteristic that makes a microcomputer different is speed. While various microcomputers have different rates of speed, early micros such as the IBM XT operated at only about 290,000 instructions per second—less than 1 MIPS. Today, that number is as high as 100 MIPS. Research has begun on the development of a microcomputer that can operate at 200 MIPS and beyond, but completion of this computer is a few years away.

Another major difference of a micro is the type of data storage devices. Microcomputers use much smaller storage devices. This is due both to need and price. Individuals using microcomputers typically do not need to store large amounts of data, as do governmental agencies and large business. There are, of course, exceptions. Also, most individuals cannot afford to spend the money to purchase such large storage systems.

Microcomputer costs range from $100 to $15,000. The price depends primarily on the computer's speed and the hardware included with the system. Speed is the most important factor in determining price. However, disk drives, printers, graphic tablets, and monitors also play a role in the cost of a computer. A full and

Teaching Tool

Classroom Recorder

For classrooms with only one computer, it is sometimes difficult to get all students involved. One solution is to assign one student per class to serve as the classroom recorder. The classroom recorder records all events during that class and reports to other class members. The class report can include absentees, assignments, hand-outs, and even class notes. At the end of each class, the student prints a copy of the report for all students to use or to include in a class notebook. The class notebook is then available for students to check on assignments, due dates, or any other topic related to that day's class.

detailed discussion of these different components, and how they affect both the cost and effectiveness of the computer, occurs later in this text.

MICROCOMPUTER FAMILIES

Microcomputers are the dominant computer in education. However, minicomputers, mainframes, and supercomputers do play roles in many settings. This book focuses on microcomputers, not because they are more important than other types, but because they are the computers most of us, as educators, use.

The term **microcomputer** represents hundreds of specific machines manufactured by several computer companies. For convenience, they are classified into families. A microcomputer is assigned to a specific family based on both hardware and how the hardware is controlled by the software. Both hardware and software ultimately play an important role in determining the family of a computer.

Hardware is easy to identify when assigning micros to a family of computers. Different manufacturers produce machines based on different computer chips—specifically, microprocessors. You can look at the hardware brand and usually determine the family of the computer. Software is another issue. All computer systems must have an initial set of controlling commands, commonly called an *operating system,* and there are different operating systems for different computer families. For example, one family includes computers that use MS-DOS as the operating system software, another family includes computers that use the System and Finder, and yet another family uses ProDOS.

Knowing that different families of micros use different operating systems is important because, with few exceptions, a computer that uses one operating system cannot use the operating system designed for a different family. In addition, the software we use to make the computer do word processing, design graphic images, and perform other applications is linked to the operating system. For example, MS-DOS (a family operating system for IBM and IBM compatibles) can only use software applications written for the MS-DOS family of computers. A computer using System 7 (an operating system for Macintosh computers) can only use software written for that family. And software written for the Apple II family will only work on Apple II computers.

As long as the microcomputer runs the same software as all other members of their family, they remain family members, for example, software written for the Apple II series will run on almost any Apple II machine. The same holds true for the Macintosh series. However, there are exceptions. Some software is written only for specific members of a family. That is, more advanced software will only operate on more advanced family members. For example, software written exclusively for the Apple IIgs will work only on the Apple IIgs, but not any other member of the Apple II family.

Another major difference among families of computers is how they read and store data. One family of computers typically cannot read disks created by another family of computers. As you will learn in later chapters, the way computers store information varies from one family of computers to another. For example, with a few exceptions, a document created with a word processor on an IBM computer cannot be used on a Macintosh or on an Apple II series computer, nor vice versa, without converting the document to the desired family format.

Now that you understand some of the basics that make up family differences, it is important to look at some of the dominant microcomputer families. The following section focuses on three traditional family distinctions.

Apple II Family

From the early 1980s, Apple Computer, Inc.'s Apple II series, or family, has been the dominant computer in schools. There are two reasons for this: one is that it was one of the very first microcomputers, introduced four years before IBM's personal computer; second, the Apple II family has supported the most educational software. It is hard to find a school that did not begin using computers with a computer in the Apple II family. In fact, many schools continue to use these computers.

Apple II, II Plus, IIe, and IIc The Apple II family started with the Apple II in the late 1970s. While it quickly captured the fancy of many people in education and brought on thoughts of revolutionizing instruction, this early machine lacked the capabilities to perform

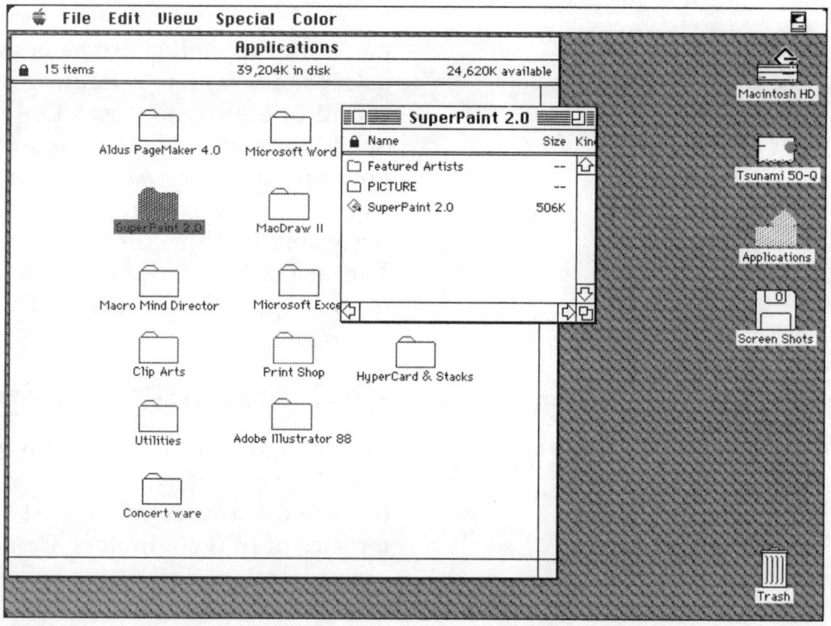

FIGURE 1-6
The software written to run on a Macintosh will only run on a Macintosh. The operating system of the Macintosh is the System/Finder, which uses a series of pictures and mouse movements to control the computer.

many important educational tasks. Even by early 1980s standards, it was a machine useful for a restricted number of tasks, such as programming and simple applications. However, schools were quick to see the educational possibilities of such a machine, and education-specific software soon followed.

The Apple II family includes the Apple II, Apple II Plus, Apple IIe, Apple IIc, and Apple IIgs. The Apple II, Apple II Plus, Apple IIe, and Apple IIc were based on a microprocessor from Motorola called the 6502. Because these computers use the same processor, software designed for one of these family members worked on others—with one exception. Apple software is normally upwardly compatible. That is, software written for an Apple II Plus worked on an Apple IIe. However, because of memory limitations, software written for an Apple IIe might not run on earlier versions of the Apple computer.

Another important factor that makes these computers all family members is the operating system used within the family. The original Apple II and the Apple II Plus used an operating system called AppleDOS. With the release of the Apple IIe, a new operating system called ProDOS (Professional Disk Operating System) was introduced. This new operating system permitted the new capabilities of the Apple IIe to be used fully and effectively. Although both the Apple IIe and the Apple IIc use ProDOS, both machines can also use AppleDOS.

Apple IIgs The most recent member of the Apple II family is the Apple IIgs. The *gs* stands for graphics and sound. In addition to offering additional memory, the Apple IIgs offered a significant enhancement—the use of graphics and sound with software. For educators requiring stimulating software, this is a major concern. Another major enhancement was the more than doubling of speed at which the computer could process data. To accomplish this enhancement, the Apple IIgs used a new microprocessor, called the Motorola 65C816, and a new operating system called GS/OS (graphics and sound operating system). Only the Apple IIgs can use the GS/OS operating system. Therefore, software written for the Apple IIgs will not run on earlier Apple II family computers. Because the Apple IIgs was a radical move away from earlier Apple computers, the designers of this computer made it capable of running ProDOS. The Apple IIgs could thus use all, or most, of the software written for the Apple IIe and even software written for AppleDOS.

IBM and IBM Compatible Family

The IBM and IBM compatible family of microcomputers includes machines manufactured by IBM. But it also includes machines made by other manufacturers that share most of the working characteristics of IBM computers. Computers that function as IBM computers are called *clones* or *compatibles.* These terms indicate that the microprocessors (the chip that controls the computer) are the same, or very similar, to the ones used by IBM. It also indicates that these computers can run the operating system used by IBM. The most common operating systems for this family of computers are MS-DOS (Microsoft Disk Operating System) and PC-DOS (Personal Computer Disk Operating System). In fact, because the operating system plays such a dominant role in determining family membership, and because MS-DOS is the undisputed leader of the field, this family of computers is often called the MS-DOS family. These include such popular computers as Zenith, NEC, Dell, Compaq, and computers made by hundreds of other manufacturers.

PC and PC/XT The oldest members of the IBM and IBM compatible family are the IBM PC, IBM PC/XT, and compatibles that have the same characteristics. IBM first introduced the IBM PC in 1981 based a microprocessor called the Intel 8088 and the original PC-DOS (or MS-DOS) operating system. This machine originally offered only floppy disk drives for storage and an operating speed of 333,000 instructions per second (.33 MIPS). The XT is functionally the same computer as the IBM PC at .33 MIPS, but it offered additional data storage capability on a hard disk or fixed disk.

Computers using the 8088 processor represent the least powerful, as well as the least expensive, members of this family. Many people choose these computers for their own personal use because they are inexpensive and there is an abundance of software available. However, by today's standards, this member of the MS-DOS family of computers is outdated and is quickly being, and in many cases has been, replaced by more advanced technology.

AT As computer users became more familiar with the capabilities of computers, they began to demand higher speed. This demand brought about the development of the IBM AT (Advanced Technology) class of computers. These computers are based on the Intel 80286 microprocessor, developed in 1982. As a class, these machines are called AT computers. However, since many compatibles use this same processor, the entire class is now more commonly referred to as *80286* or just *286* computers.

The original Intel 80286 operated at a full 2 MIPS, at or about 6 times the speed of the original 8088. Although 80286 machines brought several speed enhancements, they maintained the ability to use software designed for the XT and PC computers. The designers at Intel were very concerned about maintaining a match between hardware and the existing operating system, and so ensured that the design of the 80286 microprocessor matched the requirements of the MS-DOS and PC-DOS operating system. Because ATs could run existing software designed for PC and XT machines at a faster rate, the 80286-based computers became the choice for more serious users. Its enhanced speed and memory meant that applications could run faster on this machine than on the earlier IBM PC, XT, and compatible computers.

Teaching Tool

Classroom Newsletter

Teachers and students agree—a classroom newsletter can be a lot of fun and can be very useful for students, teachers, and parents. Having a class produce a monthly newsletter and distribute it to the students in the class, other students, teachers, and especially parents not only provides a source of useful information, but also helps students focus on classroom topics. Parents really enjoy learning about what their children are doing in class and like to stay informed. This type of project also gives students a chance to co-operate on a project, because a classroom newsletter requires reporters, graphic artists, editors, production staff, and other expertise.

80386 The next development in the IBM and compatible family came in 1985 with the Intel 80386 microprocessor. These chips offered much greater processing speed at 7 MIPS. They also offered new and improved capabilities for handling multiple tasks and improved data storage ability.

For new users of computers, speed may not be very important, especially in relation to cost. However, speed becomes very important in many applications. Consider graphic design programs, for example. These programs, increasingly popular with microcomputer users for desktop publishing, require greater processing speed because of the complexity of generating graphics. Some 80386 machines run 12 times faster than an XT. This increase in speed can make a very big difference in time—a graphic image that takes 20 minutes to draw on an XT can be drawn in seconds on an 80386. For users who require graphics and speed for other applications, the 80386 microprocessor is worth the cost.

80486 More recent IBM and IBM compatible microcomputers use the Intel 80486 processor, developed in 1989. Some machines using this microprocessor operate at more than 41 MIPS. This is clearly faster than the 80386 and offers more mathematical and memory capabilities. It also surpasses the speed of many existing mini and some mainframe computers. The 80486, like all microprocessors developed by Intel, maintains compatibility with the existing MS-DOS operating system. Virtually all software written years ago for the original IBM PC will operate on today's fast computers.

FIGURE 1-7
More complex operations require higher speed and more computing power. This is the case with Microsoft Windows. The 80386-based computers and beyond can meet these needs.

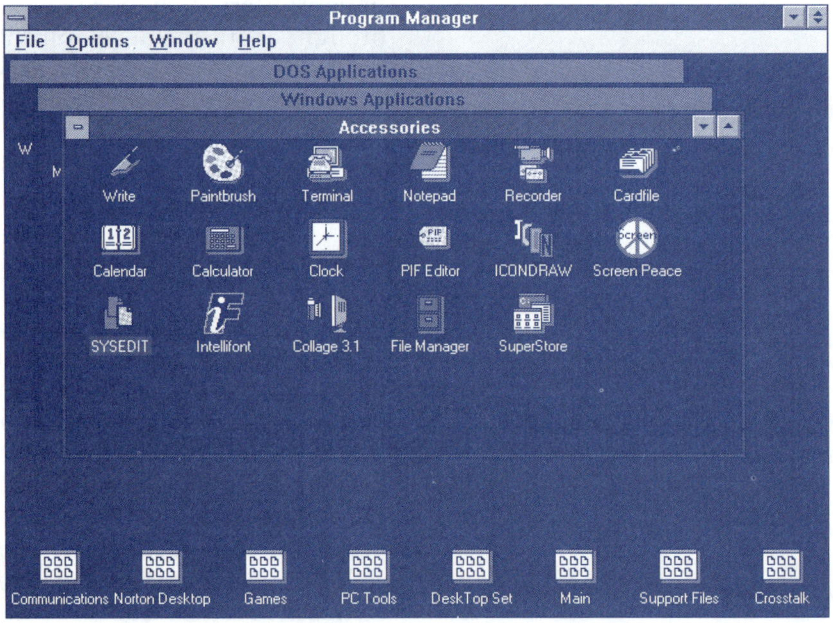

Pentium In 1993, Intel offered a new microprocessor that operates at speeds reaching 100 MIPS. Its name, Pentium, deviates from Intel's pattern of naming new processors by number. In fact, some refer to this as the "80586." Pentium is an evolution of microprocessors that enhances computing power significantly over previous microprocessors in the Intel family. Following the pattern of the 80286, 80386, and 80486, the Pentium allows software written for older processors to run on these new machines. In addition, the Pentium offers so much computing power that many have projected that these microcomputers will replace many minis and even some mainframes.

Intel Microprocessors

Year	Microprocessor	Instructions per Second	Use
1971	4004	60,000	Calculators
1974	8080	290,000	Terminals
1974	8086	333,000	AT&T 6300 PC
1978	8088	333,000	IBM PC and XT
1982	80286	2,000,000	IBM AT
1985	80386	7,000,000	386 Computers
1989	80486/25	15,000,000	486 Computers
1991	80486/50	41,000,000	486 High Speed Computers
1993	Pentium	100,000,000	Ultra High Speed Computers

Macintosh Family

Another major family of microcomputers is the Macintosh, developed and produced by Apple Computer, Inc. Like the IBM or MS-DOS family of microcomputers and the Apple II series, the Macintosh family has several members. However, unlike the MS-DOS family, which has hundreds of manufacturers producing computers in the family, the Macintosh family has only one. Apple Computer, Inc. is the only producer of Macintosh computers.

The introduction of the Macintosh was a significant break from the IBM family of computers and even from the Apple II series. Recall that the IBM family is based on the MS-DOS operating system. For IBM, the method for issuing controlling commands was to type them. That is, all commands designed to be processed on the IBM were text-based. The Macintosh was one of the first computers to popularize the use of graphics to control hardware.

Early Macintosh Computers The original Macintosh computer, introduced in 1984, used a microprocessor developed by Motorola called the 68000. This microprocessor had controlling features and requirements different from the Intel microprocessors. Even though the Motorola 68000 is roughly equivalent to the Intel 80286 processor in speed, it was not the hardware that made this family unique. Macintosh computers were complete systems that even had a small, built-in black-and-white monitor. What made the Macintosh attractive was not the hardware but the software.

The Motorola 68000 was designed to support the unique command structure that became the Macintosh trademark. The first Macintosh introduced the concept and application of using little graphics called *icons* as a means for controlling programs and data. Instead of having to remember an actual command, users look at a picture on the screen, move a pointing device called a mouse onto the picture, and click one button. Pointing and clicking were all that was and is required to control a Macintosh.

Soon after the original Macintosh was introduced, people outgrew the limitations in memory and storage. They wanted more speed and more features. So Apple began introducing a line of Macintosh computers that revolved primarily around adding memory and speeding up the internal clock (it determines the rate at which information is processed). The Mac 128 and Mac 512 model numbers indicated the amount of available memory. The Macintosh Plus introduced memory variable up to 4 megabytes (4,000,000 characters). All of these computers operated at a speed of 7.83Mhz (megahertz).

Macintosh SE The Macintosh SE was a continuation of computers based on the Motorola 68000. It offered the same basic look, with a black-and-white monitor built into the chassis of the computer, and supported the use of the same popular Macintosh software. The SE integrated the operation of nineteen separate chips into one. By reducing the number of chips needed to do the same processes, as well as by enhancing several other features, the SE ran faster and more reliably than previous Macs built using the same microprocessor.

Macintosh Classic In 1991, the Macintosh Classic replaced all previous Macintosh computers with the familiar monitor and chassis. It is a machine that is roughly equivalent in speed and memory to the Macintosh SE and takes advantage of advanced technology by packing more and more features into fewer chips. This new Mac was needed because the Macintosh hardware had changed so rapidly with the introduction of the Mac II (see next section). The Macintosh Classic was introduced to combine all previous models into one machine. Apple designated it as the low-end machine in the new Macintosh line.

Teaching Tool

Assignment Management

Managing the learning environment is the teacher's responsibility, but it also poses problems for students. In one case, students were assigned to write letters to several community leaders, community groups, and family members. Acquiring and maintaining all the address data needed to complete this assignment posed some real problems for students. Fortunately, students built mailing lists using a database. The students were able to create their own mailing list and use this data for a variety of other types of projects.

Macintosh II The release of the Macintosh II represented the first change in microprocessors for the Macintosh family. Until this new machine was developed, all previous enhancements and model changes were based primarily on how much memory was available within the computer. The original Mac II was based on the Motorola 68020 microprocessor, making for a much faster machine. One of the key ingredients in determining speed is the internal clock of the computer. The Motorola 68020 has an internal clock that allows the microprocessor to operate at twice the speed of the original 68000.

In addition to a major improvement in the microprocessor, one of the biggest differences of the Macintosh II from earlier Macs was the change to a modular computer design. Instead of a machine with a built-in black-and-white monitor, Mac II computers used separate monitors. This allowed for the introduction of color into the Macintosh family.

The Macintosh II has undergone several revisions. These include IIx, IIsi, IIcx, IIci and IIfx. Each member of this series represents different levels of speed, power, and capabilities. For example, the Mac IIx uses the 68030, equivalent to the Intel 80386; the Mac IIfx uses a Motorola 68040, which has the speed and functional capabilities of the Intel 80486.

Macintosh LC With the elimination of the Apple II family of computers from production, Apple management realized that schools and others had large investments of software that they needed to continue to use. With this in mind, Apple introduced the Macintosh LC computer to operate both Macintosh software and software written for the Apple IIe. All that is required to make the Mac LC run Apple IIe software is a special card that inserts into the Mac LC. Since the Apple IIe card only allows the operation of Apple IIe software, not Apple IIgs software, this Mac has become a favorite of many school districts.

There are many other members of the Mac family, including a series of computers called PowerBooks and Quattras. PowerBooks are transportable laptop computers that are the size of a notebook, while the Quattras are the latest in the Mac line. Like all other computers in this family, software is generally upwardly compatible but not downwardly compatible. In other words, know which Mac you are using, then select the software according to those hardware specifications.

Summary

- The definition of a computer begins with "a programmable machine that receives, stores, and processes data and outputs information."
- Computers are programmable in that they can receive and act upon a set of instructions called a program.

- A computer is also a system. Therefore, any good definition of a computer must take into consideration that a computer is made up of hardware and software.
- Hardware devices are the physical devices we can see and touch. Software is the instructions, or programs, that control the hardware.
- We often classify computers according to how fast they can complete a task, the amount of data they can handle, and the number of users that can be supported.
- Computer classifications include supercomputers, mainframe computers, minicomputers, and microcomputers.
- There are several families of microcomputers that are distinguished by the type of microprocessor and operating system software.
- The popular families in education include the Apple II family, IBM/IBM compatible computers, and Macintosh computers.
- The Apple II and II Plus use the AppleDOS operating system. The Apple IIe and IIc can use AppleDOS but also use ProDOS as the primary operating system.
- The Apple IIgs (graphics and sound) uses the Motorola 65C18 and the GS/OS operating system. This computer can also use AppleDOS and ProDOS if needed.
- The IBM family of computers uses Intel microprocessors and often uses the MS-DOS operating system.
- Macintosh computers use a microprocessor from Motorola and controlling software called System.

Fill-In Questions

1. The word ________________ is derived from the word *compute,* meaning "to count."
2. A computer is a programmable machine that ______________, ______________, and ______________ data and ______________ information.
3. The word ________________ refers to the ability to receive and act on a set of instructions.
4. ______________ is the result of the computer's processing data.
5. Computer systems are made up of both ________________ and ________________.
6. ________________ refers to the physical devices we can see or touch.

Quiz

1. A computer must receive information from a keyboard.
   a. true b. false
2. Which of the following is the largest computer type?
   a. microcomputer b. minicomputer
   c. mainframe computer d. Macintosh computer
3. The AT computer belongs to which of the following computer families?
   a. Macintosh b. Apple
   c. Commodore d. IBM
4. *Hardware* refers to the set of information or instructions a computer receives.
   a. true b. false
5. *Software* refers to the physical devices that make up a computer system.
   a. true b. false
6. Which of the following computer families uses Finder?
   a. Macintosh b. IBM
   c. IBM compatible d. Apple
7. What is the final result of data processing by a computer?
   a. instructions b. processing
   c. storing d. information
8. Which type of computer is primarily used by very large business and industry?
   a. microcomputer b. minicomputer
   c. mainframe d. personal computer
9. What are computer pictures called?
   a. cursors b. graphics
   c. paintings d. portraits
10. Software written for the Apple IIgs will work on which computers?
    a. all Apple II family computers b. only the Apple IIgs
    c. all IBM/IBM compatible d. all Macintosh

Exercises and Applications

1. Why learn about computers? Write an essay explaining why people should learn about computers. Include in your essay your expectations for this course. What do you hope to achieve at the end of this course? How can you use a computer?

2. List five common machines that resemble, but are not computers. Next to each, explain why the machine is not a computer. For example, a car receives data through the steering wheel and pedals and processes the information by performing tasks, and outputs information through the actual movement of the car. However, cars are neither programmable nor can they store information.
3. Over the next week, keep a journal of every encounter you have with a computer or with computer output. Pay particular attention to bills and bank statements, school registration, banking machines, grocery shopping, computers in cars, credit cards, controlled traffic lights, and video games. Be prepared to share journal entries with the rest of the class.
4. How have computers affected your education? Write a one-page summary of how computers have improved your education and how they have created problems. For example, in some high schools, computerized attendance-monitoring devices make calls home whenever a student does not report to school. This has made skipping school difficult.
5. Some consider the human brain to be the most powerful of all computers. Write a description of a human in terms of a computer system. Describing the hardware is easy, but what about the software?

2

ESSENTIALS OF HARDWARE

LEARNING OBJECTIVES

Learning the material in this chapter will enable you to:

- identify the critical hardware components of a computer
- explain the differences between input and output devices
- describe the CPU's function
- define bits and bytes
- list common computer peripherals
- explain how a computer uses main and auxiliary memory
- explain the role of formatting auxiliary memory

CHAPTER OVERVIEW

The backbone of any computer system is the collection of physical devices known as *hardware.* Certainly, technological advances in electronics led to the development of computers. Without hardware, there is no computer.

To use computers and related technology in schools, teachers must understand hardware. Without knowing what specific hardware does and how hardware controls information, and without an understanding of the various devices that make up hardware, teachers cannot effectively use computers in instruction. In short, you must know something about the equipment you expect to use. The focus of this chapter is on the various types of hardware found in schools.

COMMON HARDWARE

Hardware is a generic term referring to all the devices we can see and feel. These include monitors, printers, disk drives, keyboards, and the "box" we commonly call the computer. Hardware also refers to all chips, resistors, circuit boards, and wires inside the case that make up the computer. For example, the microprocessor (or

FIGURE 2-1
This message, generated from ROM, appears on IBM and IBM compatible computers using MS-DOS if the correct booting sequence is not followed.

CPU, central processing unit) that controls the computer's memory chips, the video boards, drive cables, and switches are all pieces of hardware.

Each piece of hardware contributes to operating the computer system. In fact, each piece of hardware plays a role in converting data into useful information. To do this, every computer system has three distinct pieces of hardware—input, output, and the CPU.

The type of computer doesn't matter: all computers have input and output devices and a central processing unit (CPU). An Apple II must have input and output devices and a CPU to perform any task. A supercomputer has the same requirement. Even the computer at your local grocery store is made up of input and output devices and the CPU. The differences are the type of hardware used for input, the type of hardware for output, and the way the CPU changes data into information.

FIGURE 2-2
Hardware devices are the physical devices in a computer system. What pieces of hardware can you identify?

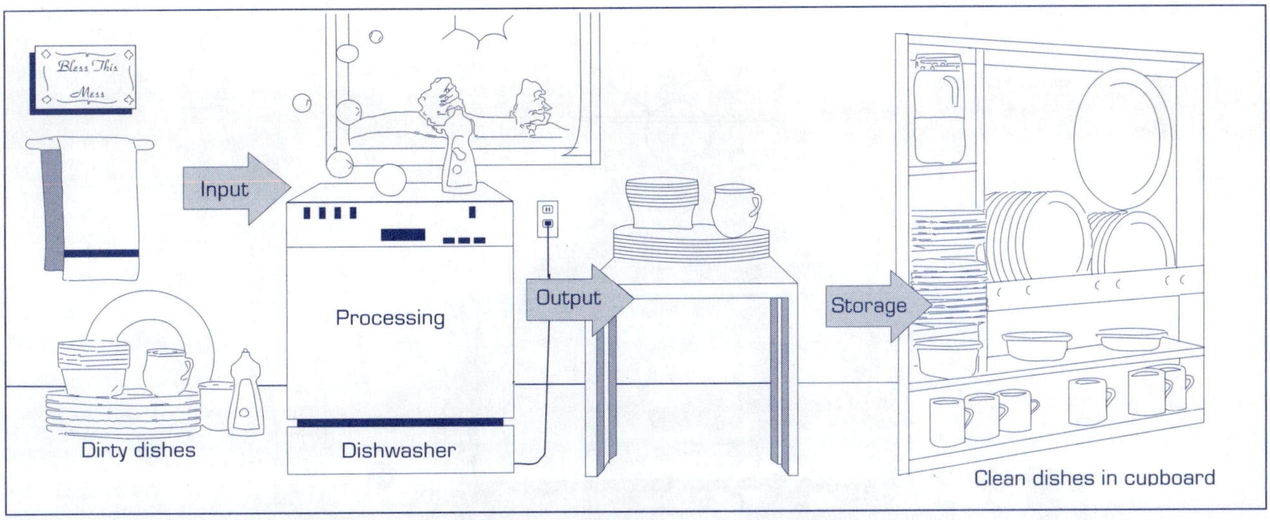

FIGURE 2-3 *Information moving from input, to CPU, to output.*

Data is what is received by the CPU. It usually has little meaning. *Information* is what the CPU processes. Data in—information out.

> *Teaching Tool*
>
> **Touch Screens**
>
> Ask even a three-year-old to identify a computer and he or she will identify the combination of a box, a keyboard, and a monitor as a computer. The keyboard puts the data in, the computer processes the information, and the monitor displays information. Each has its own traditional role. However, the division of devices into discrete units, each with one task, is quickly fading. This is best exemplified by monitors. Many monitors now allow students to touch the screen to provide input to the computer. These are called touch screen monitors. It makes a lot of sense—if you see something you want on screen, why go to the keyboard? Touch screen monitors are a logical tool. Just watch a three-year-old with a computer; when they see action on the monitor, they want to touch it.

Input Devices

An input device is any piece of hardware that passes data into the computer in a format the computer understands. In essence, input devices act as translators between humans and the machine. Keyboards, magnetic ink readers, bar code readers, tape drives, and disk drives all perform this task and are input devices.

Output Devices

Output devices display, store, or present information processed or produced by the computer itself. Without an output device, the computer would be of little value because there would be no way to use, or even see, information. Input devices translate information from human to computer; output devices translate information from computer to human or store it. Data entered into the computer would simply stay there without the use of an output device. Some examples of output devices are monitors, hard drives, and printers.

Remember, not all output devices display information that you can read. Many output devices simply store information. Disk and tape drives are examples of these types of output devices.

Also, some output devices double as input devices. For example, disks and tapes are output devices as well as input devices. The computer both sends information to them and receives data

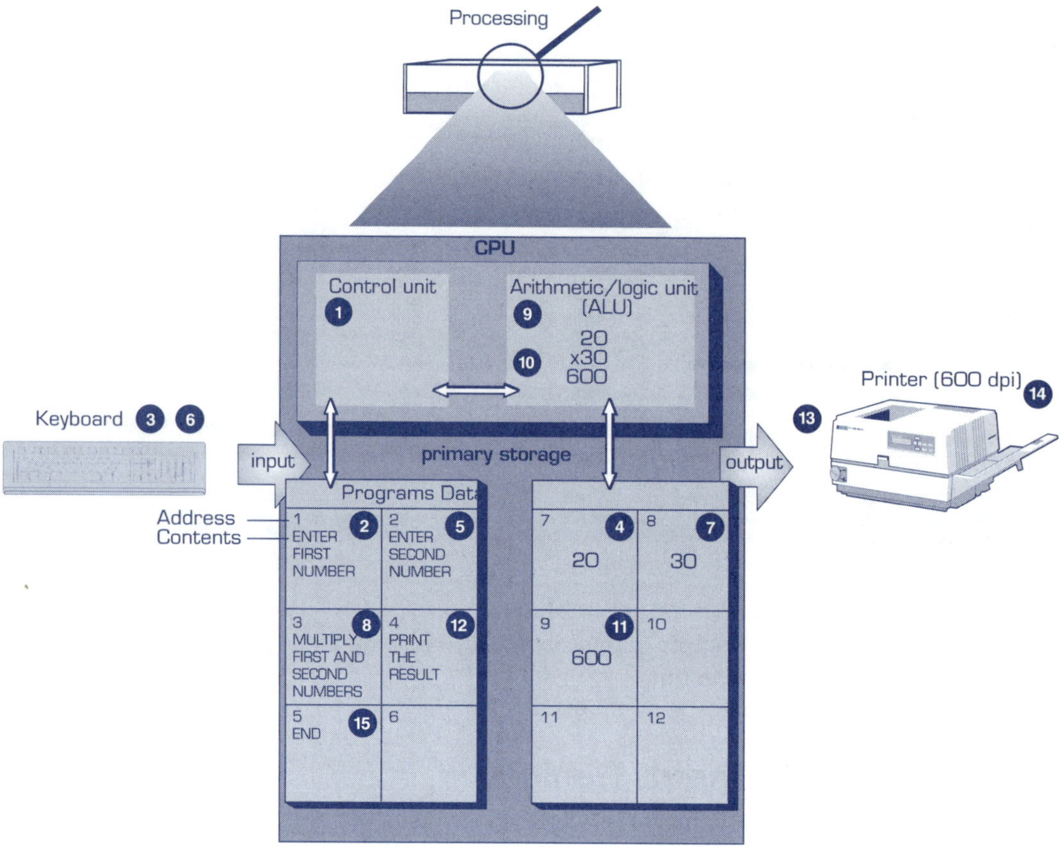

1. The control unit recognizes that the entire program has been loaded into primary storage. It begins to execute the first step in the program.
2. The program tells the user ENTER FIRST NUMBER.
3. The user types the number *20* on the keyboard. An electronic signal is sent to the CPU.
4. The control unit recognizes this signal and routes the signal to an address in primary storage—address 7.
5. After completing the above program instruction, the control unit executes the next program instruction, which tells the user ENTER SECOND NUMBER.
6. The user types the number *30* on the keyboard. An electronic signal is sent to the CPU.
7. The control unit recognizes this signal and routes it to primary storage address 8.
8. The control unit now executes the next program instruction: MULTIPLY FIRST AND SECOND NUMBERS.
9. To execute this instruction, the control unit informs the arithmetic/logic unit (ALU) that two numbers are coming and that the ALU is to multiply them. The control unit next sends the ALU a copy of the contents of address 7 *(20)* and then sends a copy of the contents of address 8 *(30)*.
10. The ALU performs the multiplication: *20* x *30* = *600*.
11. The control unit sends a copy of the multiplied results *(600)* back to primary storage, to address 9.
12. The control unit executes the next program instruction: PRINT THE RESULT.
13. To execute this instruction, the control unit sends the contents of address 9 *(600)* to the printer.
14. The printer prints the value *600*.
15. The control unit executes the final instruction: END. The program is complete.

FIGURE 2-4 *The CPU has several critical components that control the flow of data through the microprocessor.*

from them. These are only two examples of devices that serve two purposes; a closer look at some of these input/output (I/O) devices follows in this chapter.

The Central Processing Unit

Input and output devices are of little value without a device to convert data into useful information. This is the role of the CPU—to process data. The CPU is actually a single chip made up of three parts: a control unit, a memory register, and an arithmetic/logic unit.

Data coming into the CPU first enters the memory register to wait for processing. The memory register is small and holds only limited amounts of data. Once data is in the memory register, the control unit sends the data to a device that converts data into information. This conversion is the function of the arithmetic/logic unit (ALU), which performs all arithmetic and logic functions. The control unit determines when the ALU will do these functions and it manages the conversion of data and the operations within the ALU. Finally, the control unit sends the results of the ALU's work back through the memory register to an output device. To illustrate, think of a car. A car has all types of parts, but the *driver* manages the system. As the manager or control unit, the driver determines when and what to do. The engine (ALU) actually performs the work.

BINARY REPRESENTATION

The function of the CPU is to control data. But just what does that mean? What *is* computer data? To answer these two questions, you must remember part of the definition of a computer— an electronic machine. It runs on electricity that is either off or on. All data in a

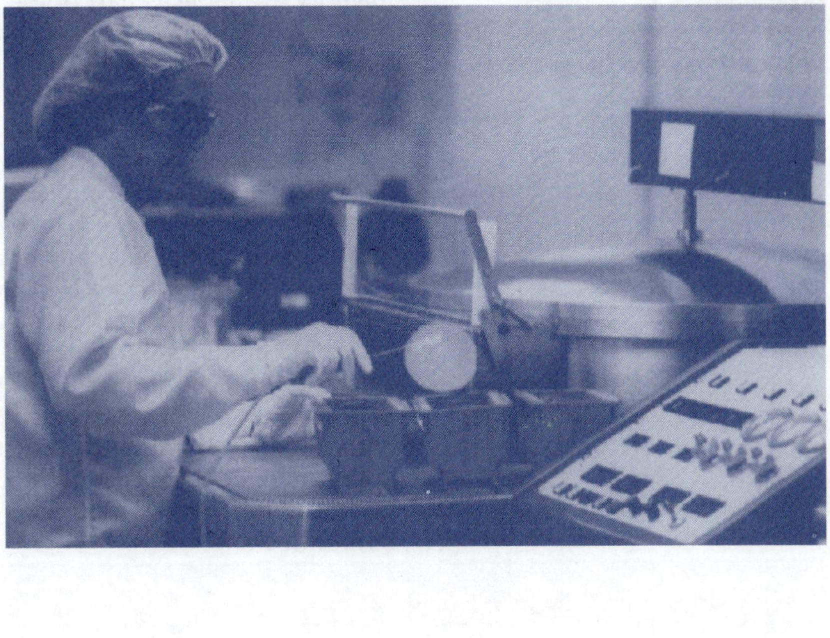

FIGURE 2-5
Manufacturing a CPU requires a sterile environment. Any imperfections in this small piece of equipment will leave a computer useless.

Teaching Tool

Videodiscs

Videodiscs have made a slow but steady progression into the classroom. Videodiscs are designed primarily to link real-time video to classroom instruction. With this type of hardware, students can watch portions of a video, answer questions on what they have seen, then watch other segments in any order. For a golf coach, this technology can be both fun and educational. Students can play different holes of golf at some of the most famous courses in the world. For a social studies teacher, important news events can be played and replayed in any desired order. An English teacher can show great plays. An art teacher's students can examine great artworks.

computer is really nothing more than a series of electronic on and off switches.

For a computer to process data, it must operate using these switches. However, it is very difficult for people to translate thoughts and ideas into simple on and off statements that a computer can understand. Imagine saying to a computer, "on on off on off on off off on on." Or, imagine asking the computer to calculate on on on multiplied by off on off. As confused as you may feel about computers now, can you imagine having to use words to represent the on off state? That would be a communication nightmare. To use computers, another system was needed to represent the two states of electricity. The binary numbering system offers a solution.

A binary numbering system uses zeros (0) to represent off and one (1) to represent on. The number 3 in the base 10 system (our everyday system) translates to the number 11 in the binary system. The 1 on the left is equal to 2 in base 10 (think of the place value), and the 1 on the right is equal to 1 for a total of 3.

It is easy to see how binary numbers can represent base ten numbers. It is simple a matter of defining place values. However, how can 0 and 1 represent the many symbols used by the computer? Computers use a series of binary numbers to represent each character needed by the computer. For example, a series such as 01000101 represents a single character. In computer lingo, each of the 0s and 1s is a *bit*. Each bit represents the on- or off-state of electricity. The combination or series of bits that represents letters, numbers, and symbols meaningful to humans are *bytes*. The most common code is called *ASCII*, American Standard Code for Information Interchange.

PRIMARY MEMORY

One of the problems with the CPU is the extremely small amount of memory available as part of the microprocessor. Because the storage is so small, other types of memory must support the large volumes of data and information that computers normally handle. Every computer has a set of memory chips, directly controlled by the CPU, designed to hold data before it enters the CPU and hold information from the CPU. This type of memory is known as *primary memory*.

The CPU does not process each byte of data as it is typed, nor does it immediately perform each instruction. Rather, the control unit holds both the data and the instructions that tell the computer what to do with the data in primary memory. The control unit may also send all or part of the instructions to the arithmetic/logic unit. The ALU holds the instructions and acts on these instructions to process data. Data remains in primary memory until the ALU is ready to process. When the arithmetic/logic unit is ready, the control unit of the CPU directs the transfer of data from primary memory to the arithmetic/logic unit. After processing the data, the control unit sends the information back to the primary memory and then to output devices.

FIGURE 2-6
To find the ASCII code for a particular character or symbol, first locate the column containing the character. Next, note the row. Remember, or jot down, the first three bits identifying the column, then jot down the last four bits identifying the row. For example, the lowercase letter j is in the column labeled 110 and the row labeled 1010. The ASCII code for the letter j is 1101010.

		First Three Bits							
		000	001	010	011	100	101	110	111
	0000	NUL	DLE	space	0	@	P	‘	p
	0001	SOH	DC1	!	1	A	Q	a	q
	0010	STX	DC2	“	2	B	R	b	r
	0011	ETX	DC3	#	3	C	S	c	s
	0100	EOT	DC4	$	4	D	T	d	t
Last	0101	ENQ	NAK	%	5	E	U	e	u
Four	0110	ACK	SYN	&	6	F	V	f	v
Bits	0111	BEL	ETB	’	7	G	W	g	w
	1000	BS	CAN	(	8	H	X	h	x
	1001	HT	EM	)	9	I	Y	i	y
	1010	LF	SUB	*	:	J	Z	j	z
	1011	VT	EXC	+	;	K	[	k	{
	1100	FF	FS	,	<	L	\	l	|
	1101	CR	GS	_	=	M	]	m	}
	1110	SO	RS	.	>	N	^	n	~
	1111	SI	US	/	?	O	-	o	DEL

The ALU rarely holds all the instructions necessary to process the data. Needed instructions are called from primary memory by the control unit and sent to the ALU through the memory register. As new instructions are needed, the control unit flushes the old instructions from the ALU and transfers in new instructions. This is followed by transferring data from primary memory to the arithmetic/logic unit for processing. Primary memory holds the instructions performed by the CPU, the data to be processed, and the results of the processing. Primary memory must therefore be large enough to hold all the different types of data, instructions, and information needed to make the computer function.

Primary memory is a series of electronic switches put together as microchips or chips. These memory chips store data, instructions, and information in a binary fashion. The easiest way to think of how memory chips work is to think of how a bank of switches works. Each switch is either off or on—sound familiar? A bank of switches forms a byte, and a byte represents a piece of information. The more bytes, the greater the capacity of the chip to store data or information. The amount of data each chip can store is reported in bytes.

Some chips store about 64,000 bytes, called 64K. *K* stands for kilobyte, or 1024 bytes. Other chips store over a million bytes, called 1Meg (for megabyte).

There is one more point to remember about the relationship between the CPU and primary memory. Within the CPU, the control unit directs the temporary storing of data to memory on the system board by placing information at a series of *addresses,* or locations in primary memory. When the CPU needs this information, the control unit remembers the addresses and transfers the information found there.

Computers need a large set of specific instructions to perform any activity. Unfortunately, most computers do not have enough primary memory to store all the instructions required for the many different operations we demand. If all instructions for all computer activities were stored in primary memory, the computer's memory would soon be full. The number of applications the computer could perform would be severely limited. It would not make much sense to have a computer that could only do a few tasks; therefore, primary memory is broken down into two parts. One part permanently stores information needed by the computer every time it is turned on. The other part temporarily stores information, so the data, instructions, and information can change as needed. These two types of primary memory are known as ROM and RAM, respectively.

ROM

ROM (Read Only Memory) permanently stores the basic set of instructions needed each time the computer is turned on. A computer cannot function without instructions. It even needs instructions to know what to do when the power switch is turned on. These initial instructions are the ones permanently stored in ROM. Data stored in ROM cannot be altered.

The instructions stored in ROM are known as *firmware,* because the information in ROM remains intact even when the computer is off. Some examples of firmware include the initial greetings, error messages, and information about the keyboard.

Teaching Tool

Sound

Throughout most of the evolution of microcomputers, sound has received little attention. People have learned to look at a monitor for the majority of output. However, over the past few years computer-generated sound has become a very hot item. Instead of reading the Gettysburg Address onscreen, students can listen to an actor read it. For young students, it's more natural to be instructed by voice than by words on a screen. The quality and use of sound is on the increase and is improving the quality of instruction.

RAM

Because ROM cannot be altered, another type of memory must store data and instructions entered by users. This type of memory is known as *RAM* (Random Access Memory). RAM stores both the software programs that provide processing instructions and the data that the computer processes.

Unlike ROM, RAM stores information temporarily. When the computer loses power or is turned off, the information in RAM disappears. The information in RAM is thus said to be *volatile.* Suppose you enter a set of word processing instructions and then type in a thirty-page paper. If the computer abruptly loses power, all the instructions and the thirty-page document will disappear. (This is why we use disk drives—to save information on disk before it is lost in RAM.)

RAM is measured in kilobytes. A kilobyte is not exactly one thousand (1,000) pieces of information, it is one thousand and twenty-four (1,024) bytes. The reason is that binary numbers do not calculate to the common base ten system. Thus, 64K RAM is actually 65,536 (64 x 1,024) pieces of information. For more specifics, look at the following table. However, for describing the size of RAM, using the concept 64K, or 1Meg, or 1Gig is accurate enough.

Memory Table

1 bit	= 1 on or off switch
1 byte	= 7 or 8 bits (or more in some computers)
1 kilobyte (K)	= 1,024 bytes
1 megabyte (Meg)	= 1,048,576 bytes, or 1,024K
1 gigabyte (Gig)	= 1,073,741,824, or 1,024Meg

RAM is one of the primary ingredients in determining the capabilities of a computer. A computer with a small amount of RAM cannot perform the same number of tasks, or even tasks of equal complexity, as computers with higher levels of RAM. Generally, the more RAM, the faster the computer is able to process data.

The amount of RAM required depends on the software one wants to use. Each software package has minimum RAM requirements. (The RAM requirements are written on the software's box.) If a software package requires 512K, then the computer must have at least 512K of RAM. Many programs require much more. Therefore, as a general rule, the larger the RAM, the better.

FIGURE 2-7
The motherboard is the platform that contains all devices controlled by the CPU. Any additional hardware must be connected to the motherboard to be controlled by the CPU.

AUXILIARY MEMORY

As mentioned in the discussion of primary memory, if power to the computer is interrupted, the contents of RAM are erased. Remember, memory chips are like a set of switches. As soon as power to the computer stops, all the switches are turned off, and all information is lost.

Obviously, losing power to a computer poses a problem. You cannot leave a computer on all the time out of fear of losing the contents of RAM. To solve this problem, an additional type of memory, external to primary memory, must be available. This is *auxiliary memory*, sometimes called auxiliary storage or secondary memory.

Several devices fall into the category of auxiliary memory. There are tape drives, removable drives, and even CDs (compact disks). However, two of the most familiar examples of auxiliary memory are floppy disks and hard disks.

The key attribute of auxiliary memory is that it can store information in a semi-permanent fashion. Auxiliary memory stores data, instructions, and information and does not need a constant source of power. This makes auxiliary memory non-volatile—an ideal place to store information created by the CPU. One of the strongest interactions in a computer occurs between RAM and auxiliary memory.

The relationship between auxiliary and primary memory normally begins with a set of instructions located in auxiliary memory. Typically, a program residing in auxiliary memory is loaded or placed into RAM. From RAM, the instructions move to the CPU. As information is produced by the CPU, it is transferred to RAM. To save this information for later use, the information in RAM is then moved and stored in auxiliary memory.

This is how the interaction works when using a word processor to type a term paper. The first step is to load the word processing program into RAM from auxiliary memory. Usually, this involves loading the software from a disk. The word processing commands are then executed by the CPU, making word processing possible. Text for the term paper is then entered from the keyboard. As each letter or character is typed, it is placed into RAM. At any point while typing the paper, it is possible to send the text from RAM to auxiliary memory (save text). One must, of course, save one's work when finished typing. After saving all text (storing it in auxiliary memory), the computer can be turned off without losing the data for the term paper. At any point from then on, it is possible to load the text from auxiliary memory and place it back into RAM for further changes or additions.

Teaching Tool

CD-ROM

One of the fastest-growing forms of electronic storage is CD-ROM (Compact Disk-Read Only Memory), the same type of data storage device used with audio CDs. There are two major advantages of CD-ROM. First, the amount of available data storage space far exceeds the amount typically found on magnetic hard disk drives. Second, data is much more stable than with magnetic devices (it can't be lost or overwritten). For teachers, CD-ROM provides access to information on a scale never before seen in the classroom. With CD-ROM, whole encyclopedia are stored on one disk. CD-ROM makes it possible for students to access pictures and sound, as well as traditional text-based data. In fact, the growing popularity of CD-ROM is now providing teachers with a whole new type of software to further enhance the quality of instruction.

Magnetic Disks

Magnetic disks are the most popular type of auxiliary memory used with microcomputer systems. One reason is that they provide a reusable medium for storing information. Since magnetic disks store information in a series of magnetic fields, it is easy to change data by changing the magnetic field. Magnetic disks are also cost-effective. A

FIGURE 2-8
The two most common size floppy disks are 3.5 inch and 5.25 inch. Many people think 3.5 inch disks are called hard disks because of the hard shell case. This is incorrect; it is not the case but the disk itself that determines type.

typical floppy disk for a microcomputer can range in price from ten cents to a couple of dollars. For these reasons, disk technology for microcomputers plays an important role in making microcomputers a popular tool.

There are two main types of disks available for use with microcomputers: floppy disks and hard disks. Floppy disks are removable and can easily be transported from one computer to another. Hard disks are typically sealed inside the computer and are not usually removable.

It may seem that floppy disks are the best choice. However, the amount of data or information a floppy disk can store is much less than a hard disk. For example, one size of floppy disk for the IBM family stores 360K of data. (*Size* refers either to physical size or storage size; for example, one 3.5-inch disk can contain 1.44Meg of storage capacity.) Some Macintosh floppy disks store 800K. Hard disks can range in storage size from 20Meg to several gigabytes. Floppy disks are also slower at moving data from the disk to RAM than are hard disks.

The typical microcomputer system consists of both a hard disk drive and one or more floppy disk drives. Since hard disks are faster, most people prefer to use them whenever possible. However, because floppy disks are transportable, the floppy disk drive enables software to be entered into RAM, then stored on the hard disk. Of course, floppy disks are also used to store information generated by the CPU to be transported to other computers.

When considering different types of floppy disks, one obvious feature is the disk itself. Disks come in different sizes. For example, many microcomputers can use both 5.25-inch floppy disk and 3.5-inch floppy disks. Disks also come in two basic types. Hard-sectored disks are prepared for use on a particular brand of disk drive on a specific computer. Soft-sectored disks can generally be used on any computer system. Most microcomputers use soft-sectored disks.

Another way of classifying floppy disks is their storage capacity. The physical size of the disk is not related to storage capacity. In fact, smaller disks typically have greater storage capability. The key is how the magnetic field is structured, and different floppy disk drives structure the magnetic field differently. For example, within the IBM family, there are four major structures: two for each size of disk. Within the Macintosh family, there are three major structures for 3.5-inch disks.

Table 2-1 Disk Storage Capacities

Family	Size	Capacity
IBM	5.25	360K
IBM	5.25	1.2Meg
IBM	3.5	720K
IBM	3.5	1.44Meg
Mac	3.5	400K
Mac	3.5	800K
Mac	3.5	1.44Meg

The magnetic structure that determines storage capacity is the *disk format*. The process of creating the structure is known as *formatting*. Because different families of computers use different disk formats, and because there are different types of disk drives within families, correct formatting is critical to using magnetic disk storage.

Formatting Disks

All disks must be formatted (sometimes called *initialized*) before being used in any disk drive or with any computer system. Software disks have already been formatted since they contain program information. However, new blank disks contain no information and do not have a magnetic structure; there are so many different types of formats that it would be difficult for manufacturers to produce the wide array of formats needed. It is easier and more cost-effective to provide blank disks and let users format them according to their computer and their needs.

Recall that a *family* includes all microcomputers that use the same operating system. This is important to formatting because all members of one family can usually use the disks formatted by other members of that family. For example, a disk formatted for an IBM will work with IBM compatibles. A disk formatted for a Macintosh will work with any Macintosh. However, in general, disks formatted

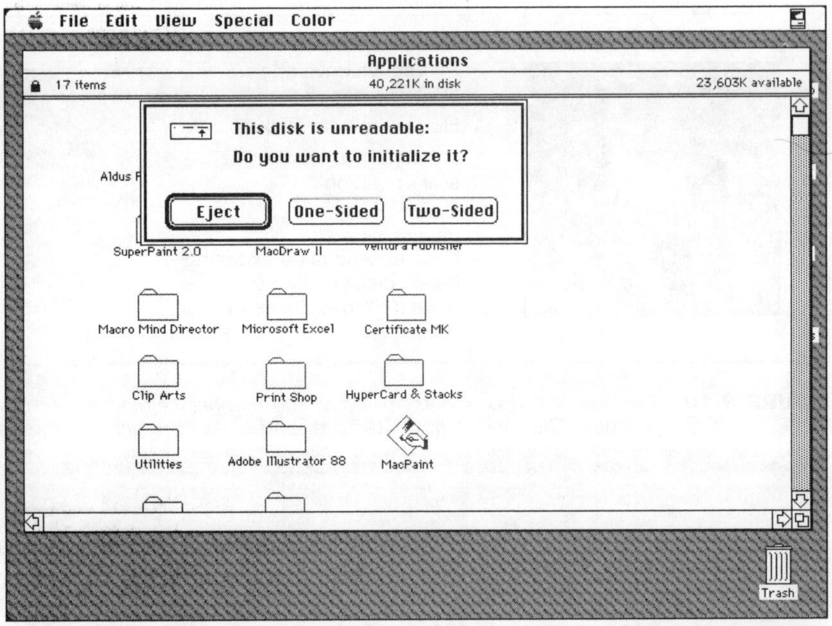

FIGURE 2-9
Inserting a new, blank disk into a Macintosh starts the initializing (formatting) process.

for IBM will not work with Macintosh and vice versa. Programs and disk drives that allow for the interchange of disks between different families of computers are now becoming more common.

One final factor in being able to use a disk formatted for one member of a family with other members is the type of disk drive on each computer. To use a floppy disk formatted for an IBM 1.44Meg drive, a 1.44Meg IBM or IBM compatible drive must be available.

Just what is the process of formatting or initializing? (MS-DOS computer users call the process of preparing disks *formatting.* For Macintosh computers, it is called *initializing.*) The process involves the creation of storage or memory cells. Memory cells are created by the intersection of sectors and tracks. Tracks are concentric circles around a disk, and sectors are similar to slices of a pie. Some disk drives format disks with 40 tracks, others have 80, and still others have more. The number of sectors also varies from disk drive to disk drive. Some have 9, some 16, and still others 18 sectors. Therefore, different disk formats can have a different number of cells.

The creation of cells is an important part of formatting. The number of cells created determines the data storage capacity of the disk. The more the cells, the greater the capacity. However, disks also store different amounts of information *within* each cell, depending on the format. Some store 512 bytes of information per cell, others 256 bytes. Another feature that affects how much information a disk can store is whether one or both sides of the disk are used. Disks formatted on both sides can store twice as much information as can disks formatted on only one side.

To get an idea of how a disk format affects the amount of information stored on a disk, consider the following example. A disk that uses 9 sectors and 40 tracks on each side, and stores 512 bytes in

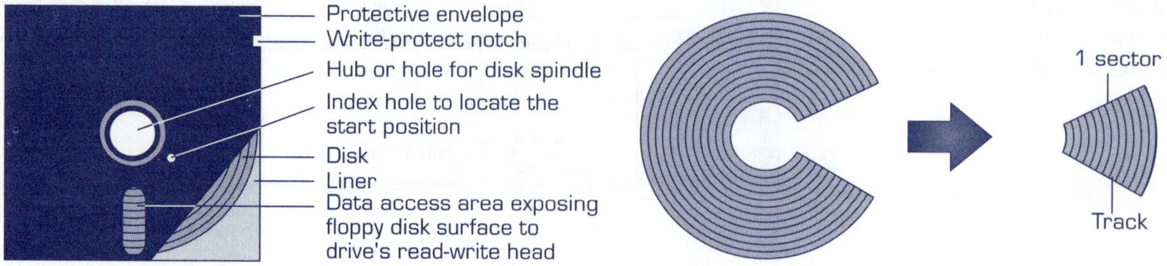

FIGURE 2-10 *The size of a disk is determined by the number of tracks, sectors, and sides used in the formatting process. The more tracks, sectors, and sides, the greater the data capacity of the formatted disk.*

each cell, can hold 368,640 bytes ($9 \times 40 \times 512 \times 2 = 368{,}640$), or 360K. This is a popular disk format for an IBM 5.25-inch floppy disk. Remember, the number of cells and the amount of information available in each cell determines storage capacity.

As mentioned earlier, one of the advantages of magnetic disks is that the magnetic structure can be changed. Formatting is not permanent. A disk can be reformatted at any time to create a new magnetic structure. Therefore, it is possible to format not only blank disks, but also disks that already contain stored information. When a disk is formatted, the first step in the formatting processes is to erase any existing magnetic structure. Thus, any time a disk is reformatted, all information and data on a disk are first erased before creating new tracks, sectors, and cells. Like a VCR tape, it can be used over and over, but each time you record, old information is erased.

PERIPHERAL DEVICES

Any device attached or connected to the CPU is considered a peripheral device. By definition, a *peripheral* is any device controlled by the CPU but external to the computer. If it is added on and plugged into a computer, it is a peripheral. Most peripherals fall into one of three groups: input (keyboards), output (monitors), and I/O (input and output) devices (disk drives). The following describes some of the more common peripherals that can be a part of a microcomputer system.

Popular Input Devices

As previously discussed, input devices are peripherals that send information to RAM for processing by the CPU. However, the type of information sent to RAM is controlled by the input device. Some are adept at sending text. Other input devices send graphic information.

Still others send specialized data required for unique applications. Today there are so many different types of input devices that it would be difficult to include them all here.

Keyboard For most microcomputer users, the keyboard is the most important input device. The computer keyboard is different from the typewriter keyboard. Both computer and typewriter keyboards allow us to enter letters, numbers, and symbols, but computer keyboards allow us also to enter commands.

Mouse In the last several years, the mouse has become very important as an input device. Now it is as important as the keyboard. A mouse inputs data simply by moving the mouse and pointing at information on the screen and clicking the mouse button. With a mouse, users no longer need type commands—they can simply point and click.

Graphics tablets A graphics tablet helps users create graphic designs. To do this, users move a stylus, or pointer, over a special board. As the stylus moves, data is sent into the computer, processed by the CPU, and displayed on an output device. Usually, stylus moves appear on a monitor in the form of a graphic design.

Optical disks (CD-ROM) Optical disks use a series of laser-burned holes to represent data. As the disk spins, a light beam shines through each hole. The presence or absence of light represents each bit. This technology enables large amounts of information to be stored on a very small disk, using the same technology that makes compact disks work. It is frequently called a CD-ROM because it can only be used as an input device. The ROM part of the term has no relationship to ROM in primary memory.

FIGURE 2-11
Interactive video workstations are popular teaching and training tools.

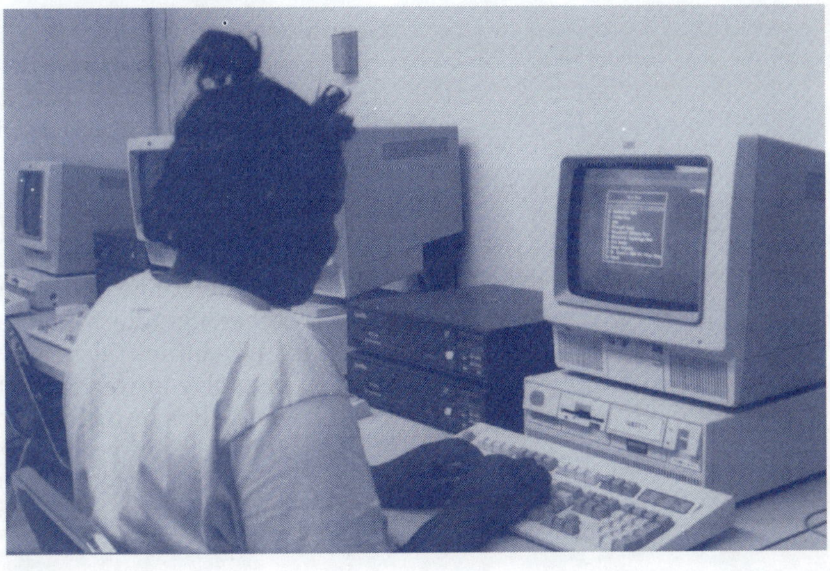

Teaching Tool

Scanners

Students often want to include more in their documents than text entered from the keyboard. Scanners make this possible. Scanners look like simple photocopy machines, but instead of making a copy to another piece of paper, scanners generate data files. Students can take a photograph, place it on a scanner, scan it, and use the photograph as part of a word processing document. Imagine the fun students will have when they can include a photograph of the Grand Canyon in a report about the Grand Canyon.

Scanners Scanners read information by passing a light over an object. They work on much the same principle as a photocopier. However, instead of making a duplicate paper copy, scanners take text from a page and send it to RAM. To do this, the scanner uses software called OCR (Optical Character Recognition) to translate what the scanner sees as images into actual characters. Using scanners, typewritten pages can be read and placed into a word processor.

Scanners can also take photographs, line art, or any other type of graphic on paper and place it into RAM. Graphics that have been scanned into RAM can be modified using graphics software.

Common Output Devices

As you know, output devices display information generated by the CPU. Because the CPU can produce a wide range of output, output peripherals have become specialized. Like input devices, there are so many different types of output devices it would be impossible to discuss them all here. However, here are a few of the most common.

Monitors Probably the most common output device for microcomputers is the monitor. Other terms for a monitor are CRT (Cathode Ray Tube), VDU (Visual Display Unit), and simply screen.

Different types of monitors are available for different uses. Two of the most popular types are color and monochrome. Monochrome monitors are dual color such as black and white, amber and black, or green and black. People who work primarily with text often find monochrome monitors a good choice. Color monitors vary according to the number of colors and the crispness, or resolution, of the display.

Graphics display adapters For a computer to display text or graphics on a monitor, information generated by the CPU must be translated into a form the monitor can use. This is the role of the graphics display adapter. Different microcomputers use various graphic adapters to control monitors. Some microcomputers, such as the Macintosh Classic, all the Apple II family, and many of the IBM PS/2 computers have graphic adapters built into the motherboard. Other microcomputers allow graphic adapters to be added to support a wider range of displays.

Whether a graphics adaptor is built-in or added on to the computer, it still requires the use of a monitor. However, monitors must be able to display the output of the graphics adapters. The two work hand-in-hand. It is impossible to have one without the other. Graphics adapters determine the type of display. For example, a monochrome graphics adaptor only produces two-color output. Therefore, only a monochrome monitor designed to work specifically with that graphics adaptor can be used.

Printers Printers, another familiar output device, produce paper copies. The common term for a paper copy is *hardcopy.* There are about as many different types of printers as there are computers. Some of the more popular printers include laser printers, dot matrix printers, daisy wheel printers, and ink jet printers. The major differences between these types of printers are the quality of output, the speed of the printer, and the price. The higher the quality and the faster the print, the more expensive the printer. Many high quality laser printers cost more than computers.

Plotters Plotters use pens to make precise drawings on paper. Typically, plotters are used in drafting.

Popular I/O Devices

One of the most important classifications of peripherals are those devices that can send data, programs, and information into RAM and receive output from RAM. These devices are called input/output devices or simply, I/O.

Floppy disk drives As discussed earlier, disk drives either load data, programs, or information into RAM or receive output from RAM or the CPU.

Hard disk drives This section also discussed hard disk drives as another form of magnetic storage. These devices operate on the same basic principle as floppy disks, since they can both load data, programs, and information into RAM and receive output. Most hard disk drives are sealed and the disk itself is not removable, but newer

FIGURE 2-12
Modems make it possible for computers to share data and information over existing telephone lines.

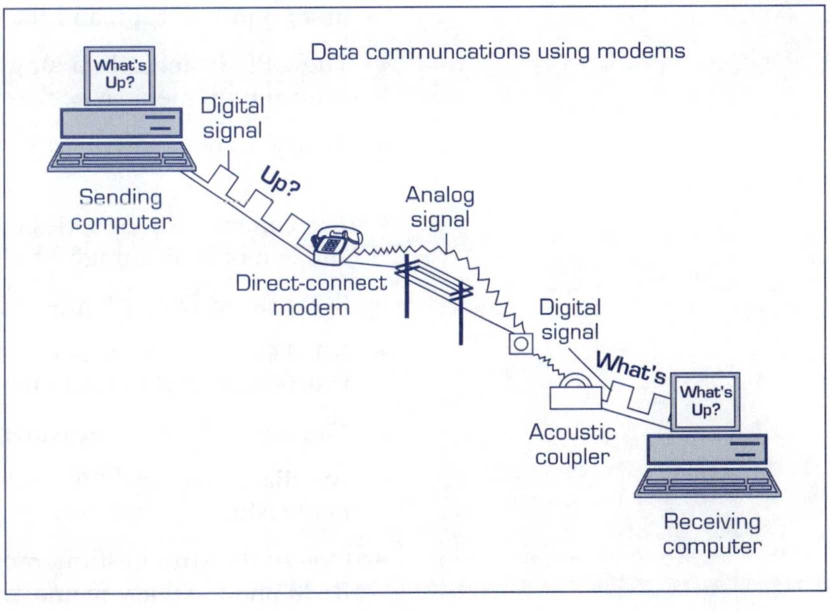

hard disk technology is creating removable hard disks. Hard disks are very precise and able to store much larger amounts of information than floppy disks.

Tape drives Tape drives are peripheral devices used for auxiliary memory. Tape drives store information magnetically on computer tape similar to the tape used in audiocassette tapes and VCR players. Tape drives can store large amounts of information. However, information is stored sequentially—that is, in one long stream. Therefore, information must be retrieved in one long stream rather than in any desired order as with disk drives. This process can be time-consuming. Because of this limitation, tape drives are commonly used as a backup device for information stored on hard disks.

Modems Modems are communication peripherals that allow one computer to exchange and share information with another computer using telephone lines. Through a modem, a microcomputer can access information from a variety of sources. Modems allow friends to share information between microcomputers over long distances and they allow microcomputer users access to large corporate data banks. With a modem, information can be sent and received anywhere there is telephone, almost instantaneously.

Summary

- *Hardware* is a generic term that refers to all the physical devices of a computer system that we can see or touch.
- It doesn't matter what type of computer, all computers are made up of input, output, and the CPU.
- The CPU is actually a single chip made up of three parts, the control unit, memory register, and arithmetic/logic unit.
- Binary numbers use a series of zeros (0) and ones (1) to represent off and on.
- The combination or series of bits that represent letters, numbers, and symbols meaningful to humans are simply called bytes.
- ROM (Read Only Memory) provides permanent storage.
- RAM stores both the software programs that provide processing instructions and the data that the computer processes.
- The size of RAM is measured in kilobytes.
- Auxiliary memory stores information and data in a more permanent fashion.
- One of the strongest interactions in a computer occurs between RAM and auxiliary memory.

- Magnetic disks are the most popular type of auxiliary memory used.
- There are two main types of disks available for use with microcomputers: floppy disks and hard disks.

Fill-In Questions

Fill in the blank for each of the statements listed below.

1. Any apparatus used to put information into a computer is called a(n) ________________ device.
2. A(n) ________________ is used to display, store, or present information processed by a computer.
3. The component within the computer that does the actual processing is called ________________ .
4. Whenever information is passed to the CPU from an input device, that material is stored in ________________ .
5. ________________ only allows sets of instructions to be read or retrieved.
6. The three major types of memory used with computers are ________________ , ________________ , and ________________ .

Quiz

Answer the following questions.

1. What type of memory is associated with a disk drive?
   a. RAM b. ROM
   c. CPU d. auxiliary
2. What type of memory is associated with a tape drive?
   a. RAM b. ROM
   c. CPU d. auxiliary
3. Which main memory device receives information from a disk drive?
   a. RAM b. ROM
   c. ALU d. INPUT
4. How many symbols in a binary numbering system?
   a. 1 b. 2
   c. 10 d. 20

5. Which of the following is the smallest piece of information a computer uses?
   a. bit b. byte
   c. RAM d. ROM

6. Which of the following occurs when a disk is formatted?
   a. files are prepared b. disk is erased
   c. main memory transfer d. secondary memory transfer

7. Which of the following is the best example of an input device?
   a. monitor b. printer
   c. RAM d. light pen

8. Which of the following is the best example of an output device?
   a. monitor b. bar code reader
   c. RAM d. ROM

9. Which of the following uses sectors and tracks?
   a. RAM b. ROM
   c. disk d. tape

10. Which type of printer produces text through the use of light beams?
    a. dot matrix b. daisy wheel
    c. laser d. ink jet

Exercises and Applications

Follow the instructions for each exercise and application.

1. Inside every computer is a CPU. If possible, open a computer, look inside, and identify the CPU. It may not be easy to locate, however a computer technician, professor, or computer dealer can point out the exact location of the CPU.
2. Create a diagram that explains how any computer operates.
3. Make a list of input and output devices. Explain why each device is an input or an output device and describe the function of each device.
4. Keep a computer notebook. This notebook may contain class handouts, definitions of important terms, and other important questions. A computer notebook will become a permanent reference guide.

3

ESSENTIALS OF SOFTWARE

LEARNING OBJECTIVES

Learning the material in this chapter will enable you to:

- describe the use and application of system software
- identify the system software for Apple II, IBM and IBM compatible, and Macintosh computers
- describe the use and operation of application software
- describe three popular types of system utility software
- identify the six major types of application software
- list possible uses for each type of application software
- list the four major types of CAI software and their uses and applications

CHAPTER OVERVIEW

As you know, computers cannot operate without instructions. It is the software in the computer system that instructs and controls the computer, enabling it to perform tasks and solve problems. There are many types of computer applications and many types of software available for educators. For problems that involve mathematical calculations, for example, there is spreadsheet software. For problems of weather analysis, there is weather forecasting software. For problems of keeping student records, there is grade book software. For almost any problem, there is some type of software.

While computer software can help solve many problems, it cannot solve all educational problems. Software, of course, cannot prevent students from getting poor grades. However, the right kind of software can offer some help. A computer with telecommunications capability and the right software can help students find sources for writing a term paper. Word processing software can help students write a paper by making it easier to edit text. Desktop publishing software can help create a more professional-looking paper, but the software cannot determine if the words are meaningful. It cannot determine if the paper is thoughtful or insightful, nor can it judge the quality of the work.

FIGURE 3-1
Software often stimulates cooperative learning.

Beginning with this chapter, the focus is on how software can affect teachers, students, parents, and administrators. However, before looking at specifics, you must get an overview of software. To gain a full understanding of the role of software in a computer system, we must examine the major classifications of software. One common classification divides software into three major areas—**system software, system utility software**, and **applications software**.

Some words of caution: throughout this chapter, there are several terms and references to software unique to the Apple II, Macintosh, or IBM/IBM compatible computers. This chapter will give you a good overview of software for all systems; the specifics for each of the three families are provided as appendices. Many of the topics presented in this chapter are precursors to later full chapters.

SYSTEM SOFTWARE

System software is the set of instructions (a program) primarily responsible for directing and controlling hardware. System software is really nothing more than the commands that allow users to control the machine. For example, it contains the commands needed to tell the computer to move data from RAM to a floppy disk. System software also contains the command to move information from a floppy disk back into RAM.

System software is known by other names including *operating system, Disk Operating System*, and *master control program*. The names are important because they show the different roles and functions of system software. Operating system describes this type of software as software needed for operating the computer system. Disk Operating

System (DOS) describes one of the primary functions of system software—controlling the flow of data to and from disk drives. Master control describes software that controls the entire computer system.

There are two main uses of system software. First, users can directly control the computer by entering commands. For example, typing DIR on a computer with the MS-DOS operating system causes a list of all files to appear. On the Macintosh, double-clicking the mouse button while the pointer is on a program icon will start the program. These tasks are directed by the operating system.

Second, system software is used by other types of software. Word processors, spreadsheets, games, and all other types of applications software use system software to interface between the applications program and the computer hardware. For example, to save a file on a disk, the applications program sends a command to the operating system instructing it to save the file. Applications software does not actually perform the task.

Because the system software does the work, applications software written for the computer must also be written for the operating system. For a program to work on an IBM computer with the MS-DOS operating system, the program must use the operating commands of MS-DOS. Every piece of applications software must be written for, and include, commands in the system software, because operating systems differ from family to family. Operating systems are the reason there are different versions of software for different computers.

Controlling Disks and Files

The operating system contains the commands that control the flow of programs and data to and from auxiliary memory. This is one of the most important duties of system software because programs and data are typically stored on disks. The operating system directs the loading of computer programs and data from disks into the primary

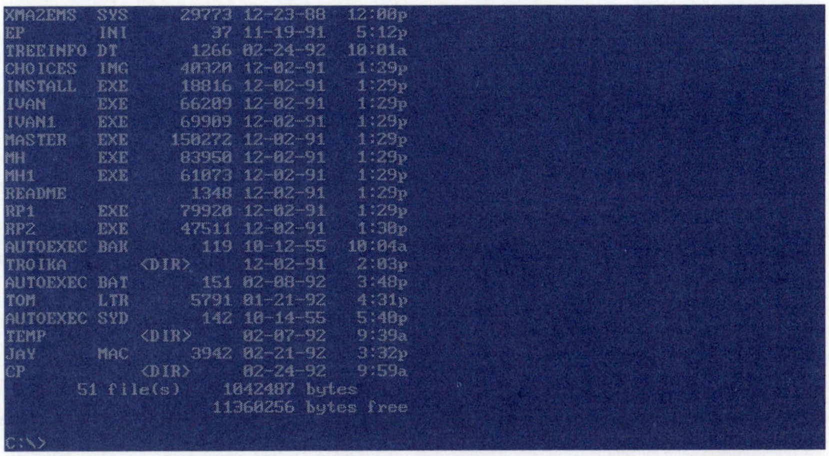

FIGURE 3-2
The most common system software for the IBM is MS-DOS (Microsoft Disk Operating System). The MS-DOS command DIR displays the contents of a disk.

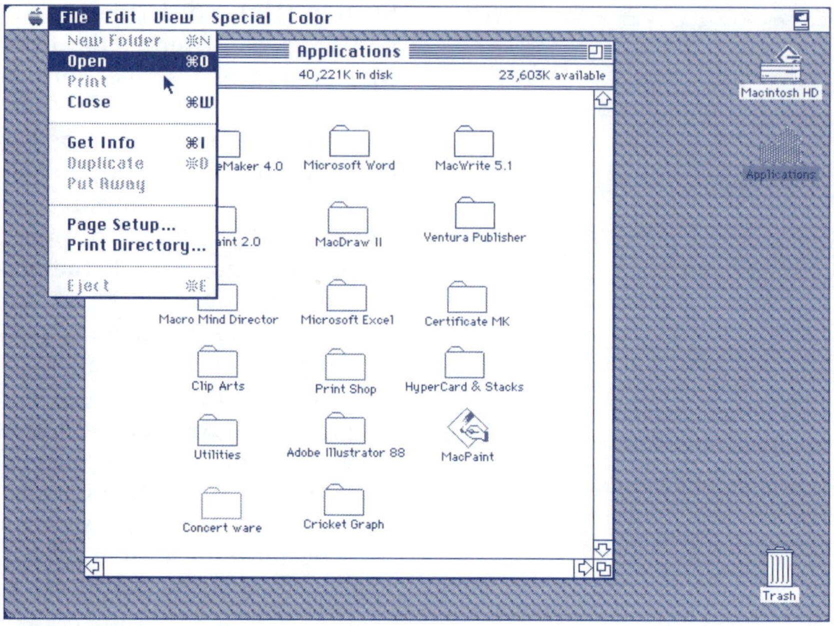

FIGURE 3-3
The Macintosh operating system, called System, uses graphics to control files on a disk. The little pictures, or icons, represent data and programs. Be sure to read Appendix A to learn about the operating system found on the Macintosh.

memory of the computer before executing program commands. Then it coordinates the computer hardware to execute program commands and controls the flow of data through an output device.

System software also controls the storage of information on disk. The operating system determines how much data to store on a disk, the arrangement of the data on the disk, and the means by which the data can be moved back to RAM for further work. Different operating systems create different organizational schemes for storing data. This is another reason why disks formatted on computers from differing families cannot be used interchangeably.

Controlling Peripherals

Another important task of system software is to control peripherals such as the monitor or printer. System software controls how data or information is sent to peripheral devices.

Controlling Program Execution

When learning to use any computer system, one of the first steps is to determine how to start a program. The command or procedure for executing (starting) software is controlled by the operating system. For example, executing a program using an IBM operating system is generally done by simply typing the name of the desired program and pressing the enter key. (Several variations will be presented later.) Executing a program through the Macintosh operating system is done by moving a mouse pointer onto the desired program icon and clicking the mouse button twice in rapid succession. Executing a program on an Apple IIe is usually part of start-up procedure.

Types of System Software

A variety of operating systems is available for microcomputers, and each family of microcomputers uses a unique operating system. For example, the IBM and IBM compatible family uses the operating systems MS-DOS (Microsoft-Disk Operating System) and PC-DOS (Personal Computer Disk Operating System). Microsoft produces MS-DOS; PC-DOS is an IBM product. Macintosh computers use a completely different operating system called System. Because Apple Computer, Inc. is the only producer of Macintosh computers, this is the operating system most commonly found on Macintosh computers. Within the Apple II family of computers, there are two popular operating systems—ProDOS and OS/GS.

These are only a few of many different types of operating systems available. For example, MS-DOS is the most common operating system for IBM, but some IBM and IBM compatible computers can use the UNIX, ZENIX, or OS/2 operating systems. System is the most common operating system on the Macintosh, but it can also use other operating systems, including UNIX.

SYSTEM UTILITY SOFTWARE

Some operating systems are difficult to use and do not provide an easy or efficient way to control the computer. System software such as MS-DOS requires users to remember many system commands to control the computer. Also, MS-DOS requires users to use these commands in a specific sequence. For example, to copy a file named *PAPER.TXT* from a floppy disk in drive A: to a hard disk, the following command must be typed in the correct order: COPY A: PAPER.TXT C:. *Any* deviation will cause the command to fail. To copy a whole set of files, there is a different Copy command. For some people, remembering all these commands and the order in which they must be entered can be difficult. For this reason, there are programs designed to help the user control the operating system. These programs are commonly known as **system utility software**.

Utility software works with the operating system to control disk drives, peripherals, and all operations normally accomplished by the operating system alone. System utility software "sits on top" or is "attached to" the operating system and makes the operating system easier to use. Utility software is not always necessary to use the computer (although some software requires its use), however, it is designed to eliminate the need for users to remember long series of commands.

With utility software, menus or hints are presented as reminders. Users choose the hint, or prompt, to use depending on what they need. For example, rather than type the command to copy a file, identify the file's location, the name of the file, and where to copy the file—in that order—system utility software provides a series of reminders guiding the user through the process of copying files from one location to another.

Some system utility software provides more control over the computer system than does the operating system alone. For example, utility software may contain options to organize programs and data on a disk drive, making the disk drive operate more efficiently. With this type of utility software, files may be located sequentially on a disk rather than being placed in different locations. Sequential placement speeds up the process of retrieving data. MS-DOS does not contain this or any similar command; it is found only on utility software. Some utility software permits the display of the contents of a disk onscreen without having to type a series of commands. For example, MS-DOS's DIR command lists files in the order they are stored on disk. Utility software can list files by the date last used, the name, the size, or several other specifications.

Shells, Program Managers, and the Graphical User Interface (GUI)

Several software manufacturers have developed menu-based programs to automate many of the DOS processes. These software packages are known as *shells.* Other manufacturers have developed more sophisticated programs to control the operating system by using pictures (icons) to represent programs and files. These are know as *program managers.* Three of the most popular types of system utility software are shells, program managers, and graphical user interfaces. Each takes a slightly different approach to making the operating system easier to use, but each does the same type of task.

Shells and program managers are most commonly associated with MS-DOS. (Operating systems such as System for Macintosh and OS/GS are not command-driven and therefore do not typically use shells and program managers.) With the more recent releases of MS-DOS, a DOS Shell is included with the operating system. DOS Shell from Microsoft uses a series of menus to execute the most frequently used commands.

Program managers **Program managers** also change the way DOS commands are issued. As with DOS shells, program managers permit control of the operating system. However, program managers often add several enhancements. One popular example of this type of software is Microsoft Windows for MS-DOS computers. Windows, as it is commonly called, adds the ability to run more than one application program at a time. This process, known as **multitasking**, makes it possible to work with several programs simultaneously and move data between programs quickly and efficiently. For example, with Windows it is possible to receive data through a modem while working on a word processing document.

> *Teaching Tool*
>
> **Staff Development**
>
> Most school districts require teachers to spend several days per year learning new teaching techniques, developing strategies for better classroom management, studying parent-teacher relations, and a host of other teacher training topics. The problem is that teachers often need further training, or training at a different time than the allotted in-service days. The solution for many teachers is for administration to develop customized in-service programs.
>
> Customized in-service programs provide teacher training specific to the teacher. With a computer and selected software, teachers can make training time more flexibly meet their schedule. If a teacher needs to learn to use a new classroom grade book, or even learn about techniques involved in implementing a cooperative learning model, learning by doing with special training software provides a customized solution. Computer-based training programs fulfill the needs of individual classroom teachers, provide scheduling flexibility, and allow teachers to work at their own pace.

FIGURE 3-4
One of the many features of Windows is a help screen that guides users through controlling the computer.

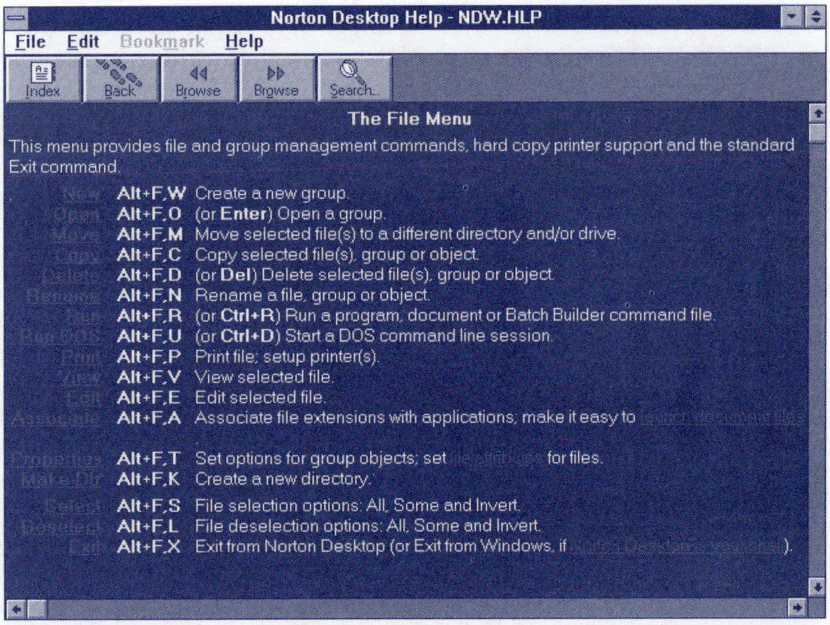

With MS-DOS, the keyboard is used to enter and issue all operating system commands. The command structure of Windows, in contrast, is graphics-based—a **graphical user interface**. Windows converts many text-based commands to easy-to-follow graphic pictures known as *icons*. Windows provides screen displays containing a variety of icons through which one can control the operating system. Simple mouse movements execute the commands.

For the Macintosh computer, a very special type of user interface is required to make System work. This interface is Finder. Like Windows, Finder is a graphical user interface; in fact, Macintosh made graphical user interfaces popular. However, unlike Windows, Finder *must* be working to control the operating system. System and Finder are so closely interrelated that many people identify the operating system on the Macintosh as System/Finder.

The Apple IIgs also uses a Finder to control its operating system. In fact, the Finder for the Macintosh and the Finder for the Apple IIgs are very similar.

Other System Utilities

Besides adding controlling features to operating systems, there are hundreds of other utilities dedicated to making a computer operate more efficiently. There are programs that manage computer memory. There are programs that help protect programs from viruses that destroy programs and data. There are programs that condense the size of hard disk files, resulting in more room for additional files. There are even utilities that cause the screen to look like a fish tank to protect the monitor if it is on but not being used. It would be impossible to list all of the different types of utilities in this text. Just be aware that utilities are available for a wide range of uses.

APPLICATIONS SOFTWARE

System software and system utility software make the computer work, but system software and utility software do not make the computer do the types of tasks most people need. In fact, most users do not pay much attention to system software unless there is a problem. What concerns most users is the software that makes the computer do the tasks they want. This software is known as applications software.

Applications software are those packages that make the computer process text (word processors), manipulate numbers (spreadsheets), store and locate large sets of data (databases), connect the computer to others through telephone lines (modems), generate graphic images (graphics software), produce high quality documents (desktop publishers), and more. However, before looking at each of the major types of applications software, keep in mind that it is the system software that allows an application to work and utility software that makes accessing the application easier. Still, it is the application itself that makes the computer valuable to users.

In education there are many types of applications software. There is software to provide students with drill and practice activities on concepts taught previously. There is tutorial software to provide direct instruction. There is software to help teachers manage and compile student grades. In fact, the list is almost endless. However, a group of applications software is common to both education and to the general business community. In fact, this software is so common that it makes up as much as 80 percent of all the work done on all computers. The group is known as the Big Six.

The Big Six

Most microcomputer users work with one or more of the six most common types of applications software. These are word processors, spreadsheets, databases, graphics programs, telecommunications, and desktop publishing. Because each of these applications plays such an important role in the use of computers, a separate chapter is devoted to each. However, understanding each type should make understanding any application software easier.

Word processing A **word processor** is a program designed to manipulate text. It permits users to enter, edit, and change text. The basic use of a word processor entails three important steps. First, text may be entered directly. After entering text, the second step is to edit it. The third step is proofreading the printed document for mistakes and correcting the original word processing file.

Using a word processor makes editing much easier than using traditional pencil and paper. After typing a document with a word processor, retyping the entire document is not required, no matter how substantial the changes. It is possible to correct mistakes, move sentences and large blocks of text, and even check the spelling of a document before printing a copy.

There are many varieties of word processors. There are as many brands of word processors as there are computer manufacturers—maybe more. To give you some idea of the features of word processors, read the following list. These features allow users to:

- automatically check the spelling of an entire document.
- automatically check the spelling of a single word.
- create an index and table of contents.
- generate outlines.
- boldface, center, and underline text.
- sort alphabetically.
- use several different typefaces or fonts.
- consult a thesaurus.
- incorporate graphics into a document.
- work on more than one document at a time.
- use automatic headers and footers.
- automatically number pages.

Word processing has become such a popular application that this software, more than any other, has motivated many people to become computer-literate. Because word processing makes writing easier, many people have reason to use word processors.

Spreadsheets Businesses need to know what they must do to survive and grow. This calls for business forecasting, and business forecasting requires the manipulation of numbers. Spreadsheets, the second most popular type of applications software, help users manipulate numbers.

A spreadsheet is a large grid made up of several columns and rows that intersect at cells. Cells are spreadsheet locations for entering and storing information. Each cell may contain a number, a label identifying the number, formulas for mathematical calculation, or even dates. For example, a label may identify the amount of sales referred to by a number, or it may identify the number of hours worked by an employee. Spreadsheets use formulas to perform mathematical operations. For example, an addition formula sums the values in any column or row. An averaging feature automatically averages a column or row. Virtually all forms of arithmetic operations are available in most spreadsheet applications.

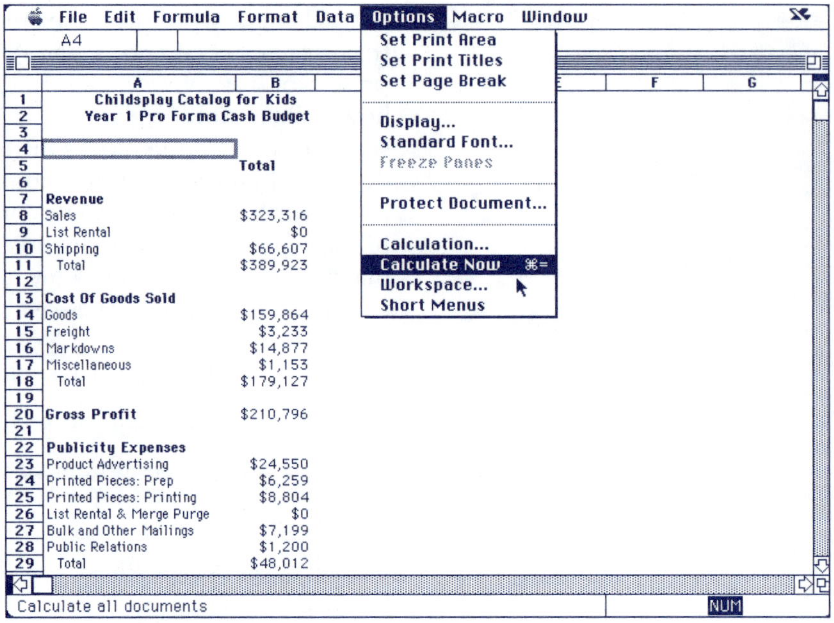

FIGURE 3-5
Microsoft Excel is a spreadsheet popular with Macintosh users.

All spreadsheets allow users to enter and manipulate numbers within a grid, and many spreadsheets offer a variety of additional features. Common features allow users to:

- print spreadsheets in a variety of formats.
- do statistical calculations.
- chart and graph information.
- move a spreadsheet into a word processing file.
- automatically change entire series of data.
- copy, cut, and move information to a variety of locations within the spreadsheet.
- format text for a polished look.
- make changes in one file and have the changes recorded automatically in other files.

Databases One of the strengths of computers is the ability to store and recall large amounts of data. In addition to storing data and quickly recalling it, computers can sort through data to locate specific types of information. Databases can store form letters from word processors, mailing lists, accounting information, personnel records, salary schedules, social security numbers, places of birth, credit histories, military service records, high school and college grades, political party affiliations, and much more. After storing data, database software can retrieve it in a variety of different ways.

As with all software, database software comes with a variety of features and capabilities. A few of the most common features allow users to:

- enter information in a variety of forms.
- sort information alphabetically or numerically.
- retrieve all or part of the information in the database.
- locate information that matches specific characteristics.
- isolate information not consistent with the structure of the database.
- generate detailed reports about all or selected information within the database.
- chart and graph information within the database.
- send information to other database software or other applications software.
- print information in a variety of forms.

Graphics Graphics software allows users to create visual displays. These include pie charts, bar graphs, and histograms generated from data, as well as pictures and other graphic representations designed by a graphic designer. Graphics software also helps those with limited artistic skills create a variety of visual displays.

Some graphics software makes pictures of information generated by a computer. For example, a spreadsheet may report school budget information as a list of percentages for different expenses. Computer graphics software can create a pie chart depicting each of these expense categories. The pie chart makes the abstract percentage information concrete.

Computer graphics software can also help produce television and movie titles, create company logos, and produce visual images. These programs can also produce and control video segments. Many professional artists use graphics software to produce cartoons, create commercials, and animate advertising. Art created with computer graphics software is also becoming a genre in its own right.

The following lists a few of the most common features of graphics software. These features allow users to:

- create lines of different size.
- type and alter type.
- change colors in specific areas.
- import graphics from other programs.
- draw circles, squares, rectangles, and rounded rectangles, and draw freehand images.
- rotate graphic images.

Teaching Tool

What's My Grade So Far?

These words are spoken in almost every class. The problem is not the question, but the answer. It can take a teacher a great deal of time to calculate just one student's grade. Having to calculate grades each time that question is asked can take away from the time a teacher has for instruction. The answer for many is the classroom grade book. With grade management software, teachers can answer these and many other questions with a simple press of a button. Teachers can also produce monthly, weekly, even daily report cards for any or all students.

- automatically scale graphics to different sizes.
- use a wide range of drawing tools, such as a computer "paint-brush" or "spray can."
- cut and copy different parts of a graphic image.

Telecommunications The fifth major software application type is telecommunications software. With this type of software, computers can share data or information through telephone lines. Using telephone lines for telecommunications requires software and a modem (MOdulator-DEModulator). **Modems** work by translating digital computer information to a continuous (analog) signal that can be sent over telephone lines, then translating the analog signal back to a digital signal at the receiving end. When computers communicate, both computers need modems—one modem to send and one to receive. Telecommunications software controls information transfer through the modem.

Computer telecommunications ability offers exciting possibilities. One possibility is having students gather research information from data housed in a distant computer. Imagine a student wanting to learn about Native American history. Telecommunications software enables the student to examine articles and reference material from almost anywhere in the world. A student may use telecommunications software to review a number and variety of periodicals to find information for a term paper.

Computers can access other computers if both computers have a modem, telecommunications software, and the user has permission. Unfortunately, computer information is not secure. Some unscrupulous individuals use telecommunications to get private

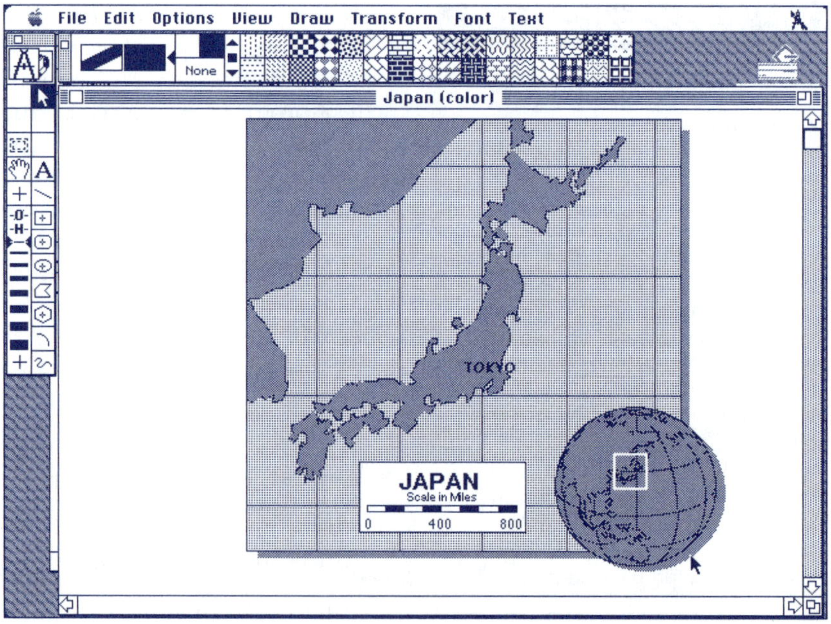

FIGURE 3-6
Drawing programs make it easy to produce high-quality graphic displays.

information. For example, during the recent Persian Gulf War, several Dutch youths used computers to access confidential Pentagon information. Doing so is unethical, illegal, and legally punishable in many states.

Desktop publishing Although word processing software enables users to enter, edit, and print text very easily, most word processing software packages have several limitations. One of the major limitations of word processing software is they cannot produce stylish publications such as magazines or brochures, nor can they easily format lengthy publications. Because of the limitations of word processors, another type of software, desktop publishing software, has become popular.

Desktop publishing software performs four important tasks. First, it is possible to use desktop publishing software to enter text as with a word processor. Desktop publishing software, however, is not a very efficient word processor. Second, it can take a document created on a word processor and automatically change the type's attributes (style, size and so on) and alignment on the page. Third, it can integrate text and graphics within a single document. Fourth, the software can easily publish lengthy documents, books, and even series of books.

There are many different types of desktop publishing software available, from the simple and easy-to-learn to the more complex and sophisticated programs. The following list contains a few of the most common features of these programs. These features allow users to:

- import and combine text and graphic files from a variety of sources.
- edit text and change its appearance.
- use a full range of type faces (fonts) and sizes, and control typography.
- adjust the sizes of graphic images.
- draw lines, circles, squares, rectangles, and rounded rectangles.
- use color as a part of the graphic design.
- re-create a wide range of graphic designs.

Computer Assisted Instruction (CAI)

One popular group of software in schools helps students learn conceptual information. **Computer assisted instruction**, or CAI, comes in many forms, but all share the same goal—to help students learn.

CAI software is difficult to classify. Because it is software designed to enhance the learning process, the many different programs take a variety of approaches. Some CAI software simply drills students on concepts taught previously. Other software provides direct instruction. Still other software combines these two. One reason CAI is difficult to classify is the crossover between major types. Nevertheless, many educators classify four major types of CAI software—**drill and practice, tutorial, simulation**, and **problem-solving**.

Drill and practice Drill and practice software is the most widely-known type of CAI. Briefly, it provides problems or questions for students to solve, but does not help solve the problem. Rather, it prompts a student for an answer to a question or problem, then informs the user whether their reply was correct or incorrect. For example, math drill and practice software may provide fifty addition problems for students. If students answer correctly, the software provides a positive reply. If the answer is wrong, a negative reply comes from the software.

Many educators incorrectly equate drill and practice software to old-style ditto sheets. While both encourage practice, there is a big difference between drill and practice software and ditto sheets. Ditto sheets do not offer immediate feedback. It is possible for a student, thinking each answer is correct, to answer innumerable math questions incorrectly on a ditto sheet. This is not possible with drill and practice software. Drill and practice provides immediate response and reinforcement. Dittos don't.

Tutorial Direct instruction is the primary characteristic of tutorial software. Its goal is to present new concepts and new ideas. Unlike drill and practice software, tutorials often determine a student's level of knowledge, then present new information to build on that existing knowledge. For example, a tutorial designed to teach students about Native American history may begin with an overview of major historic events and personalities, then offer a chronological discussion of the major events. Tutorial software may use graphics and sound for more appealing learning, or it may be completely text-based.

Two common uses of tutorial software are for reinforcement and remediation. If a student has trouble comprehending a specific lesson, teachers can use tutorial software for a different mode of instruction. If a student misses a class on two-digit addition, instead of moving on to three-digit addition, the student can use tutorial software to cover the missed material. Teachers often have a difficult time helping students make up missed class lectures. Tutorial software can help.

Simulation Teachers try to give students real-world experiences in the classroom. After all, experiencing a situation, making decisions, and seeing the results of those decisions can be a valuable learning experience. However, it can be difficult, dangerous, or impossible to provide students with some real-world decisionmaking experiences. Simulation software helps bring real-world situations into a safe and controlled environment.

Teaching Tool

Test Generation

Writing tests is not one of the tasks that many teachers enjoy. In fact, many teachers avoid giving tests just so they do not have to create them. The solution to this problem lies with a group of educational software tools commonly called test generators. Test generators, as their names imply, make it easier for teachers to create tests. The process of generating test items, however, is not much different than the traditional method. The time-saving occurs with test generators in two ways. First, many test generators come with a test bank—a list of test questions. Test banks are usually provided with accompanying text books. In college courses, many introductory course texts provide the instructor with hundreds of test questions. Second, many test generators store items from which the teacher can select. The teacher can then select the items to use for each test. Test generators also make it easy to generate several different versions of a test by changing the order in which test items are presented, or even change the items from specific groups. For example, a test generator may store 20 items on hardware and randomly pick 5 for form A and 5 for form B.

Teaching students about the process of nuclear power generation often involves a lecture on how rods control the amount of steam generated in a power plant. A teacher may show a film or take students to a power plant for a field trip, but no nuclear facility lets students control the rods to see what happens. Simulation software can put students at the controls of a nuclear power station. With this type of software, students can simulate a nuclear meltdown without releasing a radioactive cloud.

Problem solving Problem solving software gives students a problem and offers several alternatives for solving it. This type of software is *open-ended*, meaning that multiple solutions exist for a single problem. For example, problem-solving software may ask students to draw a hexagon. One student's hexagon may be small, and another student's hexagon large. One student may draw hexagons to the left, another draw them to the right. Although different in all these situations the answer is correct.

Some problem-solving software tries to teach students a process for problem solving. These programs may teach students to break a problem into several very specific phases. For example, this software may teach students to apply the phases for solving problems (recognition, planning, work, and action phases).

Other Types of Applications Software

There are so many types of applications software we cannot begin to describe them all. However, the following should give you some idea of the wide variety of available software.

Games Microcomputer games can be an important part of a teacher's educational repertoire. Many games challenge the intellect; others enhance manual dexterity. For example, current microcomputer chess games play almost as well as a grand master. They can offer a stiff challenge for most chess players and improve the average player's skills. Chess games are particularly appealing to young and older adults, but even younger children become skillful when playing chess against a microcomputer. Still other games can develop good hand-eye coordination. Many of these types of games require moving little screen figures and coordinating their movement with "hazards" built into the game. These types of games are certainly fascinating to younger microcomputer users.

CAD/CAM This software is commonly used in Technology Education and Industrial Technology programs in high school and adult education classes. **Computer aided design** and **computer aided manufacturing** programs allow users to make electronic blueprints and designs of a wide range of products. For example, a telephone installation company may use a CAD program to help design the proper locations for placing telephone wires in buildings under construction. Automobile manufacturers use CAD software

FIGURE 3-7
Bulletin board software makes it easy for many users to have access to a wide range of information.

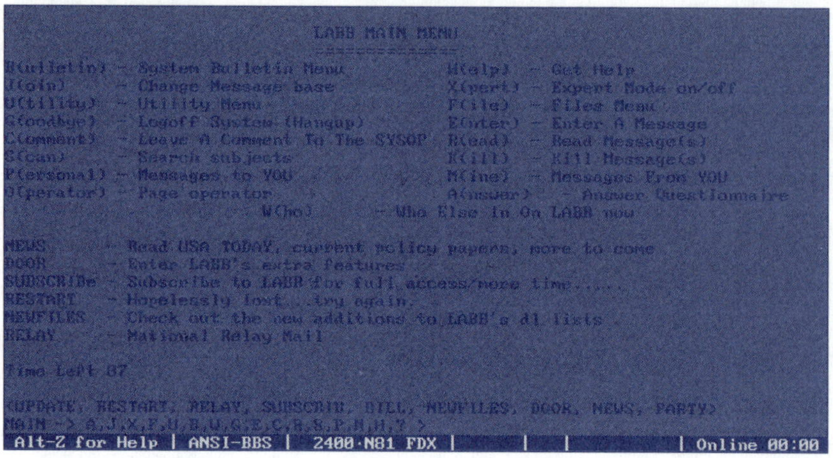

to design new models of cars. Computer aided manufacturing software allows computers to control the production of new products. For example, a CAM program can direct the exact placement of automobile parts as part of the machining process.

Electronic bulletin boards Teachers often use bulletin boards to share instructional ideas with other teachers. Electronic bulletin board software lets users share information with other users. Using a modem, microcomputer users can call a bulletin board service (BBS). There are many free electronic bulletin boards in most cities. These free bulletin boards may be sponsored by computer clubs or retail computer sales outlets. People who use bulletin boards can leave public messages, available to anyone using the service. This is very similar to posting a notice on a bulletin board. With many bulletin board services, users can also leave private messages for other users, provide software and hardware tips, and download or upload public domain software. In addition to free bulletin boards, there are commercial bulletin boards such as Dow Jones' and bulletin boards provided by software publishers.

Tax preparation In high school business courses, learning to prepare taxes can be a valuable skill. Not only can tax preparation software help students learn to file taxes, it is a great tool for teaching the impact of legislation on individual taxation. Many people find income tax preparation software a valuable tool. Every year software is redesigned to take advantages of new tax legislation. This software helps users prepare their annual income tax statements. In addition, the IRS accepts electronic income tax filing, since it reduces the amount of paperwork for the IRS. After filling out an electronic income tax form, the microcomputer operator uses a file transfer program to send the electronic income tax form to the IRS. For the filer, it speeds income tax returns.

Weather forecasting For the science teacher, weather forecasting software can be both entertaining and a great tool for teaching meteorology. With this software, students can generate their own forecasts based on data provided by the teacher or weather service bureaus. Students can then compare their forecasts with those on the local news. Weather forecasting software allows both professional and amateur meteorologists to store large amounts of data on weather patterns and make predictions based on that data. Of course, national weather forecasters use supercomputers to plot the enormous amount of data on atmospheric conditions when forecasting weather. However, many microcomputer programs allow users to generate forecasts based on smaller amounts of data provided by the National Weather Service. This allows smaller communities and amateur meteorologists to make weather predictions.

Statistical programs Statistical calculations involving large amounts of data are difficult and time-consuming to perform by hand. Statistical programs available for microcomputers can provide a variety of statistical analyses with ease. With these statistical programs, researchers can analyze their data at home or in their office with a small microcomputer. They no longer have to go to a large university or research organization to use a mainframe computer.

Image-generating programs Image-generating programs generate visual displays of various kinds. One very common type of image generating program is the ultrasound software used by physicians to display fetuses. Using ultrasound, physicians can diagnose medical problems and recommend treatments. Geologists also use visual images to analyze geological formations. Image-generating programs are used to reconstruct a picture of rock and soil formations. This can help determine what is below the surface of the earth. Meteorologists and astronomers use visual images to provide representations of radar data. For example, radar may detect certain types of atmospheric conditions. Image-generating software translates this data to a graphic display.

Music composition Music composition software automatically generates sheet music from music entered on a digitized keyboard or some other digital instrument. For example, a user can play a song on a keyboard. The software can display this digitized data as musical notes on a screen. The software can also transcribe music to different keys, times, and staffs, and allows musicians to experiment with an assortment of different musical controls.

Summary

- Three major types of software are system software, system utility software, and applications software.
- System software is the set of instructions (a program) that has primary responsibility for directing and controlling hardware.
- Applications software written for the computer must also be written for the operating system.
- The operating system contains the commands that control the flow of programs and data to and from auxiliary memory.
- Three of the most popular types of system utility software for operating systems are shells, program managers, and graphical user interfaces. Shells and program managers are most commonly associated with MS-DOS.
- Most microcomputer users spend their time working with one or more of the six most common types of applications software. These are word processors, spreadsheets, databases, graphics programs, telecommunications, and desktop publishing.
- Computer assisted instruction software is difficult to classify. Nevertheless, many educators feel there are four major types of CAI software—drill and practice, tutorial, simulation, and problem solving.

Fill-in Questions

Fill in the blank for each of the statements listed below.

1. Software can be placed into three major categories:

   _______________ , _______________ , and _______________ .

2. _______________ are programs that enhance the efficient operation of hardware.
3. _______________ provide users with several important system controls that either are not part of an operating system or are enhancements of existing operating system procedures.
4. Software that permits users to perform specific productive

   tasks are known as _______________ software.
5. _______________ software is written to solve a specific problem or perform a specific task for users of a certain family of computers.
6. _______________ software is designed to manipulate and control text.

Quiz

Answer the following questions.

1. Another term for system software is:
   a. utility software
   b. applications software
   c. operating system
   d. system control
2. All system utility software is text-based operating system software.
   a. true
   b. false
3. Spreadsheets can process:
   a. text
   b. numbers
   c. formulas
   d. all of the above
4. A menu program, known as a shell, is:
   a. system software
   b. utility software
   c. applications software
   d. financial software
5. The type of software that makes a microcomputer valuable to most users is:
   a. systems software
   b. utility software
   c. applications software
   d. word processing software
6. The most common software applications fall into a category known as:
   a. the big four
   b. the big five
   c. the big six
   d. the big seven
7. A thesaurus is found in which full featured applications software?
   a. word processor
   b. spreadsheet
   c. database
   d. graphics
8. What type of software would you use to locate a virus?
   a. systems software
   b. system utility software
   c. graphics software
   d. spreadsheet software
9. What type of software is a program manager?
   a. systems software
   b. utility software
   c. graphics software
   d. spreadsheet software

Exercises and Applications

Follow the instructions for each exercise and application.

1. Obtain a user's manual for a word processing program (e.g., WordStar, WordPerfect, Word) and create a list of the available features (e.g., spelling check, moving text, merging text). Next to each feature, place a Y for yes if the feature is important to

you or an N for no if it is not. Be ready to share your responses and explain your decisions.

2. How can educators use database software? List ten possible uses in education, and next to each describe how that use can benefit teachers, parents, students or administrators.
3. Collect ten different publications produced with desktop publishing software. Consider newsletters, manuscripts, resumes, brochures, or any other document that is visually appealing.
4. Imagine that you, as a new teacher, are asked to integrate computers into the classroom. Describe the types of computer software you would use and how they would benefit you and your students.
5. Video games are computer programs that entertain. Take some time to play a video game. Describe what features make the game fun and what features might improve the game.

4

ESSENTIALS OF INSTRUCTIONAL SOFTWARE

LEARNING OBJECTIVES

Learning the material in this chapter will enable you to:

- identify the major types of educational software
- describe Computer Assisted Instruction
- identify major educational paradigms
- describe six processes of information-processing theory
- discuss attention in learning
- discuss meaning in learning
- describe the uses of, and the major issues in, drill and practice software
- describe the uses of, and major issues in, tutorial software
- describe the uses of, and major issues in, simulation software

CHAPTER OVERVIEW

Chapter 3, Essentials of Software, introduced the basic types of software. While this introduction is important, to really understand computers in education you need to be familiar with the four major types of educational software—Computer Assisted Instruction, computer tools (applications), management, and computer science. This chapter will address Computer Assisted Instruction software.

LEARNING THEORIES

How do people learn? After innumerable debates and research projects by hundreds of philosophers and researchers, the answer is—we don't have a definitive answer. This does not mean that teaching and learning is a hit-or-miss proposition. Fortunately, we do know something about learning. Over the past 200 years, researchers have given us a great deal of insight and a foundation for understanding the teaching and learning processes. From this research, we can improve teaching and learning, so it is important to examine a bit of learning theory before looking at the issues of instructional software.

As with all endeavors that seek to expand knowledge, research into teaching and learning is based on sets of fundamental beliefs. In the discipline of education, there are several different belief systems known as *paradigms*. Different education paradigms provide different overall views of the teaching and learning process. The collection of related theories bases each paradigm. Some of the more popular educational paradigms include behaviorism (Skinner, operant conditioning, classical conditioning, reinforcement, and so on); developmental (Piaget, stages of development, conservation, moral development, and so on); and human cognition (Gagne, information processing, and so on).

While one can justifiably examine learning from each of these paradigms, in this book we will use the theory of human cognition as the paradigm of learning when examining instructional software. This is not to suggest that other theories and paradigms are not important. In fact, when appropriate, we will intersperse basic concepts of several other paradigms to help you develop an overall understanding of the teaching and learning process as it relates to instructional software.

An Overview of Human Cognition

Human cognition is the notion that learning is made up of approximately six distinct processes—reception, attention, short-term memory, encoding, long-term memory, and retrieval. Of course, theorists use a number of deviations and terms for these processes, but most include these six fundamental processes.

Each process plays a distinct and meaningful role in the outcome of learning; however, each process does not act in isolation.

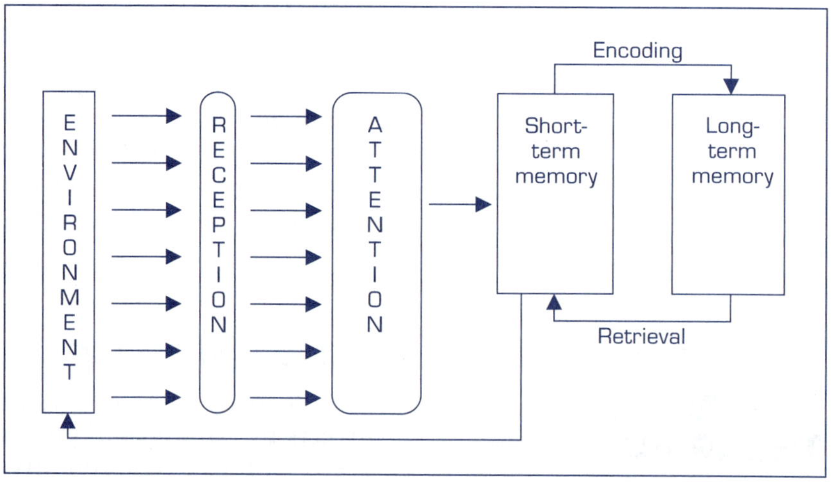

FIGURE 4-1
This is a simple model of a complex human operation. See if you can construct a model for learning to ride a bike.

Teaching Tool

Assessment

Teachers, school psychologists, school counselors and social workers often spend a great deal of time assessing students. Assessment can be for academic potential, social and emotional development, or diagnosis for specific types of problems. Computer software often makes this task much easier. There are computer programs available that will assess a student's reading ability, attitudes towards others, self-concept, even his or her personality traits. When used correctly by trained evaluators, this assessment software can provide an efficient tool.

Each of these processes, while independently important, combine to produce a specific learned capability. These types of learned capabilities include verbal knowledge, intellectual skills, cognitive strategies, motor skills, and attitudes. To understand human cognition one has to look at the six different processes, then examine how each process works within a prescribed model.

Reception The process of reception begins as our senses receive outside stimuli. Our senses, known as sensory receptors, not only *detect* stimuli, they *transform* stimuli into neural codes. These neural codes are impulses that carry information in a useable form. Information carried by neural codes resides, for very short time, in a store called the sensory register. In the short time it takes for information to be translated and put into the sensory register, usually only a few hundredths of a second, information is preserved in a near-exact state. In other words, all information received through our senses is stored exactly in our sensory register.

The most important aspect of the sensory register, other than receiving stimuli, is its volatility. While the sensory register stores virtually everything detected by our senses for a brief instant, the vast majority of information quickly decays or leaves the sensory register. Another process known as attention (discussed next) is the mechanism for moving information out of the sensory register to awareness.

Obviously, reception plays an important role in learning. While it may sound apparent, it is not possible to learn what is not received through the senses. All too often we assume learners receive information when in fact they do not. A student who is looking out the window cannot absorb what is written on the chalkboard. A computer program that does not attract the attention of at least one of the senses will not help students learn.

Attention Attention moves information from a very temporary state to a state of awareness. In its simplest form, it is only possible to learn what we attend. Conversely, anything that detracts our attention from the information, detracts from learning. Listening to a radio while reading a chemistry text is fine if you don't focus attention on the music. However, as soon as you focus attention on the music, the information from the book is lost.

Many people falsely assume that the more attention we pay, the more we learn. Not so. The lack of attention is as important as attention. If we paid attention to every piece of information received by our senses, we couldn't function. As soon as you wake, each of your senses is bombarded with stimuli. If you stop to pay close attention to all the sounds, smells, and sights, you would have little time to do anything else. Therefore, attention must be, and fortunately is, selective.

Think of attention as a filter that restricts the amount of information contacting the information and knowledge we already maintain. Information filtered out will not be learned. Information that makes it through the attention filter has a chance.

Focusing attention is, of course, a critical component of learning. Think of a student who sits through every class, yet fails the final. It is not enough to simply receive the information. Attention must be given for learning to occur.

Short-term memory Short-term memory, sometimes called working memory, is where most mental activities occur. Of course, only information that passes through the attention filter makes it into short-term memory. However, that alone does not ensure that learning will occur. Short-term memory has its own limitations.

One of the most important limitations of short-term memory is size. Short-term memory can contain about seven distinct pieces of information, plus or minus two. The second most important limitation is information maintenance in short-term memory. Only by continual attention will information remain in short-term memory. Try to recite the following letters: FLGASCNCVAMDDENJNY. Can you remember these without memorizing them? How about if you knew that they are state abbreviations from Florida to New York? Giving meaning makes it easier.

Many strategies help maintain information in short-term memory. The practice of *chunking,* or logically grouping pieces of information together, helps. For example, if the letters above represent the initials of family members, recall is easy. Nevertheless, the key to keeping information in short-term memory is attention.

Long-term memory Information in short-term memory must either be discarded or moved to permanent storage. Permanent storage is called long-term memory. *Encoding* is the process by which we move information from short-term memory to long-term memory.

Long-term memory is the final destination. Once information is in long-term memory in such a way that it can be recalled, learning has occurred; therefore, storage and retrieval of information into long-term memory is the goal of learning. (Recalling information from long-term memory is called *retrieval,* discussed in the next section.)

How information is stored in long-term memory is critical. Long-term memory is not like computer disk storage, on which information is stored without logical connection. Rather, long-term memory requires information have meaningful connection. Think of your kitchen; the appliances, the smells, the activities, and the furniture are all stored as meanings in your long-term memory. You can recall even the smallest "fact" of your kitchen because it has meaning. Take a few minutes to see how much detail you can recall.

For information to be meaningful, it must be linked or integrated with information already residing in long-term memory, commonly called prerequisite knowledge. If you want to "learn" someone's name it is much easier to link the name with the person's physical appearance. If you want to "learn" that a chicken is a bird you must first "learn" what a bird is. The lack of prerequisite knowledge may be why it is so difficult for many students to excel in chemistry.

Memorizing is often not an effective way of learning, because it does not provide meaning. If you write a series of notes that do not link the new knowledge to existing knowledge, learning will be very difficult. However, if you take new knowledge and apply it to what you already know, then learning will be much easier.

For teaching, either with software or by traditional instruction, understanding the role of meaning can be very critical. First, teachers must make sure students have the prerequisite knowledge needed for the new information. Second, providing students examples based on what they already know helps to establish the link. Writing a list of facts on a chalkboard will not help students connect new knowledge to existing knowledge. Third, asking students to verbalize what they have learned helps students make knowledge connections.

Besides meaning, information organization is of critical concern. It is generally believed that information is stored in an organized form of patterns or propositions, ideas, and concepts. Each independent proposition, idea, or concept is connected to others by relationships; learning best occurs when having organized links to existing knowledge. Presenting information randomly can be very confusing. Presenting information in a well-organized, logical sequence can be profitable.

One of the major distinguishing differences between long-term memory and short-term memory is size and consistency. Short-term memory is very limited in size. Long-term memory is considered unlimited. While information in short-term memory is ephemeral, once information is placed in long-term memory it may last indefinitely. Some believe that once information makes it to long-term memory, it is there forever. In other words, once you learn something you will never forget it. You may have a hard time recalling that information but you will never forget. This makes the process of retrieval critical.

Retrieval It does very little good to have large amounts of information in long-term memory if you cannot recall that information. Retrieval is the process by which information is recalled. If you see a robin and recall that it is a bird, retrieval from long-term memory has occurred. In many cases, retrieval is much more than simply recognizing information. Retrieval often generates a specific response to a stimuli. The response act occurs through what is known as the response generator. For example, if someone throws a ball at your face, you will do much more than recall the information "ball, face, pain." More than likely you will duck. The ducking occurs through the response generator.

Why do people forget things? The answer goes back to how you originally stored information in long-term memory.

As mentioned earlier, information is stored in an organized fashion, with each piece of information related to other information. If you think of these relationships as paths, retrieval means finding the correct or desired path to the information. Because we have so many paths, it is easy to become confused and lost in the "maze." When we first learn the information, the more paths we create, the easier it will be to recall. If you have but one path to the knowledge it will be very difficult to recall. If you build multiple paths by verbalizing the information or by linking the new information to several pieces of existing knowledge, it makes recall easier.

COMPUTER ASSISTED INSTRUCTION

There are two reasons why it is important to understand a bit of learning theory before examining the different types of available instructional software. First, good instructional software is based on sound research into the teaching and learning process. After all, what good is educational software if it is not an effective teaching tool? Second, understanding learning theory guides the effective integration of instructional software into a teaching and learning environment. Software may be designed to be instructionally effective, but if it does not link to other information in a classroom, the software will not be effective. Educational software does not work in isolation. It works best when fully integrated into an effective learning environment.

Computer Assisted Instructional (CAI) software is software designed either to assist a teacher in delivering content or take on the task as the primary content-delivery tool. As briefly discussed

FIGURE 4-2
Instructional software provides a valuable teaching and learning vehicle. Here a teacher and student work together to solve problems posed by instructional software.

Teaching Tool

Focused Drill and Practice

Some types of drill and practice software allow the teacher to generate customized drills. Instead of the software generating ten math problems or using the same ten problems for every student, customized drills enable the teacher to select which problems the students will receive. This makes it possible for a teacher to focus on both the strengths and weaknesses of individual students.

in Chapter 3, there are four major types of Computer Assisted Instruction—drill and practice, tutorial, simulation, and problem-solving. This chapter deals with the first three.

Drill and Practice

Drill and practice software does not teach new concepts or ideas, nor does it provide students with an independent vehicle for learning new information. But good drill and practice software does help students review, remediate, rehearse, and practice. The software does not teach, but provides the opportunity to ensure understanding of concepts.

A number of general criticisms have been levied against drill and practice software. As with most criticism, some is warranted, some is not. One of the principal criticisms is that drill and practice software does not fully use the capabilities of the computer system. Many examples of drill and practice software are said to act as electronic ditto sheets. That is, many of the types of drill that occur on screen could be accomplished just as easily with pen and paper.

Those who criticize drill and practice software on these grounds fail to consider two critical points. First, good drill and practice software provides immediate and effective feedback to students. It is not uncommon, for example when teaching math, to assign a large number of problems from a ditto sheet for students to practice two-digit addition. The hope is that through repetition, students will fully grasp the concepts taught in class. If the first problem of the ditto is 12 plus 19, and the student answers 211, the ditto gives no immediate feedback. In fact, a student who has a conceptual misunderstanding is likely to do all 50 problems incorrectly, believing they are all correct. At the very least, drill and practice software's corrections help prevent students from "learning" concepts incorrectly.

Good drill and practice software, as opposed to traditional ditto sheets, can reduce unnecessary redundancy. Many children grow up hating math. For some, it may be because they were assigned endless problems to complete, even after they fully understood a concept. Instead of having students complete large numbers of problems without knowing whether they are doing the work correctly, good drill and practice software can identify mastery when students complete 10 consecutive problems without error. Instead of doing innumerable problems, drill and practice software requires students do only enough problems to ensure understanding. Drill and practice software can help avoid overkill.

Another criticism of drill and practice software is it does not teach concepts. Of course not; that is not what the software is intended to do. The problem is not the software, but the reasons that teachers employ the software. If a teacher uses drill and practice software in the hope that students will learn two-digit addition, or any other concept, the teacher and students are doomed to failure.

The following are some of the major features available within the realm of drill and practice software.

Student control Giving students some control over the software can be very beneficial. However, software that provides too many options and too much control over the presentation of information can be detrimental. The key is to find a balance. In general, good drill and practice software does not allow students to decide how many problems or items are presented. If students are given the choice, they may choose far too few problems. It is better to have the software (or better still, the teacher) determine how many problems each student must complete to achieve mastery of a particular concept. One area of appropriate student control is the selection of general concept areas. For example, it is appropriate for students to select one-, two-, or three-digit addition problems, but not how many problems they will receive within each group.

It is generally appropriate for students to control the rate of presentation. This is commonly known as *pacing.* Students are naturally more receptive to information presented at a comfortable rate. Some students prefer a faster presentation, while others prefer to move more slowly.

Problem selection How a piece of drill and practice software selects problems to present to students can be critical. It does very little good to present problems that are too difficult or too easy for students. It is also inappropriate for the software to present such a limited selection of problems that the software can be mastered too quickly.

There are several methods that drill and practice software uses to generate problems, including random selection, organized queuing, flashcard queuing, and variable interval performance queuing. Random selection is probably the simplest. The software randomly selects the problems to present to students from a constant pool of problems. In some situations, this is appropriate; in others it is not. Random selection neither gives students control of the software, nor does it offer practice in a logical or sequential fashion.

Organized queuing is a method of selecting problems for a specified list. In this method, the drill is a sequence of problems often based on level of difficulty. Students are presented with easy problems first, leading to more difficult problems.

Flashcard queuing is an organized queuing method that works like flashcards. When a student is presented with a problem and answers it correctly, the problem doesn't recur. However, if the student fails to correctly answer the problem, it is returned to the end of the "pile" and presented again to the student. Mastery occurs when all problems are answered correctly.

In variable interval performance queuing, when students fail to answer a question, the problem is returned to the queue of questions at a location appropriate for the next presentation of problems. In other words, the presentation order or problem queue changes after each question. This constant adjustment causes the presentation of items to remain appropriate to the student. This is far more complex than the other methods of problem presentation.

Feedback Feedback is one of the most important aspects of any drill and practice software. Without appropriate feedback, drill and practice software is not much different or much better than traditional ditto sheets. But feedback is much more than saying "correct" or "incorrect." In fact, there are many different aspects of feedback.

The first type of feedback occurs with format errors. These are errors made in the presentation, rather than the content, of answers. For example, a format error may occur when a student enters a T for true instead of the letter A from a multiple choice list. It is unhelpful if the software views this as an incorrect response, rather than a format error. The correct type of feedback should be something like "Press the letter that corresponds to the correct answer" rather than "Wrong."

Positive feedback is most desirable, even for incorrect student responses. Negative statements, even ones done in a joking fashion, can be very offensive and do not enhance student learning.

Corrective feedback is much more helpful than pointing out errors. Software that uses the statement "Incorrect" is neither positive nor corrective. Imagine a student presented with the problem 19 plus 4, and the student responds with the answer 113. Drill and practice software often replies "Incorrect. The correct answer is 23." Unfortunately this is neither positive nor effectively corrective and is of very little value to the student. A more appropriate software response would be to analyze the student's answer and state "Not quite. Remember to carry."

With drill and practice software, discrimination errors are among the most common. These errors occur when students fail to identify items. For example, mistaking a square for a circle is a discrimination error. Feedback for discrimination errors should indicate that the answer given is the correct answer for a different problem. For example, if the software displays a circle and the student responds with "square," the appropriate feedback might be something like "Good try, but a square has four sides."

Student motivation Motivating students to learn is an important part of any good educational material. It is especially important with drill and practice software. Contrary to popular belief, drill and practice software does not have to be boring. Students can actually have fun using this software, thereby motivating them to learn.

There are many techniques to motivate students. One is through some form of competition. This can be competition against oneself, against others, or even against the computer. Of all these, competition against the computer can be very effective. The computer is a good loser, whereas competing against other students will always mean someone fails.

Changing the displays and varying the modes of presentation can also be valuable motivational tools. The same presentation over and over can become boring and cause students to lose concentration. Motivation can also be achieved by providing some form of reward at the end of the drill. Often some form of game or other fun activity is the reward for successfully completing one or more sections of the lesson.

Good Drill and Practice Software

The key with drill and practice software is to determine if the drill is necessary and appropriate to learning objectives. For a teacher making decisions about the use of drill and practice software, the question that should always be asked is "Is this the best for students given my desired learning outcomes?" If the answer is yes, then the software is likely to be appropriate. If no, then the teacher should look for other types of software or other types of educational material.

If the software is appropriate for learning objectives, there are several questions that a teacher should ask to determine if the software is any good. These questions are based on learning theory and the peculiarities of drill and practice software, and are listed below.

- Does the software clearly define the task at hand so students will be able to easily operate the program?
- Does the software use effective feedback?
- Does the software provide effective motivation?
- Does the software allow students to control appropriate portions of the software?
- Is the pacing appropriate?
- Does the software provide enough information for students to answer each problem?
- Does the software make sure students have the requisite knowledge to proceed successfully?
- Does the software determine mastery?
- Does the software focus on one concept at a time?
- Does the software provide an appropriate method of problem selection?
- Does the software monitor student performance and provide selective repetition and feedback?
- Does the software provide varied contexts of encoding and retrieval of information?
- Does the software help students link new information to existing knowledge?

- Can the software diagnose student errors and provide appropriate corrective feedback?
- Does the software allow students to practice the whole skill, rather than each individual component?
- Can the software be used in small cooperative group settings?

Tutorial Software

Unlike drill and practice software, tutorials are designed to teach new concepts and ideas. In their simplest form, tutorials are designed to present information to facilitate student learning. In general, tutorial software does not seek to provide prolonged practice, nor does it rely heavily on student assessment. These are found in other types of software. What tutorial software specializes in is providing students with another medium for the delivery of instruction.

Tutorial software is among the most commonly used software in schools. There are tutorials in virtually every discipline and at every grade level. Teachers use tutorial software for a host of instructional applications.

Imagine reviewing elementary math concepts. On Monday, you review single-digit addition. On Tuesday, you review two-digit addition. On Wednesday, the review covers three-digit addition; Thursday is set aside for an overall review. Quiz will be on Friday. Of course, math is not really taught in this manner, but let's assume, for this example, that three students miss school on Monday and Tuesday. Obviously, when these three students return to class, they will have missed information critical to the Wednesday lesson. In short, they may not have the knowledge necessary to be successful in three-digit addition. The three students may become hopelessly

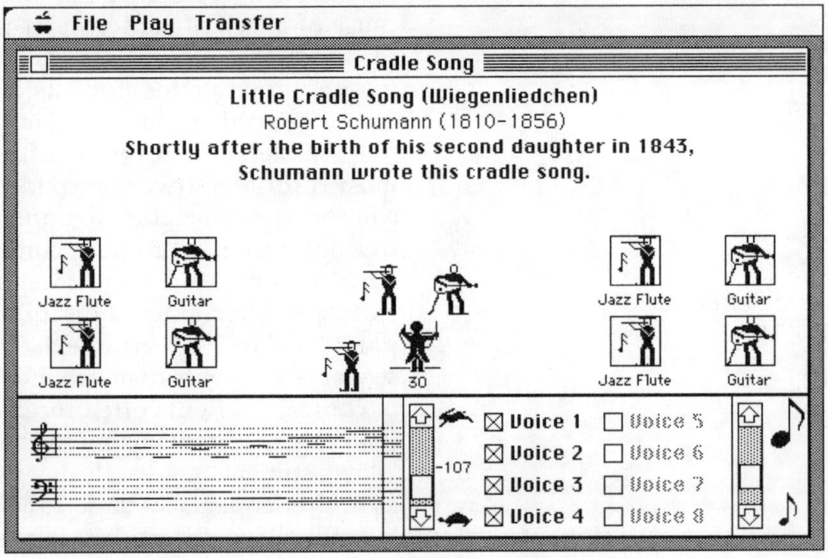

FIGURE 4-3
The program ConcertWare+ Music Player allows students to examine musical concepts.

Teaching Tool

Absentees

One of the most popular uses of tutorial software is for absentee students. Imagine a student missing two days of instruction on nouns. He or she will clearly have a difficult time without some type of additional instruction. Unfortunately, teachers don't always have the time to focus on one or two students when there are 28 others. Tutorial software provides a great alternative. If students miss a class covering vital information, they can be assigned portions of tutorial software for support. At the very least, they will get some exposure. At best they will have enough information to stay up with the rest of the class.

lost; unfortunately, most teachers haven't the time to provide the necessary make-up instruction. Fortunately, good tutorial software can provide an instructional alternative, so the students can receive much-needed instruction.

Now imagine teaching the same three lessons over three days without anybody missing a class. It is likely that some students will have a difficult time with some of the concepts. Again, the teacher may not have the time to provide the additional instructional help. Again, tutorial software can be a valuable tool. Instead of leaving students to flounder, a teacher can use tutorial software as a remediation tool, or even use it to provide students with an alternative method of instructional delivery.

Another problem for the teacher may be some students will quickly understand the concepts. As a teacher, you do not want to bore the students. Again, this type of software can allow students to learn new material by themselves.

Finally, there are some schools that find it economically impossible to offer all of the different courses that students need. For example, in many small high schools, students want and need a course in Organic Chemistry. Unfortunately, the school may be so small that the district cannot afford to hire another teacher for a specialized course. In this case, tutorial software can provide a vehicle for instructional delivery.

As with drill and practice software, many different features and facets make up good tutorial software; the following are some of these.

Student control Appropriate student control of the software is critical with tutorial software. Some suggest that students are better able to make decisions about the sequence of a tutorial presentation than are teachers. Others suggest that the more control a student has over the delivery of instruction, the less effective that instruction. Because of a lack of consensus regarding student control, the safe bet for successful tutorial software is to balance the control. It may be most appropriate for students to control the overall sequence rather than the specifics of instruction.

While some tutorial software permits total student control, most tutorial software provides one of three additional means of control. These include program control, adaptive control, and adaptive advisement. Program control exists when the program limits student control to mere direction (forward and backward). The software determines the sequence of events and the completion points. Adaptive control exists when the software determines the sequence of events to match individual student needs. With this type of control, students often receive instruction and content different than other students using the same software. Adaptive advisement allows students a great deal of control over the delivery, but advises as to the sequence. Adaptive advisement suggests what to do next, but still allows the student to make the final decision.

Sequencing Whether control over events is primarily with the student or with the computer, the sequencing of concepts is important with tutorial software. In general there are three sequencing techniques—linear sequencing, branching, and difficulty leveling.

Linear sequencing is the simplest of all. Concepts are presented one after another with no deviation in order. Typically, linear sequence tutorials present information in a step-by-step format where students provide limited responses. In most cases, linear tutorials use a hierarchical model. The software author takes a particular task, divides the task into components, and presents the components in the order needed to ultimately complete a task.

Branching takes student performance responses and determines, based on those responses, the next concept or idea. A tutorial that uses menus to allow students to select content is an example of a very simple type of branching. Branching also occurs when students answer a question. If the question is answered correctly, the student goes to a new question. If the question is answered incorrectly, the problem branches to an area of remediation.

Difficulty leveling adjusts the sequence of presentation based on the performance of the student. If a student is given a presentation on single-digit addition, then provided a ten-question quiz, difficulty leveling occurs when the program assesses student performance on the quiz, and determines the next question based on that performance.

Pretesting Pretesting is an important consideration with tutorial software. Unless the software is able to determine if students have the necessary prerequisite knowledge, then some students will likely find the content much too difficult, while others find the content

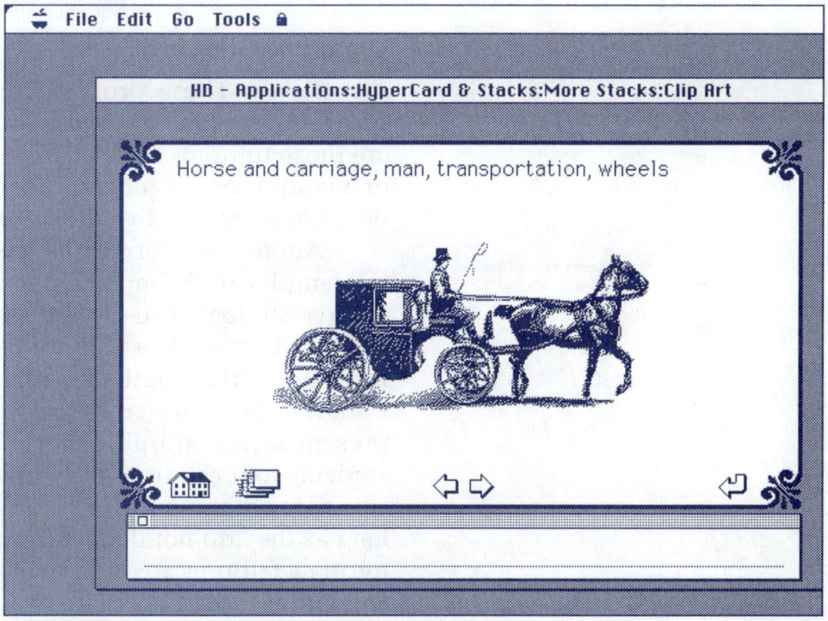

FIGURE 4-4
With HyperCard, teachers can develop their own instructional packages, customized for their own classrooms and students.

much too simple. Good tutorial software can make a determination and, using difficulty leveling, provide instruction tailored to the student's existing knowledge.

Motivation Motivation is also an important consideration. Students bored with the task will see the software and the method of instruction negatively.

There are two major types of motivation—intrinsic and extrinsic. Intrinsic motivation occurs when a student has an inherent desire to learn the subject of the software. For example, if a student is interested in sailing, almost any sailing software will be interesting enough for the student to explore. Extrinsic motivation is motivation external to, or independent of, the instruction. Sometimes this type of motivation can be in the form of a student reward. Of the two types, intrinsic motivation is far more desirable. Some suggest that with extrinsic motivation, student interest is only for the reward, not for the learning's value.

There are several ways to develop intrinsic motivation in students. If the tutorial is fun, motivation is likely to be very high. Also, providing student control, challenging students, developing curiosity, and encouraging students all help to further intrinsic motivation. Also, visually appealing software can be beneficial (more on this later).

One final issue of motivation is especially important with tutorial software. Motivation must be provided in moderation. Some tutorial software is designed to be so much fun that the student loses sight of the goal of increasing knowledge. Evaluate software carefully to see that it teaches what is necessary.

Modes of presentation Some software presents only text-based instruction. These programs can look very much like electronic books ("electronic page turners"). At the other end of the spectrum are those tutorials that fully use the graphics and sound capabilities of a computer. In general, the more diverse the mode of presentation, the more effective the tutorial software.

Another concern is the length and layout of the tutorial. Tutorial length can be important for many reasons. If a teacher's goal is to have students use the software in class, software that requires 54 minutes to complete will not be very effective in a 50 minute class. In addition, the length of components within a tutorial is important. Usually, the more complex the tutorial, the greater the need to present information in short spurts, with ample opportunity for students to break from the software.

Graphics, sound, and animation are also very important as long as they do not detract from the objective of the software. Many tutorials fall prey to overuse of these features. Graphics, sound, and animation should illustrate or further important concepts.

Assessment and evaluation An important part of any tutorial is its ability to evaluate a student response. However, evaluating student responses is much more involved than determining if the answer to a question is right or wrong. Teachers often judge responses based on inflection, expression, failing to include important concepts, and recognizing rational decisionmaking. These are all difficult tasks for any computer program to undertake. However, some types of evaluations and assessments are appropriate for a tutorial.

Simple answers are the easiest and most common evaluation forms within tutorial software. There are single-selection answers, in which the tutorial judges if the answer is correct or incorrect. There is no gray area. Multiple-choice answers are much the same. Numeric answers, such as with problems, are also easy to judge as being correct or incorrect. However, it is difficult for a tutorial to consider the process used to obtain the answer. Normally, there are usually no points for partially correct answers.

String answers are somewhat common. String answers occur when a computer is able to judge if a set of characters (a string) is correct or incorrect. For example, if a question asks for the capital of Colorado, Denver is the correct string. The problem with string answers occurs if someone answers "Denever." Is this an incorrect answer? Unless the program is designed to accommodate certain spelling errors, most software will judge "Denever" as incorrect.

Good Tutorial Software

As with drill and practice software, the most important consideration with tutorial software is to determine if the tutorial is necessary and appropriate to learning objectives. Again, teachers should always ask "Is this the best for students given the desired learning outcomes?" If the answer is yes, then the software is likely to be appropriate. If no, then the teacher should look to other types of software or other types of educational material.

Given that the software is appropriate to the learning objectives, there are several questions that a teacher should ask to determine if the tutorial is appropriate. These questions are based on learning theory and the peculiarities of tutorial software. These are listed below.

- Does the software clearly define the task at hand so students will be able to easily operate the program?
- Does the software use effective feedback?
- Does the software provide effective motivation?
- Does the software allow students to control appropriate portions of the software?
- Is the pacing appropriate?

Teaching Tool

Graphing Math Data

In the teaching of math, graphing numeric data often poses instructional problems. First, students must understand the concepts involved in generating the graph. This is what teachers need to focus on most. Second, students must be able to convert data into a graphic representation. Again, this is often difficult for students if they do not have the necessary drawing skills. Some instructional math software is especially well-suited to helping students graph while supporting the conceptual development presented by the teacher.

- Does the software make sure students have the requisite knowledge to proceed successfully?
- Does the software determine mastery?
- Does the software focus on one concept at a time?
- What type of sequencing is employed?
- Does the software provide an appropriate method of problem selection?
- Does the software monitor student performance and provide selective repetition and feedback?
- Does the software provide varied contexts of encoding and retrieval of information?
- Does the software help students link new information to existing knowledge?
- Can the software diagnose student errors and provide appropriate corrective feedback?
- Does the software allow students to practice the whole skill, rather than each individual component separately?
- Can the software be used in small cooperative group settings?

Simulation

Simulation software is designed to approximate real-world experiences in a safe, controlled environment. Simulations are designed to provide students with experiences they might not otherwise have, allow them to make decisions, and permit them to see the consequences of those decisions. The ultimate goal of simulation software is to help students develop a mental model.

Like other types of software, there are several categories of simulation software. These include procedural, situational, physical, and process-oriented simulations.

Procedural simulations are designed to teach the procedure for accomplishing a specific goal. There are many examples of procedural simulations, including operating a nuclear power plant, flying an airplane, and building a house.

Situational simulations deal primarily with attitudes, behaviors, and beliefs. They differ from procedural simulations in that the goal is not to learn a specific skill but rather to examine social or behavioral issues. A common example might include role playing, management situations, or confrontational situations. A simulation designed to teach issues of classroom management to prospective teachers is an example of a situational simulation.

Physical simulations are commonly associated with scientific experimentation. They enable students to conduct experiments, modify variables, and judge the results of an experiment. Included in this type are simulations of mathematical or statistical modeling.

Process-oriented simulations are closely related to physical simulations. The major difference is that process-oriented simulations teach major concepts associated with an experiment, rather than only providing an experimental tool. These types of simulations are common in the social sciences. A sociologist may use a process-oriented simulation to forecast group behaviors. An economist might use a process-oriented simulation to forecast economic trends. They are called *process-oriented* because, in most cases, the user can modify a single variable and process the simulation based on a single modification. They also make it possible for students to accelerate or slow down a particular process to gain additional insight. For example, a student may act as the mayor of a city. In a matter of a few moments, the student is able to see the effect of taxes on municipal revenue, population growth, crime, and other factors over a ten-year period.

As with all other types of instructional software, there are several issues relating to the quality of simulation software. A few of these are listed below.

Motivation Simulation software is among the most enjoyable for students. Often they are presented in a game-like format, and students may not even realize they are learning sophisticated material. Of course, different types of software tend to be motivational for different types of learning outcomes. For example, physical simulations tend not to be game-like, but they can be very motivating in that students can develop complex experiments not normally available.

Process and situational simulation often are very motivational because they can resemble the electronic games that so many students play. In fact, some of these are so much fun that it is hard to get students to leave the software and discuss material.

Safe and controlled environments Many teachers look to simulation software to give students a learning opportunity that they could not normally offer. For example, a teacher interested in teaching the concepts of aerodynamics cannot take students up to fly a jumbo jet; a marine biology instructor cannot take students to the bottom of the sea. Obviously, process simulation provides a safe, controlled environment for this type of learning.

Practical All of the different types of simulations offer a very practical approach to teaching. Teaching students the variables involved with economic forecasting can be an exhausting experience. Further, teaching different economic trends and how to measure the effect of these trends adds to the difficulty. Because simulation software builds in the mathematical models, students do not need to spend as much time performing calculations when considering which variables to modify.

Sequence Issues of sequence are as important to simulations as they are to other types of software. Depending on the goals of the program, some simulations may be linear while others may use a branching technique. Still others may use recursive processes. The more complex the relationship of variables in the simulation, the more the issue of sequence plays a vital role in determining the simulation's effectiveness. It is important to remember that a simulation is only as effective as the programmers' design.

Good Simulation Software

As with other types of software, the most important consideration with simulation software is that it be necessary and appropriate to learning objectives. All too often, teachers select a simulation because it is fun and interesting, but it may have no bearing on the instructional goals of the classroom. There are several questions that a teacher should ask to determine if the software is appropriate. Many are the same as those that apply to other forms of instructional software.

- Does the software define the learning objectives?
- Is the software easy to use by students?
- Does the software provide a realistic set of controls over selected variables?
- Does the software motivate students?
- Does the software provide appropriate student control?
- Is the pacing appropriate to individual student needs?
- Does the software determine mastery?
- What type of sequencing is employed?
- Are there various levels of difficulty?
- Does the software monitor student performance and provide selective repetition and feedback?
- Does the software provide varied contexts of encoding and retrieval of information?
- Does the software help students link new information to existing knowledge?
- Can the software diagnose student errors and provide appropriate corrective feedback?
- Does the software allow students to practice the whole skill?
- Can the software be used in small cooperative group settings?

Summary

- A collection of related theories is a paradigm.
- Some of the more popular educational paradigms include behaviorism, developmental, and human cognition.
- Human cognition is the notion that learning is made up of approximately six distinct processes—reception, attention, short-term memory, encoding, long-term memory, and retrieval.
- Our senses, known as sensory receptors, not only detect stimuli, they transform stimuli into neural codes. Information carried by neural codes resides, for a very short time, in a store called the sensory register.
- It is the process of attention that moves information from a very temporary state to a state of awareness.
- Short-term memory, sometimes called working memory, is the location where most mental activities occur. Only information which passes through the attention filter makes it into short-term memory.
- For active information in short-term memory, a decision must be made to either discard the information or move it to permanent storage. Permanent storage is called long-term memory.
- Encoding is the process by which we move information from short-term memory to long-term memory.
- Retrieval is the process by which information is recalled or recorded.
- Drill and practice software does not teach new concepts or ideas.
- Tutorials are designed to teach new concepts and ideas.
- Simulation software is designed to provide students with an approximation of real-world experiences in a safe, controlled environment.
- There are several categories of simulation software including procedural, situational, physical, and process oriented simulations.

Fill-In Questions

Fill in the blank for each of the statements listed below.

1. Some of the more popular educational paradigms include

   _______________ , _______________ , and _______________ .

2. Our senses transform stimuli into _______________ .

3. Information carried by neural codes resides in a store called the ________________ .
4. Short-term memory is also known as ________________ .
5. With drill and practice software, selecting problems from an organized list is known as ________________ or ________________ .
6. One of the most important aspects of any drill and practice software is ________________ .

Quiz

Answer the following questions.

1. A collection of theories or belief systems about learning is often referred to as:
   a. legitimating ideologies
   b. educational objectives
   c. paradigms
   d. building blocks of learning
2. Human cognition is the notion that learning is made up of ________________ distinct processes.
   a. two
   b. four
   c. six
   d. eight
3. Most of the processes of human cognition operate in isolation.
   a. true
   b. false
4. The most important aspect of the sensory register, other than receiving stimuli, is its:
   a. volatility
   b. long term effects
   c. action
   d. encoding action
5. The more we pay attention, the more we learn.
   a. true
   b. false
6. The best way to think of the process of attention is to think of it as a:
   a. skill
   b. filter
   c. large receptor
   d. delimiter
7. As a general rule, short-term memory can contain about ________________ distinct pieces of information, plus or minus two.
   a. 3
   b. 5
   c. 7
   d. 9

8. Drill and practice software provides the opportunity to ensure understanding of concepts.
   a. true b. false

9. With drill and practice software, ______________ errors are among the most common.
   a. omission b. commission
   c. typing d. discrimination

10. Tutorial software seeks to provide prolonged practice as well as relying heavily on student assessment.
   a. true b. false

Exercises and Applications

Follow the instructions for each exercise and application.

1. Pick five pieces of instructional software. Identify which type of CAI the software represents. What makes the software that type? Does the software have elements of other forms of CAI?
2. Develop an instructional plan for incorporating one piece of educational software into classroom instruction. Which type of software will you select? Why did you choose that software? Are there other software options?

5

ESSENTIALS OF WORD PROCESSING AND DESKTOP PUBLISHING

LEARNING OBJECTIVES

Learning the material in this chapter will enable you to:

- describe word processing and desktop publishing
- identify the major controlling features of word processing software
- list the major rules for using word processors
- describe why desktop publishing is more than a series of typesetting tools
- identify the major page layout features of word processing and desktop publishing software
- identify the differences between a work processor and a desktop publisher

CHAPTER OVERVIEW

To be an effective teacher, you must communicate effectively. As most professionals know, there are two issues involved with effective communication—content and style. Content is the meaning of the message. Style is the presentation and appearance of words. (Some argue that the two are inseparable, but we'll accept the distinction.)

As most college students quickly learn, content and style work hand-in-hand. A well-conceived and well-written term paper, full of good ideas, but handwritten on a yellow legal pad is likely to be perceived as a poor term paper. The same paper, neatly produced, is likely to be perceived much better. In other words, looks are important. After all, why do students put their papers in plastic binders?

Most college students also know that good style is not enough. Content is critical. No matter how attractive or how effective the style, a term paper that is poorly or awkwardly written will always be perceived as a poor paper. Style cannot hide content.

For microcomputers, two types of software support content and style. Word processing software is designed to help teachers and students write effectively. Desktop publishing software is designed to help teachers and students effectively present their messages.

As you read this chapter, focus on the concepts of word processing and consider how these concepts can make writing easier, more efficient, and better. After considering issues of word processing, focus on the concepts of desktop publishing to enhance the appearance and presentation.

WORD PROCESSING

Word processing software permits users to type words into a computer, make changes, determine the appearance of the words, then store the whole document as a file in auxiliary memory. This is a different process than using a standard typewriter. While a typewriter puts words directly on a sheet of paper, a word processor stores words electronically. Because words displayed on a computer screen are easier to change than permanent words on a piece of paper, revision is much easier. Making changes with a typewriter requires retyping the entire document. Making changes with a word processor entails typing only the desired changes.

Interestingly, typewriters are beginning to look more and more like word processors. Many typewriters have electronic storage. Small screens display typed words before they appear on paper, allowing the user to correct mistakes before they are printed. Newer-model typewriters have features, such as automatic centering, that are routine on word processors. Because of these improvements in typewriters, it is more appropriate to say that typewriters have become less sophisticated word processors.

Teachers, Students, and Word Processors

So much of a teacher's and student's day is spent writing. For a teacher, a day's worth of writing may include a letter to parents, a note to the principal and, of course, grading essays, reports, and other forms of writing. Prior to the advent of word processors, for teachers to send a personal letter to parents involved a great deal of writing and typing. Although the basic content of the letters to parents may be the same, having to type letters individually is at best cumbersome. Word processing software makes this task very easy. Many word processors allow teachers to develop a list of parent names and addresses. Based on this list, teachers can type one letter, then merge parent names and addresses with the text of the letter. This gives the appearance of a personal letter.

For students and teachers alike, writing is an acquired skill. People improve their writing as they improve any other skill—through practice. Until word processors became available, practicing writing skills involved the tedium of retyping the entire document after each edit. By eliminating the drudgery of frequent retyping, word processors have made editing and rewriting easier. When it is easy to go back and improve a piece of writing, we are more likely to do it, and we are more likely to produce a better document.

For students, writing with a word processor is fast becoming a fundamental skill. In fact, more and more teachers require their students to submit writing created with a word processor. There are two main advantages. First, using a word processor makes writing easier. Students can spend more time on the message than the mechanics. Second, grading written assignments onscreen can be easier and more effective. Some word processing programs allow teachers to make suggestions directly on a student document. From these suggestions, students can improve their writing without having to redo the entire work.

Teachers and students (mostly teachers) who have never used word processors often express four basic fears: 1) I cannot type; 2) Computers and I don't get along well; 3) What if I don't like my changes and I want my original work back?; and 4) I have been writing with a pencil and paper all my life—why should I change now? Any one of these fears may keep a person from using a word processor, but they don't have to.

1. *I cannot type.* Typing is a necessary skill for using a word processor. However, good typing skills are not required to make word processors work effectively. In fact, word processors' features make producing a final document easier. Making typing mistakes

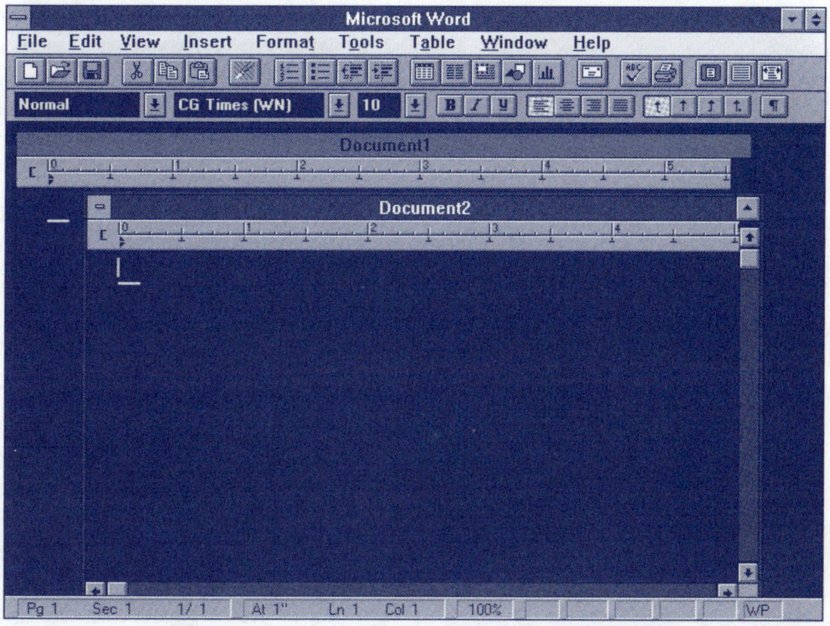

FIGURE 5-1
Some word processors provide controlling commands onscreen that make editing a document very easy.

Teaching Tool

Voice Typing

For many students, the process of typing as a means of creating text in a word processor creates a difficult challenge. Students who are dyslexic and students with other special challenges are at a clear disadvantage when using a keyboard. Today, voice recognition systems are becoming more common and useful. Students can dictate to the word processor, which will "type" the student's words onscreen. Not only does this means of data entry offer real advantages for students with special challenges, it offers all students the opportunity to develop a new method of "writing."

should not be a concern, since typing errors can be easily fixed before printing. Also, as with writing, the more teachers and students type, the better they get.

2. *Computers and I don't get along well.* Most people are cautious about computers at first. Unfamiliar technologies can be intimidating. Unfortunately, this fear of the unknown keeps many teachers from taking advantage of using a word processor or, worse, keeps them from teaching students to use a word processor. However, this anxiety soon disappears with practice and the realization that, with normal use, the computer will not break.

3. *What if I don't like my changes, and I want my original work back?* Editing with pencil on paper makes it easy to compare changes in a document with the original draft. If the changes are not needed, they do not have to be included during retyping. When editing a document on a word processor, the words on the screen change, as well as the appearance of the original document. Is the original lost forever? Not necessarily. Because word processors save documents electronically, it is possible to leave the original version intact and store a modified document as a new and separate file. If you don't like the changes made to the document, simply exiting the software without saving the revised document causes all changes to disappear. It is also possible to save several versions of a document (under different file names) and compare them later.

4. *I have been writing with a pencil and paper all my life. Why should I change now?* The habit of using pencil and paper when writing may be difficult to overcome. We tend to do things in familiar ways regardless of whether they are the easiest or most efficient. To break the pencil and paper habit, we must convince ourselves that word processing is actually easier than using the familiar pencil and paper. At first it may take more time to create text on a word processor, and so the benefits may look chimeric. But the benefits of word processing come after one has mastered the software. Only after learning the rules and the skills necessary to operate the word processor is it possible to gain the advantages of word processing. Fortunately, doing so is not difficult.

Procedures of Word Processors

Many word processing programs exist for a variety of computer families. As with most types of commercial software, word processors vary in capability. However, all word processors deal with the manipulation of words. Differences among word processing programs are mainly differences in the fine points of manipulating text.

Most word processors use three basic procedures to create a document—enter and edit, format, and print. The structure and capabilities of a word processor determine the precise strategy for entering and editing, formatting, and printing procedures. For example, many word processors can automate form letters, but precisely how to create these form letters, format the letter on a page, and then print them varies from one word processor to another. Similarly, differences between entering procedures and formatting procedures may vary from one word processor to another.

WORD PROCESSING CONCEPTS AND TERMINOLOGY

Learning the concepts and terminology used in word processing should make learning the actual commands for creating a document clearer. Since processors use enter and edit, format, and print as the major procedures, the terms and concepts described in this chapter follow that same structure. Remember that some concepts or terms may apply to more than one procedure.

Enter and Edit Procedures

You begin a document by *entering* text into the computer. When entering text with a word processor, the look of the final document is unimportant. Worries about spelling, grammar, and even sentence structure can wait. When entering text, the most important point is to get initial ideas into words and concentrate on the content of a document. (Incidentally, this is also good writing practice.) During this process, minimal attention is paid to correcting mistakes. However, after text is entered in the word processor, *editing* text is easy. Word processors make it easy to add or delete text as desired, or move text within a document or from one document to another.

Block Blocking text is done in all three procedures. A block of text is a selected portion of text. Users can select any amount, from one character to the entire document. The text selected—say, one paragraph—is called a block. Most word processors permit changes to text attributes for the entire document or change a selected block of text within the document. For example, a block of text can be selected for single-spacing, double-spacing, moving, printing, indenting, deletion, or having a different appearance (such as italics), depending on the limitations of the word processor. So a block of text, then, is nothing more than one or more characters identified for manipulation.

Cursor The location for text entry is identified by a blinking symbol called the *cursor.* Pressing a character key (letter, symbol, or number) on the keyboard causes the character to appear onscreen at the cursor location. For most word processors, commands entered from the keyboard begin their effect at the cursor. For example, if the cursor is in the middle of a single-spaced document and the author issues a double-space command, only text after the cursor will double-space (only the second half of the document). All text preceding the cursor remains single-spaced. The cursor must be at the proper location before entering a command.

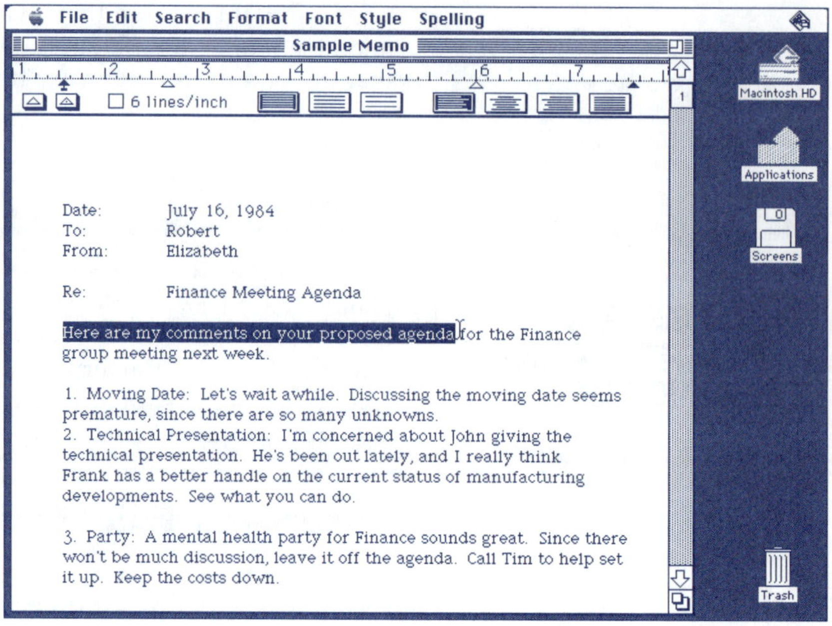

FIGURE 5-2
Selecting a block of text permits one to change text attributes. In this case, the selected text is the text in the black box.

Delete Deleting erases or removes text or characters from a document. Most word processors make it easy to delete single characters by pressing a single key (delete or backspace). However, whole words or entire blocks of text can also be deleted using simple procedures.

Editor Some word processors use a special portion of the software for entering and editing text. The common term for this part of the word processor is the *editor.* Although not all word processors have a discrete editor, they include the capabilities for deleting, inserting, moving, and replacing text without retyping.

Files Documents created with a word processor are stored electronically as a *file* in auxiliary memory. Therefore, saving a word processing document is called saving a file. All word processors require that each file be given a file name. It is a good idea to give each document a file name that is meaningful to you. For example, creating a term paper file for a history class and saving it as "PAPER" could be confusing—especially if you create more than one paper. A better name might be "H1PAPER" or "HISTORY." Using a name that makes it easy for you to remember the contents of the file will save a lot of time when you need to retrieve and use the paper.

Hard return, soft return, and word wrap On a standard typewriter, the return key ends each line and moves the carriage to the beginning of the next line. This is an inappropriate method of starting new lines with a word processor. Instead, word processors automatically move the cursor to the beginning of the next line with

FIGURE 5-3
MacWrite list of files. Word processing software makes it easy to store and retrieve files.

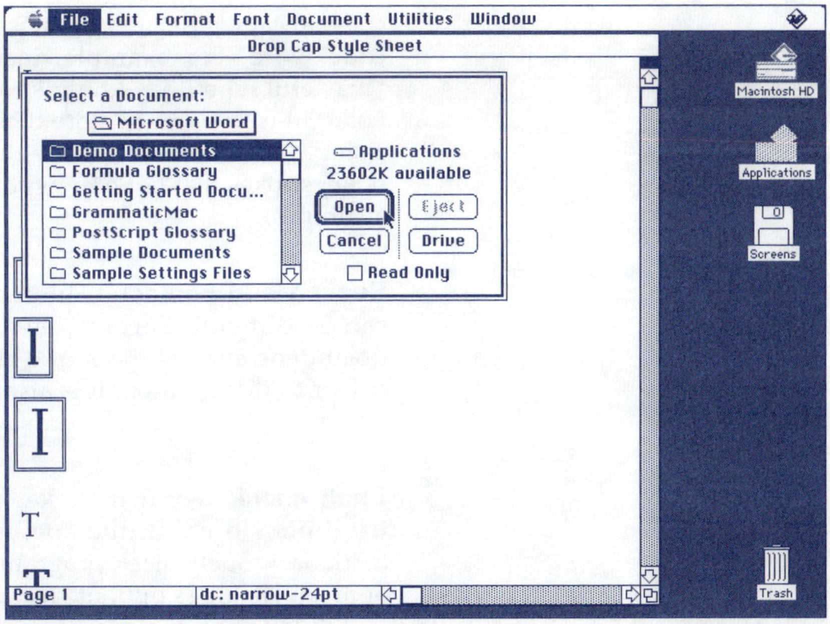

the **soft return**, or **word wrap**, feature. This is only for lines *within* a paragraph. To end a paragraph and force the cursor to begin a new line, the user must press the Return or Enter key. Pressing a Return or Enter key on the keyboard is a command that goes into effect at the location of the cursor. This command is known as a **hard return**. Be sure to read the Rule of Return later in this chapter for additional information about how to use hard returns and soft returns.

Hyphenation Most word processors automatically hyphenate words at the end of a line. This saves the user the trouble of hyphenating. It can also alter the amount of space between words in justified text (justification is discussed later). Many word processors allow users to specify the number and occurrence of hyphens.

Insert Text appears onscreen at the location of the cursor. It is possible to move the cursor to any point within a document to insert new text. "New text" may be text newly-typed or a block of text copied from elsewhere in the document (or, of course, another document altogether). Inserting causes the new text to appear between existing sentences or paragraphs. The word processor shifts all existing text to the right of the cursor to make room for the new text. This is an important feature in the editing process. If a writer wishes to move, for example, the last paragraph of a document to the first paragraph, he or she would use the Insert command.

Macro A macro allows users to "program" a single keystroke to execute an entire set of keystrokes. In fact, macro is an abbreviation of the term macrocommand. Programming a macro begins by defining frequently-recurring text, then storing it with a special code. Recalling the text, then, is as simple as pressing the code key or code word. For example, instead of having to type the words "wasteful repetitive administrative duties" in a letter to the school board, it is possible to store these words as a macro once, then press a single command to retrieve the text. Macros can include hundreds of keystrokes that not only type text but move the cursor and set text attributes.

Search and replace Finding a single word in a long document can be difficult. Fortunately, most word processors can **search** a document for instances of a word, then automatically move the cursor to that location. It is also possible to have the word processor find a word or series of words and **replace** them with new text.

Spell check For many, a key reason for using a word processor is its ability to check the spelling of words against an electronic dictionary. Spell-check programs are part of many word processors, or are available as optional features or add-on programs with others.

Spell checking compares each word in a document to a list of words in an electronic dictionary. If a word in the document does not match any word in the dictionary, the spelling checker marks, or flags, the word. Many of the more sophisticated spell-check programs stop at each potentially misspelled word and offer one or more possible corrections. Correct the spelling by choosing the correct word from the list. It is also possible to add words to the dictionary.

Spell-check programs do not guarantee correctness. Because these programs check only spelling, not meaning, they do not identify correctly-spelled, but misused, words. Using "weather" for "whether" will not be identified as a mistake. In addition, proper nouns are not part of most dictionaries (although many spell-check programs allow us to add proper names and other words to the dictionary).

Text Text includes letters, spaces, words, and other characters. While computers deal with both text and graphics (pictures), most word processors deal primarily with text.

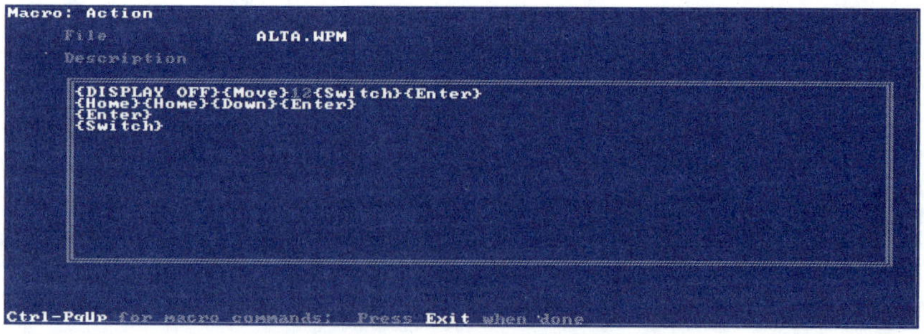

FIGURE 5-4
Macros combine several different commands, mouse movements, and keystrokes into a single command.

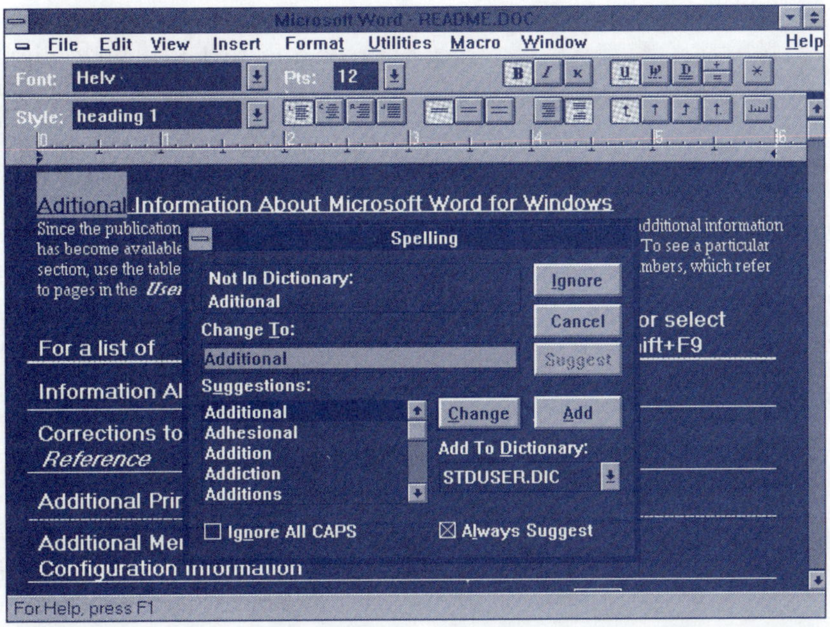

FIGURE 5-5
The ability to check the spelling of all words in a document has made word processing software indispensable for many writers.

Thesaurus Just as many word processors have electronic dictionaries for spell checking, it is common for word processors to have an electronic thesaurus. Thesaurus programs work much like spell-check programs.

Format Procedures

After creating the words with the enter and edit procedures, the second process is to set the basic appearance of the document. This is the role of the **format** procedure. Using this procedure, it is possible to create headings or sections, change margins, or to single-space or double-space a document. Here users may consider the content of the document a little bit, but primary attention is directed to how the document will look on a printed page.

Center **Centering** is a command in most word processors that places text equal distances from left and right margins. Keep in mind that centering text does not always cause it to appear in the center of the printed page if the margins are not equal.

Headers and footers A **header** is words placed at the top of every page. A **footer** is words placed at the bottom of every page. Headers and footers help organize word processing documents. For example, a term paper may have the author's name or the title of the paper at the top of every page and the page number at the bottom. Most word processors make it easy to generate headers and footers in a variety of formats.

Teaching Tool

Bilingual Writing

As many schools face the problems of how to better serve all students, one method of helping Spanish-speaking students learn English is to use a bilingual word processor. Bilingual word processors make it easy for students to translate between Spanish and English. Some of these types of programs provide a menu of pictures for helping students locate words and phrases, offer spell checking and thesauri in both English and Spanish, and even provide exercises for helping students build both their language and writing skills.

Indent and tab **Indent** and **Tab** are commands that move the cursor and text to a new alignment relative to the margins. Tab causes the cursor to move a specified distance. For example, pressing Tab in some word processors causes the cursor to move the equivalent of five spaces. The word *equivalent* is important, because many word processors move the cursor a specified number of inches. Tabs are not the same as pressing the space bar (be sure to look at the Rule of the Space Bar.)

Indent causes an entire paragraph to move in a specified distance from the left or right margin. Indent affects the entire paragraph; Tab only affects an individual line. These terms may vary with different word processors. Some Macintosh word processors use the term *indent* to refer to indenting just the first line of a paragraph. *Tab* refers to entering text in a tabular format.

Index and table of contents Many word processors make it easy for users to generate an index and table of contents. Users mark words that will appear in the index or table of contents. The listing always reflects the current page numbers of the marked words, so it is always up-to-date, no matter what changes occur in the document.

Justify Typewriter pages are left-justified—that is, the left margin is aligned in a straight line and the right margin appears jagged. Word processors can **justify** both the left and right margins. Using right justification is a matter of taste and the ability of your software and printer to proportionally space between letters and words. However, because it is easy to change the format of a document, some users print a copy of a justified and an unjustified document, then choose the one they like most.

Margins A **margin** is the distance from the edge of the paper to the beginning of text. On a page, there is a top, bottom, left, and right margin. For early drafts, it is a good idea to have wide margins on each side of the page so that reviewers can make comments in the blank spaces. When the final draft is ready for printing, it is easy to alter new spacing and margin settings.

Page numbering Word processors can put page numbers in different locations on the pages of a document. While page numbering is usually automatic, the author must make certain choices, such as where to place the page number (upper right hand corner, lower left corner, centered on the bottom of the page), whether to suppress the page number for a specific page (such as the title page), and whether to combine headers and footers with the page numbers.

Spacing Word processors make it easy to change line spacing. With most word processors, it is possible to change the entire document by executing a spacing command at the beginning of a document. It is also possible to change the spacing of only part of the document.

Suppress Placing headers, footers, and page numbers in a document causes them to appear on every page; however, it is inappropriate to have these on a title page. To keep headers, footers, and page numbers off the title page in some word processors requires the use of a **suppress** command. Suppress prevents the command from being issued on specified pages.

Underline, boldface and italics Underlining, boldfacing, and italicizing are text attributes designed to provide emphasis. Because word processors make underlining, boldfacing, and italicizing easy to accomplish, it is tempting to overuse them. When used too much, boldfacing, underlining, and italics lose their effect.

Teaching Tool

Administrative Word Processing

Everyone who writes can benefit from word processors. This is especially true for teachers and administrators who write large amounts of correspondence to parents, administrators, teachers, and others. For a teacher sending notes home to parents, the ability of a word processor to create a form letter and reproduce that letter with each child's and parent's name not only saves time but keeps parents informed.

Of course, the same uses are valuable to administrators, only on a much larger scale. Word processors may be used to create a "personalized" letter for every parent of every child in school. Many word processors can also be used to automatically generate an addressed envelope. By keeping a current mailing list of parent addresses, word processors make it very easy to communicate with all parents.

Print Procedures

The third and final procedure for using a word processor is to send the document from the computer to a printer. This process is called the **print** procedure. Printing a document produces a **hard copy**. So, a hard copy is a printed page sent by the word processor. It is easy to issue a command to make a hard copy of a document, and there are many options and selections available with most word processors. For example, the print procedure determines the number of copies, which printer will print, the print quality, and other options.

Copies One useful print feature is the ability to print multiple copies of a document. Unlike a typewriter, which produces only one copy of a document, word processors can print several copies at the same time. In fact, word processors can even collate copies.

Orientation Many word processors can print text either across the width or the length of the page. The direction of printing is known as the page **orientation**. The orientation across the width of the page (called a *portrait* orientation) is the most common orientation for letters, papers, and most other documents. The lengthwise orientation turns a page sideways. This is a *landscape* orientation. Brochures, banners, flyers, and other special types of documents may use this orientation.

Selected pages Word processors offer the flexibility of printing only chosen pages. Imagine creating a fifty-page document that has a typo on page 31. Instead of reprinting all pages after making the correction, word processors permit users to print just one page.

Text quality Different printers offer different levels of print quality. Some printers only offer one level, while others provide for a range of text quality. For example, dot-matrix printers can print very fast but not very beautifully. On the other hand, these printers can print better but more slowly. The determination of speed and quality is usually controlled through the printing procedure.

FUNDAMENTAL RULES

Because word processors are different in their operation from typewriters, there are a few rules that should be followed to make the use of a word processor even more efficient.

Rule of Return

With a word processor, it is very important to press the Return or Enter key *only* to start a new paragraph. Never press the Return or Enter key at the end of a line within a paragraph as you would on a typewriter. To remember this rule, imagine that the computer screen is two feet wide. With this in mind, enter text as though it will go to the right edge of the screen. The word processor will automatically wrap words around to the beginning of the next line. It is very important to let the word processor wrap words whenever possible.

Rule of the Space Bar

Most word processing software makes it easy to change the appearance of a document through a variety of commands. However, this flexibility does pose some problems, and one common problem is the overuse of the space bar. The space bar moves the cursor one space to the right each time it is pressed. While this seems simple enough, depending on the situation, different spaces can have different sizes. For example, with a proportional font, a space can vary depending on the characters preceding or following the space. In these situations it is impossible to use the space bar to align text. Pressing the space bar five times does not always create the same blank space as pressing an equivalent tab or indent. For this reason, avoid using the space bar to align text on a page. The Rule of the Space Bar is: *Never insert more than two consecutive spaces.* When adding more than two spaces, it is best to use the tab or indent functions. Remembering this simple rule may save hours of editing.

Rule of Saving

As text is entered into a word processor, it is stored in RAM. While this is very useful for making changes to a document, there is one major concern. Turning off the computer or suffering an interruption to the power causes all information in RAM to disappear. In other words, losing power means losing words. To obviate such a loss, it is a good idea to save the document whenever you have entered more text than you care to lose. For some this may mean saving the document every hour, for others it may be every 20 to 30 minutes.

Rule of Backup

The reason to save a file to disk is to make it available to load back into RAM for further editing. However, if the disk that stores the file becomes damaged, all information is lost. Of course, taking care of the disk helps prevent damage. However, even the most careful precautions cannot guarantee the data's safety. Therefore, it is a good idea to save important files on more than one disk. Saving multiple copies of the same file on separate disks is called *making backups*. The more important the file, the more important it is to make several backups, and often, to keep them in separate places. It is easy to see why keeping all the copies of an important file in the same carrying case is not wise. Backups are of little value if the carrying case with all the files is lost or damaged.

DESKTOP PUBLISHING

One of the major reasons word processors have become so popular is their ability to produce good-looking documents easily. And although word processors have adopted many of the features of desktop publishers, few enable users to produce a full range of visually appealing documents. Word processors are effective tools for producing attractive letters and some documents, but are not very practical for producing sophisticated designs. To have the design tools necessary to produce attractive, typeset documents, desktop publishing software is available.

A simple definition of desktop publishing (DTP) is "software that allows basic typesetting." Typesetting transforms the appearance, location, and size of text. However, desktop publishing software is more than a set of computerized typesetting tools. It is also a tool of expression. The software provides a medium for expressing ideas through the design and style of text.

Understanding desktop publishing begins by looking at the capabilities common to most desktop publishing software. Although desktop publishers perform many of the tasks of word processors, this software provides several advanced features in the control of type, use of graphics, and control of page layout. Each of these is discussed later.

A Tool of Expression

Desktop publishing software helps create attractive documents. It gives users many choices not found in word processors. However, the user must make the correct choices. Simply because desktop publishing provides many different typefaces, it does not guarantee a high-quality document. The choice of a typeface is as important as the choice of a word. For example, most software provides both a high-tech and an Old English typeface. A document in a high-tech typeface looks up-to-date. A document in an Old English typeface conveys a much different message.

Desktop publishing software also provides control over the placement and format of graphics, but it cannot tell users where to place a graphic to convey a specific message. And it does not tell users how to design an effective page layout for a particular graphic. This knowledge must come from the user.

It is relatively easy to learn to use the tools of desktop publishing software. It is much more difficult, and takes much more time, to learn to use those tools in a graphically appealing way. Many people spend years learning how to combine text and graphics in a way that makes for graphic art. They must guard against using the wrong typefaces for the wrong reasons, misplacing graphics, and making a document hard to read. Desktop publishing software is not a technological substitute for human creativity or good taste, but a versatile means of expressing creativity. Because it is both a set of typesetting tools as well as a tool of expression, learning to use it is more than learning the method of selecting a typeface or placing a graphic image. Learning desktop publishing requires learning how to use these tools in an effective and visually pleasing way.

Teachers, Students, and Desktop Publishing

As a tool of expression, desktop publishing makes a wealth of uses possible for both teachers and students. While a list of every possible use of desktop publishing software would more than fill the pages of this book, the following are a few educational applications:

- student and teacher letterheads.
- brochures for dances, fundraisers, and other special events.
- flyers for musical and theatrical programs.
- classroom attendance sheets, lunch-money forms, and other types of forms.
- classroom and school newsletters.
- classroom rule books.
- classroom and school newspapers.
- student and class books of creative writing assignments.

- special event signs.
- teacher and student resumes.

The four most common types of publications produced with desktop publishing software are flyers, newsletters, brochures, and manuscripts.

DESKTOP PUBLISHING SOFTWARE

Many programs fall within the category of desktop publishing software. As with all software, some, such as PageMaker, are fairly easy to learn but can be somewhat difficult to use with very long documents. On the other hand, those like Ventura Publisher are complex and take considerable time to learn, but offer features that enable users to create virtually any type of document of any length. There are two basic types of desktop publishing software—command-driven and wysiwyg.

Command-driven desktop publishing software requires the user to insert print command codes into a document. When the document is printed, the codes control the printer and produce the desired typographical effect. With command-driven software, you see the type changes only on the printed page.

The second type is known as *what you see is what you get* (wysiwyg). This type of software allows users to see changes on the screen as they will appear on the printed page. Of the two, wysiwyg is much more popular, because you can see what you create as you create it.

Desktop publishing programs focus on **page makeup**. They take text files generated with a word processor and graphics files generated with scanners or graphics software, and combine these files to produce a new document. Unlike word processors, desktop publishing programs are not useful for adding and editing large segments of text. Rather, they emphasize importing text generated on a word processor and graphic images generated by graphics software.

TEXT AND GRAPHICS

Many desktop publishing programs permit text entry and text editing. However, in most cases, entering large amounts of text is cumbersome. The same limitation holds true for graphics. Many desktop publishing programs provide tools for creating graphics, however, these graphics tools lack the sophistication of true graphics programs. As a general rule, it is best to compose text on a word processor, create graphics with a graphics program, and import the text and graphics into a desktop publisher.

Teaching Tool

Desktop-published Books

Students may be much more inclined to write if they know their work will be produced in a high quality form and shared with others. Many teachers use desktop publishing to create a classroom creative writing book or a classroom newsletter. Desktop publishing software allows students to import text created on a word processor, import graphics generated with a graphics drawing program, and combine the two to produce a document with the professional appearance of published books.

Typographical Controls

Typography is the art of using type to send a message. The three major type controls include typeface, typestyle, and typesize. Again, many of these features are found in good word processing software. However, desktop publishing software usually provides many additional sophisticated typographical controls.

Typeface Typeface identifies the appearance of type. It is sometimes used interchangeably with the word *font* to indicate the size and face of the type. In handwriting, for example, there are two major "typefaces"—print and cursive. Yet within those two, there are several hundred variations. In fact, everyone's style of printing is different. In desktop publishing, there are two major categories—serif and sans serif.

The selection of the typeface depends on the message. In general, within a document, the large body of text is in serif typefaces (to make reading easier). Sans serif faces work well for titles that stand out from the rest of the text. However, there may be occasions when a sans serif typeface is most appropriate for the body of text while, from time to time, serif fonts work out well as titles.

Typesize Typesize, commonly measured in *points,* is also a critical concern. **Point sizes** range from very small (2 points) to very large (128 points and up). Figure 5-7 illustrates the differences in point sizes.

Type styles

Normal

Bold

Italic

Underline

~~Strikethru~~

Outline

Shadow

Reverse

FIGURE 5-6
Typestyle refers to different type appearances within the same typeface.

Typestyle *Typestyle* refers to variations on type within a typeface. Examples of typestyles include bold, underline, double-strike, strikethrough, subscript, and superscript. For most applications, the three most common styles are normal, bold, and italic (see Figure 5-6).

Drop shadows, drop caps, and other special effects Drop shadows give a three-dimensional appearance to a box. Two sides of the box have heavier lines to give the illusion of depth. A drop cap is the first letter of a paragraph, enlarged and dropped below the baseline of the rest of the line.

A raised cap is a large first letter of a paragraph that extends above the body of the paragraph. Like drop caps, these are used to show the beginning of a chapter. Reverse type is an effective method for drawing attention to text because the color of the type and the background behind it are different from the body of text. However, reverse type should only be used for small amounts of text that use a large point size. Reversed small text is hard to read, and if the type is a serif face, can lose its serifs.

A shaded background isolates text by adding a background color or pattern behind the text. Shading backgrounds is different from reverse type, because the color of the text remains the same as

FIGURE 5-7
Different point sizes have very different uses in a published document.

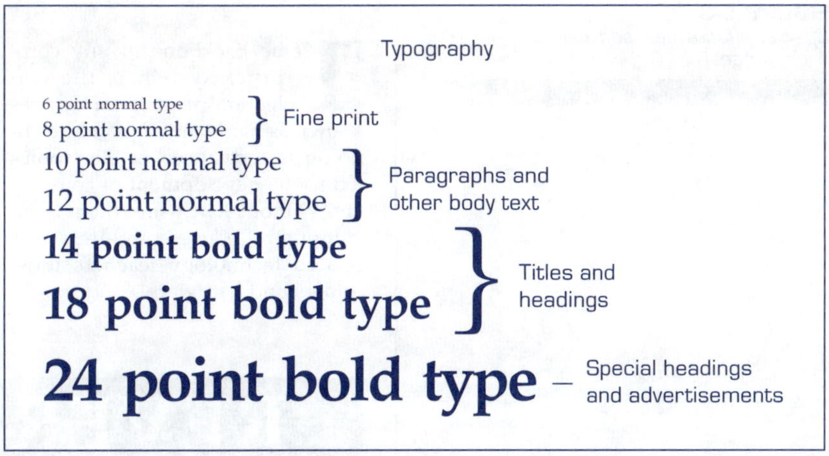

the body of the document. Reverse type changes the color of the text, generally from black to white, while shaded backgrounds leave the text black.

Deviant text separates very small amounts of text to create a visual cue. Two common deviant text techniques are compressing text and expanding text. Stretching text causes text to appear wider, while compressed text causes text to appear narrow. In either case, the text is used to create a different visual effect.

Paragraph styles and tags Suppose you are designing a newsletter, and decide that the headlines for each article will be in 24-point, Helvetica, boldface type. You could specify all these text attributes for each heading separately. But many desktop publishing programs allow users to set type specifications for text elements that fit an entire category or set of related paragraphs. **Tagging** is the term used to describe this process.

Tagging is similar to using macros in word processing software. The attributes of a tag can be applied to any paragraph in a desktop publishing document by simply selecting the desired paragraph, then selecting the tag name. Usually, tag names are listed for easy access.

Spacing Spacing between letters in a word, or between words, is controlled by two different strategies. With fixed spacing, the amount of space is constant between one letter and any other letter. With proportional spacing, different letter combinations use different amounts of space, and different letters use different amounts of space. For example, the letter I will take less space than the letter M or the letter W. In fixed spacing, if an I occurs between two Ms, it appears that there is extra space around the I. Proportional spacing reduces the amount of space around the letter I to give a balanced appearance. Controls can be set automatically for proportional spacing.

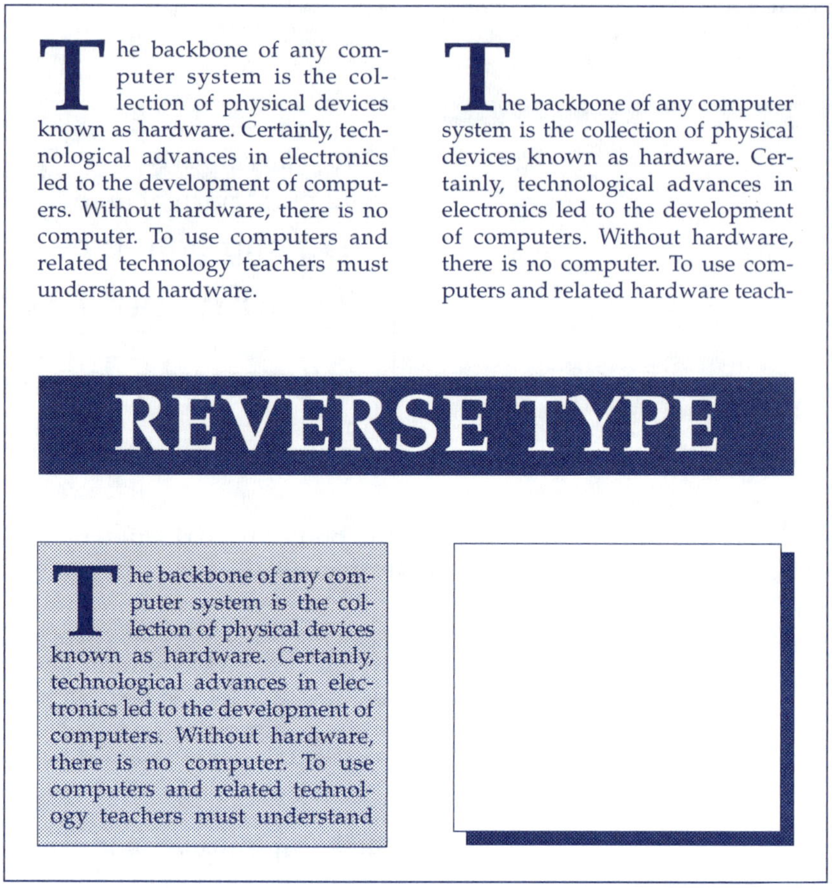

FIGURE 5-8
Special effects can add flair to a document.

For a few letter pairs, the normal amount of space between the letters also gives the appearance of extra space. Consider the letter pair AW. The angle of the A next to the angle of the W gives the appearance of extra space. *Kerning* causes these letter pairs to move closer together to reduce the extra space. It is possible to automatically kern these letter pairs, but the user can also manually adjust this space, if desired.

Leading is a publishing term that describes the amount of space between lines in a paragraph. Precisely, leading is the distance in points from the bottom, or base, of one line to the next. If text in a paragraph is at 10 points and the leading is also 10 points, the paragraph appears single-spaced. Of course, combinations of text size and leading can create a variety of effects. For example, using 10-point text and a 20-point leading doubles the space between lines. Using 24-point text with 18-point leading squeezes lines together (and creates a serious typographical blunder).

Graphic Controls

While several sophisticated word processors allow users to incorporate graphics, desktop publishing software provides a much higher level of control and precision. You can adjust the size of a graphic image to fit a particular location, trim the edges of graphic images, edit and change graphics, and create drawings. Graphic controls also permit the user to rotate images, copy images to multiple locations, add captions, and flow text either around or through a graphic image. Most of these features are not commonly available with word processing software.

Sizing and scaling Graphics *sizing* refers to the ability to change the size and amount of the graphic that appears on a page. *Scaling* refers to altering the height and width ratios. That is, by adding to the height ratio, one can make a picture appear taller and thinner; by adding to the width ratio, the picture appears squat and "fat." Sizing and scaling allow users to make imported graphics fit a specific space.

Line art Most desktop publishing software provides a set of tools for placing lines, squares, circles, and other forms of line art into a document. While many of these graphic drawing tools are similar to those found with graphics software, they are very limited. Only a few simple drawing features are available.

Graphics and text An important consideration for the use of graphics is how graphics relate to text. This includes the amount of space between text and graphics, *if* text and graphics share the same space. Some software allows users to vary the amount of space around different parts of a graphic to create a different effect.

Along with controlling the amount of space, it is also possible to determine if text will flow around a graphic, through a graphic, or

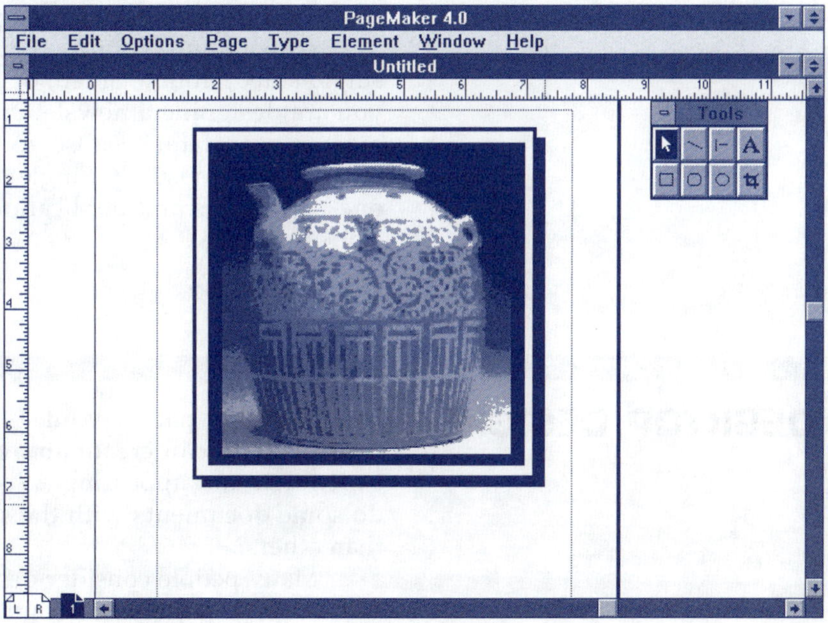

FIGURE 5-9
Programs such as PageMaker make it easy to place a graphic image into a desktop publishing document.

above or below a graphic. This is known as **text wrap**. Text wrap can create a variety of effects. For example, a large graphic on a page with text flowing through the entire graphic has a different look than a single graphic in the middle of a page with text flowing around it.

Page Layout

The overall design has the greatest influence on the effect of a document, and there are several considerations. If the document is a newsletter, how many columns will there be on a page? If the document is a flyer, what are the margins? If the document is a manuscript, what is the consistent design of each page? Design begins with page layout. The following list describes some of these controls.

Page size The first consideration in page layout is to specify the size of paper and the page size of the document. The size of the paper must correlate with the paper sizes supported by the printer. The page size refers to the area available for type—this will be determined largely by margin size.

Number of Pages, Double-Sided Pages, and Facing Pages

Page design affects the number of pages in a document. For example, if you have 5,000 words in 10-point type, you will naturally have fewer pages than with 5,000 words in 72-point type, all other specifications being the same. With multiple-page documents, it is possible to have double-sided pages or facing pages. Double-sided pages simply have type on both sides of the page. Facing pages' design is a mirror design; the left page mirrors the right page.

As with most features, you control the page layout by selecting single-sided, double-sided, or facing pages. For example, suppose you are designing a newsletter. Double-sided and facing pages are most appropriate, because you want pages that face each other to work together visually. Single-sided pages are most appropriate for one-page flyers and publications that must be printed on only one side of the page.

DESKTOP DESIGN

By combining page layout, typographical controls, and graphics controls, you can create an overall document design that is both functional and appealing. What makes an effective design? Why do some documents with the same text convey the message better than others?

Many people consider designing documents to be an art form. In fact, some document designers are highly paid for their talent in

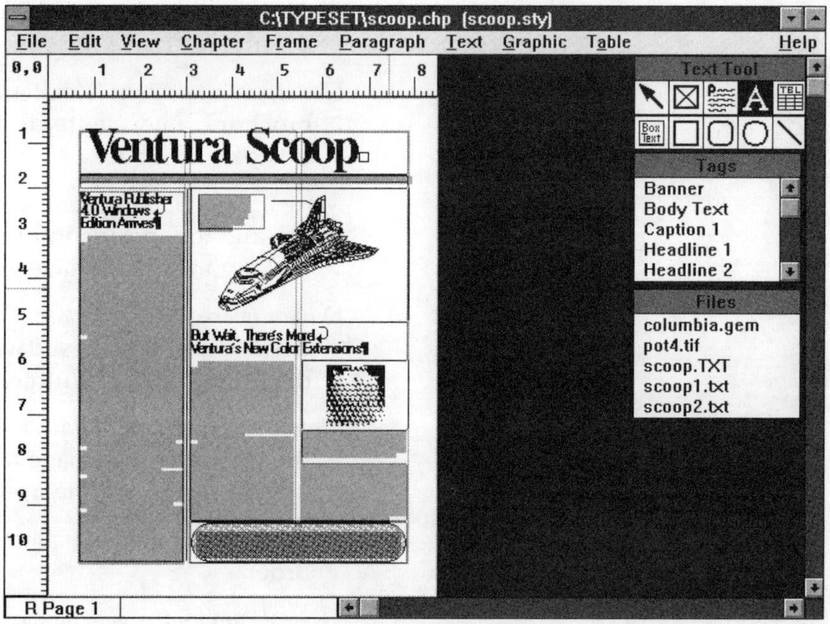

FIGURE 5-10
Ventura Publisher is a popular desktop publisher.

combining graphics, typography, and page layout. However, you do not need to be a professional designer to create good documents. You do need to be aware that graphic design is a learned skill—a skill that develops with time, practice, and experimentation.

The best way to learn how to design documents is to get a book on the basic elements of graphic design. Many bookstores carry such books in their computer software sections. Another source of ideas is the design of other documents. For example, if you are going to design and create a newsletter, look at the designs of several other newsletters. Ask yourself what makes them effective. Does the design enhance or detract from the message? Is the document easy to read? To help get you started in good graphic design, there are a few design rules to consider. The following is a list of very general design considerations.

Plan the document first. Planning provides organization and structure.

Consider the audience. Fit the design to the target audience.

Make the design enhance the content. Good design helps readers understand the message of the document.

Use the design to focus attention. Focusing attention on major points helps readers remember important information.

Avoid detractors. Detractors cause readers to focus attention on unimportant information.

Use variety. A boring design makes boring reading.

Be consistent. Once a design is established, stick to it.

Make documents warm and friendly. Warm and friendly documents make for warm and friendly reading.

Use standard designs. Readers expect a brochure to look like a brochure, a newsletter to look like a newsletter, and a book to look like a book.

Make information easy to find. Readers often scan documents looking for specific information. Help the reader by making information easy to locate.

Do not overuse the software. Do not overuse the features of desktop publishing software. It will only make the document appear cluttered.

Flow from upper left to lower right. Since English is read from the upper left of a page to the lower right, documents should flow from the upper left to the lower right.

Follow a logical sequence. Sequence parts of a page in a logical order.

Use column and page balance. Facing pages and columns should end within one line of each other.

Consider proportion. Size of a component is relative to surrounding components.

Use contrast. Use light and dark areas to focus attention.

Sometimes surprise the reader. A bit of surprise keeps a reader's attention.

Avoid excesses. Do everything in moderation.

Avoid widows and orphans. Never end a page or begin a page with one line of a paragraph.

Limit the number of typefaces. Limit a page to two or three typefaces.

Don't justify text in narrow columns. Justification causes space to be added between words. The shorter the line, the greater the effect of added space.

Try different paragraph alignments. Unusual paragraph alignments focus attention on unusual paragraphs.

Create ample white space. White space is the most common implicit graphic design tool available. However, other than breaking different sections apart on a page, white space is also used to add contrast and make a document more readable.

Use appropriate margins. Margins determine the white space in the border.

Use appropriate columns. The size of the columns influences readability.

Summary

- A word processor is software that permits users to type words into a computer, make changes, set the appearance or format of the words, then store the whole document as a file in auxiliary memory.
- When entering text, the most important point is to put ideas into words and concentrate on the content of a document.
- In word processing, the four most common processes are enter, edit, format, and print.
- Desktop publishing software is software that provides typesetting capabilities.
- The three major type features are typeface, type size, and typestyle.
- What you see is what you get (wysiwyg) software allows users to view document changes as they occur.
- Desktop publishing programs are not designed to be word processors.
- A typeface is a named design that identifies the appearance of type.
- The two major type styles are serif and sans serif.
- *Typestyle* refers to variations in a typeface, such as boldface, italic, double-strike, strike-through, and underline.
- Type size refers to the size of the type as measured in points.
- Drop-shadows give a three-dimensional appearance to a box.
- Sizing determines the space taken up by a graphic.

Fill-In Questions

Fill in the blank for each of the statements listed below.

1. What reasons do people give for not wanting to learn to use a word processor? ________________ , ________________ , ________________ , and ________________ .
2. The term ________________ generally refers to the text that has been selected for change.
3. A small symbol, such as a blinking line or box, usually indicates the location of the ________________ .

4. In word processing, procedures of setting margins, line spacing, and setting headers and footers are called ________________ procedures.
5. We use a ________________ only at the end of a paragraph.
6. A ________________ desktop publishing program displays onscreen how a document will appear on paper.

Quiz

Answer the following questions.

1. Which of the following should be suppressed on occasion?
   a. fonts　　b. spacing
   c. tabs　　d. page numbers
2. A device for storing repeated keystrokes is:
   a. an orientation　　b. a format
   c. a macro　　d. a block
3. With a word processor, we place hard returns at the end of any important line of text.
   a. true　　b. false
4. The term that describes how text will appear on paper is:
   a. a font　　b. a macro
   c. a block　　d. a format
5. A portrait orientation is equivalent to turning a page sideways.
   a. true　　b. false
6. A spelling checker will not check for the use of correctly-spelled but misused words.
   a. true　　b. false
7. Which type of desktop publishing software displays a document on the monitor as it will appear on paper?
   a. command-driven　　b. mouse-driven
   c. full page display　　d. wysiwig
8. When using desktop publishing software, it is best to enter large amounts of text directly rather than import them from a word processor.
   a. true　　b. false
9. The term *point* in publishing means:
   a. the exact location of type　　b. the size of type
   c. the amount of space required for certain text　　d. the appearance of large type

10. Which type of font is easiest to read in the body of a document?
    a. serif
    b. sans serif

Exercises and Applications

Follow the instructions for each exercise and application.

1. The best way to learn how to use a word processor is to use one. However, it is important to select a word processor that fits your needs. Most word processors perform the same basic tasks, but many differ in how they perform these tasks. Locate a word processing program and identify the commands necessary to perform the following tasks: center text; boldface text; underline text; change font; check spelling; use thesaurus; select text; change margins; set spacing; create a header and footer; change page numbering.
2. Spell-check programs are becoming very popular features of word processors. However, not all agree that using a spell check is a good idea. Write a brief essay on the limitations of spell check programs. At the end of the paper, discuss your personal preference. Will you use a spell check? If so, how?
3. How is written communication important to you? On a sheet of paper, briefly describe the importance of written communication in your life (both your own writing and the writing of others). Think, for example, about how advertisers present information that affects your buying decisions and how newspapers present information.
4. Get a flyer, a sign, or some other notice that has not been typeset (that is, typed or handwritten). On a sheet of paper, sketch a new graphic design to convey the message of the document. Then create two alternative designs and analyze what makes each effective or ineffective.
5. Compile a notebook of sample graphic designs for future reference. Your notebook should contain at least five examples of newsletters, brochures, and flyers. However, the more examples included, the more useful the notebook.
6. Select one typeset newsletter, brochure, or flyer, and critique the design. Does the design help convey what you think should be the intended message? Are there design components that distract from the message? What suggestions would you offer to make the document more effective? Write out your responses and be prepared to share your knowledge with the class.

6

ESSENTIALS OF SPREADSHEETS

LEARNING OBJECTIVES

Learning the material in this chapter will enable you to:

- describe the purpose of spreadsheet software
- identify how spreadsheets create worksheets
- describe how a worksheet organizes data
- list the major data types
- describe how to enter data into a worksheet
- define data formats
- describe the calculation options
- define absolute and relative cell reference
- use a template
- define print options
- describe how to use graphics to present data

CHAPTER OVERVIEW

Most computer users work with words or work with numbers. Word processors make it easier to work with words, and spreadsheets make it easier to work with numbers. In fact, spreadsheets are often called "word processors for numbers." Many of the same techniques for entering, editing, formatting, and printing used in word processing software are used with spreadsheet software.

Spreadsheets offer teachers and students the ability to manipulate numeric information in a variety of formats. Teachers may use spreadsheets to calculate student grades, determine eligibility lists, maintain inventories, and a host of other activities. Students may use this software to solve a variety of mathematical problems, maintain club record information, and analyze data.

The true strength of a **spreadsheet** lies in its use of mathematical formulas. A formula manipulates numbers or values contained in other cells. Changing a value in one of those cells causes the formula to recalculate to account for the change. This very powerful feature allows teachers and students to ask the question 'what if.' For example, what if you receive a 25 cent per hour raise? How much extra money will you take home each payday? With a spreadsheet program, you can place your old hourly pay in one cell, and in another cell enter the number of hours worked. In a third cell, you can write a formula to multiply the hourly rate by the number of hours worked. This third cell will display your total wages. If you go back and add 25 cents to the hourly rate in the first cell, the cell with the formula will automatically display the new total wages. You could also ask, if you work more hours, what will the effect be on wages? A change in the cell containing the number of work hours will also automatically be reflected in the cell displaying total wages. This is a simple example, but you can see that it is possible to ask several "what if" questions of spreadsheet programs and see the effect of the change almost immediately.

This chapter focuses on the concepts and processes basic to most spreadsheet programs. Understanding these concepts and processes will make learning the keystrokes and commands of a specific spreadsheet program easier.

SPREADSHEETS

Suppose you are teaching students to develop and maintain a family budget. One common approach to this task is to take a sheet of paper and, in one column, list all household expenses and sources of income, with the word *balance* at the end of the list. Months' names go across the top of the page. After setting this initial structure, students would write income and expenses for January, and so on. At the end of the column next to the word *balance,* students would subtract the total payments from the total income for each month.

One problem with this method of developing a family budget occurs when students have entered an incorrect expense or payment amount. After discovering such a mistake, students must recalculate the balance. A second problem is the lack of flexibility. What if the family needs a new car? How large a monthly payment can they afford? Answering such "what if" questions requires making many additional calculations. Spreadsheets are an alternative to creating a family budget on paper or an accounting sheet. They perform the same task more quickly, easily, and efficiently.

While a word processor allows us to place text anywhere in a document, spreadsheets require that information be entered in precise locations. These locations are cells. The intersection of **column** and **row** precisely defines the location of a cell. The entire worksheet is a series of cells—a computer-generated grid. What makes the grid a true worksheet is the type of data inside selected cells. Cells may contain **labels** (words), numbers, or formulas to perform calculations. The flexibility to use labels, values, and formulas makes spreadsheets powerful tools, because they can perform extensive calculating tasks.

Teachers, Students, and Spreadsheets

Working with numbers and calculations is a common educational task, making spreadsheet programs popular educational tools. The following is an introduction to the potential uses of spreadsheets to help solve problems.

Schools must maintain an assortment of student, budget, personnel, and administrative information. Administrators can use spreadsheets to plan and track budgets. Administrators can also project changing enrollment and monies available for student support.

Teachers may keep attendance, track lunch monies, student activity funds, inventory, and other similar tasks. Teachers also use spreadsheets to log and maintain classroom grades. A spreadsheet can store scores on a test and other assignments and can automatically calculate grades after each entry.

Spreadsheet software is very flexible, so it has a number of uses for the student. Students can use this software for mathematical operations. Spreadsheets are also useful in the science lab for tracking experimental data. Spreadsheets can also be used by students to monitor their own progress and determine their own grades. Students can use the software to develop a full understanding of budgeting. Sports enthusiasts use spreadsheets in a variety of ways, ranging from tracking baseball and softball statistics to keeping handicaps for the golf team.

FIGURE 6-1
Spreadsheets make it easy for teachers to maintain and calculate grade information about students.

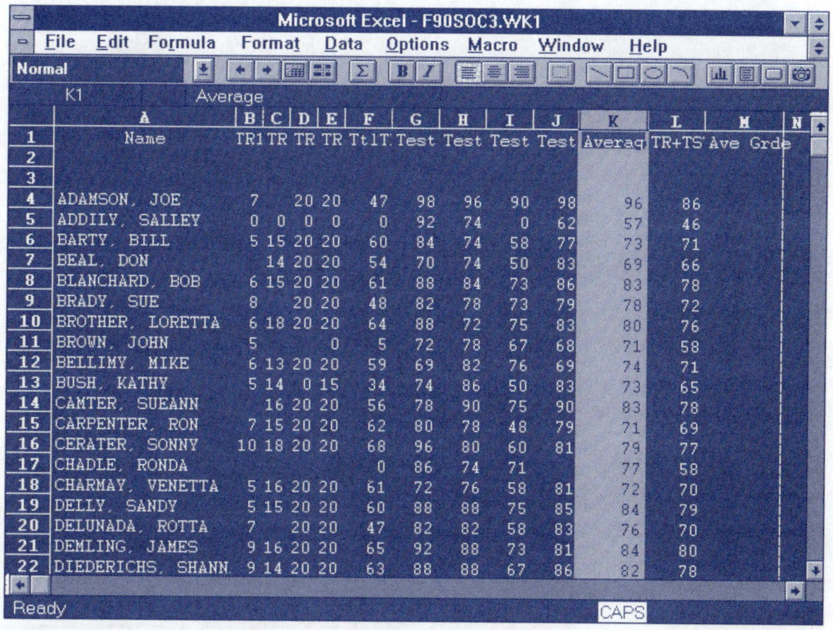

Spreadsheet software is very popular with students in business courses. Businesses use spreadsheets to develop budgets, analyze and plan sales, inventory, and many other purposes. Because they are a fundamental business tool, understanding and using spreadsheets is a requirement for many business courses.

Students can use spreadsheets when studying government. City and community planners use spreadsheets to ask "what if" questions about population. What if the population of a city increases by one percent, three percent, or nine percent? Will the city need new facilities? What if the community shrinks in size? What if birth rates increase? The answers to such questions can lead to understanding of governmental issues.

WORKSHEET LAYOUT

Understanding spreadsheet software begins with an examination of how it organizes information. Based on this organization, several important concepts and terms apply to building a successful worksheet. Although specific commands are likely to vary somewhat among different software packages, the basic capabilities, concepts, and terminology are similar.

A *worksheet* is an electronic grid consisting of rows (which run from side to side) and columns (which run up and down). Columns are identified by letter and rows by numbers. A letter and number combination identifies the *address* of each cell. For example, the first cell under column A in row 1 is cell A1. Several cells in sequence are called a *range*. For example, the range of cells A1 to E1 is five cells, all in row 1. The range of cells A1 to A5 describes five cells in column A. Many programs use a colon (:) to show a range. For example, A1:A5 refers to the cell range A1 to A5. Other programs use dots, as in A1..A5.

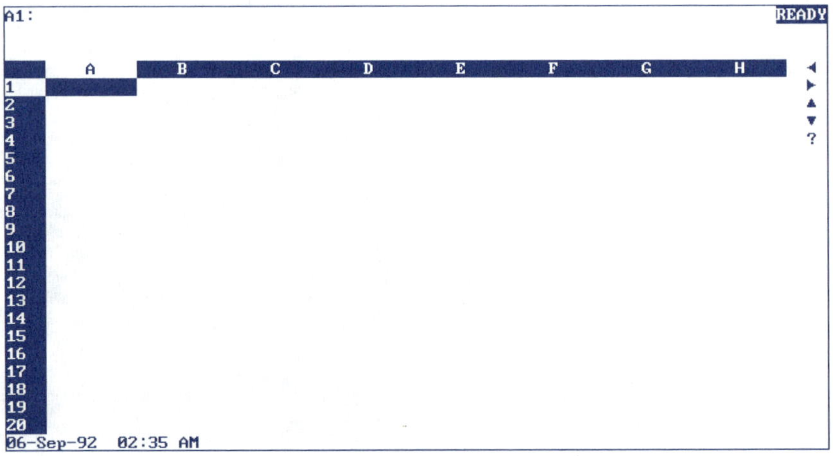

FIGURE 6-2
An empty spreadsheet screen.

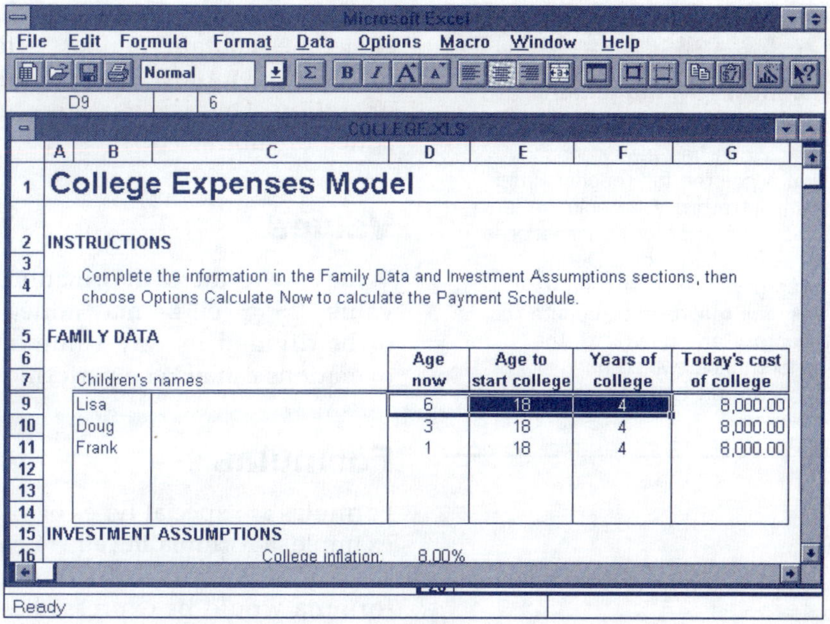

FIGURE 6-3
Notice the cell range D9 to F9.

Cell Cursor

The **cell cursor** identifies the active cell for entering one of the three types of data. (The *active cell* is the cell in which the user chooses to act next.) While there is some variation from one software package to another, typically the cell cursor fills the entire cell. The first step in entering any information into a worksheet, then, is to move the cell cursor to the desired cell. It is very important to be aware of the cell cursor's location before entering data. Probably the most common mistake is to forget the cursor location and accidentally enter data into the wrong cell.

Worksheets often consist of more than 150 columns and several hundred rows. Naturally, only a small area of the worksheet appears on screen. This visible area is often referred to as the worksheet *window.* To view different areas in the worksheet, most worksheets scroll, or move, through the window.

TYPES OF DATA

The type of **data** entered defines the type of operations performed. There are three basic types of data: **labels, values**, and **formulas**.

Labels

Labels are text entries that describe the content of other cells. For example, in the household budget mentioned earlier, the income

Teaching Tool

Inventory Management

Maintaining accurate school inventories has always posed real problems for teachers and administrators. One solution is to create an inventory spreadsheet for each classroom. During inventory time, it is then very easy for teachers to update the inventory and pass it to the school office, which can generate an updated school-wide inventory.

and expense categories and the month names are labels. Labels sometimes contain numbers— for example, social security numbers for a list of employees—but labels cannot be part of a mathematical operation. That is, characters, such as the word *January,* cannot be added or subtracted.

Values

Values are numeric information, usually numbers. For example, the value 123 in cell B4 may added to, subtracted from, multiplied by, or be divided by any value in another cell. Other mathematical operations can also be performed.

Formulas

Formulas are special types of values that manipulate cell values. For example, a formula in cell N4 can automatically add the 12 monthly car payments in cells B4 through M4. For most spreadsheets, this formula would be expressed: +B4+C4+D4+E4+F4+G4+H4+I4+J4+K4+L4+M4. Formulas begin with a special character, here, a plus sign (+). The plus sign tells the program that the B is not a label, but a cell address in a formula. Some spreadsheets use an at sign (@), and still others use an equals sign (=), to indicate the beginning of a formula.

As suggested earlier, the strength of spreadsheet software is in its use of formulas. A formula automatically performs the specified mathematical operation, no matter how cell values change. Suppose your students want to know how an increase in the car payment—say, to $165.00, would affect the budget. Changing the value in cells

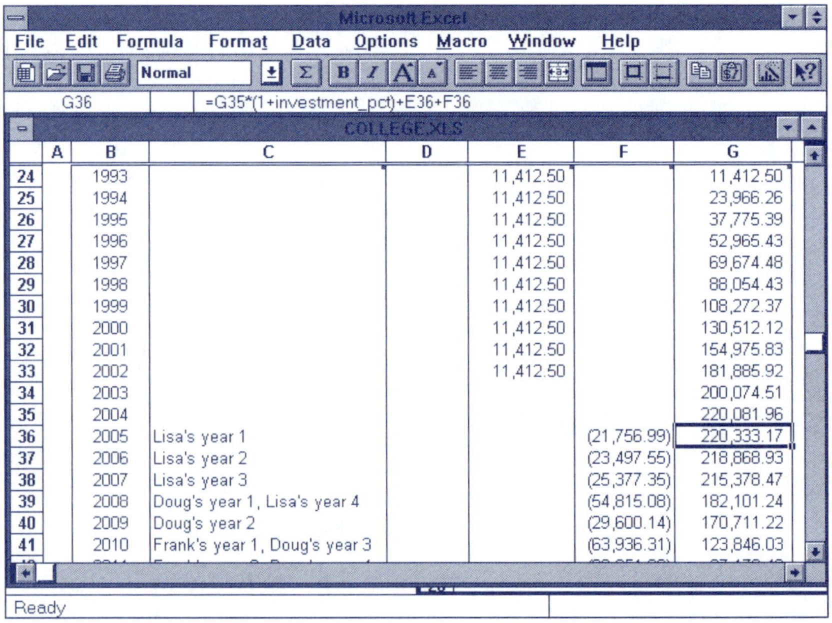

FIGURE 6-4
The spreadsheet formula displays the results of the formula's calculations in the cell. The formula is displayed in the status line.

B4-M4 to $165.00 would automatically cause the total (in cell N4) to reflect this change.

Functions A potential problem with entering formulas into cells is formula length. The formula just used as an example is fairly long. Imagine adding 200 cells. Even if you have the patience to enter long formulas, most spreadsheets do not accept formulas that exceed about 250 characters in length. To address this problem, spreadsheets have *functions* as alternatives to standard mathematical formulas.

Most functions identify specific operations by name and the range of cells on which the operation will be performed. For example, @ SUM(A1:A5) is an addition function that totals the values in all cells beginning with A1 and ending with A5. As a rule, the range of cells selected may not include the cell containing the function. The at sign in this function works as the plus sign in the formula considered earlier. It defines the letters that follow as part of a function. Table 6-1 gives examples of some of the types of functions available.

Table 6-1 Some Common Spreadsheet Functions

Function	Description
@ AVG(A1:A5)	Averages the values in cells A1:A5
@ SUM(A1:A5)	Adds the values in cells A1:A5
@ SQR(x)	Finds the positive square root of x
@ RAND	Generates a random number between 0 and 1
@ DATE(yr,month,day)	Gives the date number of year, month, and day
@ VAR(A1:A5)	Finds the population variance of values in cells A1:A5
@ STD(A1:A5)	Finds the standard deviation of the values in cells A1:A5

Placing Data in a Cell

As mentioned, entering data always begins by moving the cell cursor to the desired cell, then entering the data. Most spreadsheets determine the type of data by the first character entered. For example, when a letter is typed first, the spreadsheet automatically assumes the entry of a label. When a number is typed first, the program assumes a value. While the assumption is usually correct, there are exceptions. You have already seen that a formula or a function must begin with a symbol such as + or @ . Without the symbol, the program would see SUM, for example, as a label, and would not try to calculate in that cell.

Most spreadsheets have default cell widths. That is, they predefine cell widths to limit the number of characters one can enter, usually up to nine characters. As you might expect, many times a cell will not be wide enough to display all the data in the cell, or the cell may be much larger than needed. Either way, it is easy to increase or decrease the width of a column. You may also opt to leave the cell at the default width; all of the data in a cell may not be visible to you, but it is all in the cell, even if it doesn't display. It also appears on an edit line, or entry bar, usually near the top of the worksheet. Formulas or functions display on the edit line or entry bar but are not executed until pressing the Enter or Return key, or moving the cell cursor to a new location. In either case, it is important to finish data entry before pressing Enter or Return or by moving the cell cursor.

DATA FORMATS

The values in budget worksheets are normally expressed in dollars and cents, but it is not necessary to type in dollar signs. Most programs allow you to format numbers in a variety of ways. It is possible to choose whether or not to display dollar signs, where to place commas, and the number of decimal places. These number formats can vary from cell to cell or be set for an entire worksheet.

In addition to specifying number formats, it is possible to specify type fonts, styles, and sizes for both numeric and label data. Using these options helps create visually appealing worksheets. As

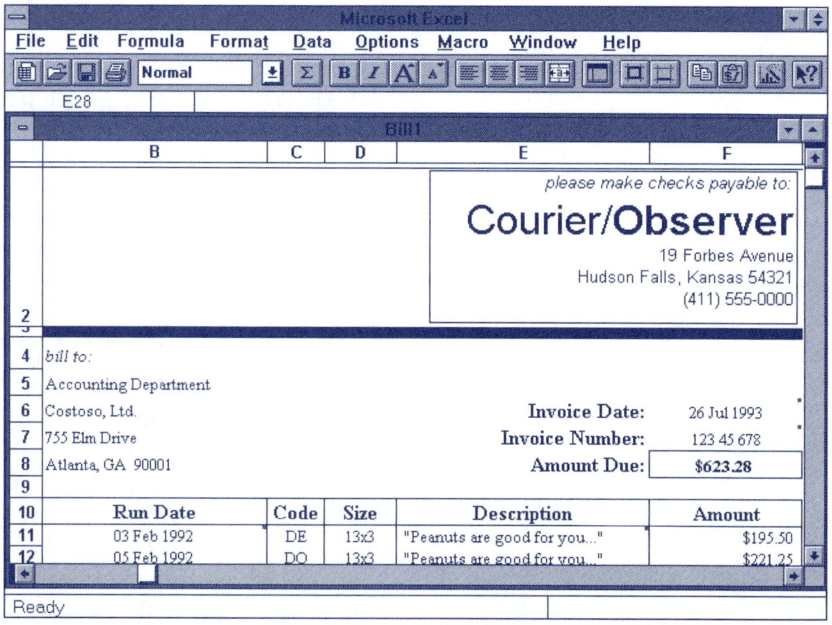

FIGURE 6-5
Many spreadsheets make it easy to format for visual appeal.

Teaching Tool

Spreadsheet Team Statistics

One popular use of spreadsheet software is to maintain full athletic team statistics. A spreadsheet can track a basketball team's shooting percentages, shot location, free throws made, and almost any other type of scoring and shooting data. For a golf team, spreadsheets make it very easy to maintain handicap information.

with word processing programs, however, be judicious in using these options. Overuse of type changes for emphasis can cause distraction and confusion.

The alignment of data in columns and rows can also be adjusted for both numeric and label data. Data can be aligned at the left, right, or center of the cell. Numeric data can also be aligned along decimal points. The process for setting or changing the format will vary from one brand of software to another. However, the first step in formatting is to select cells to change, then specify the desired format characteristics.

Editing Cell Data

Editing the contents of a cell is similar to editing a document on a word processor. While typing a cell entry, but before pressing the Enter or Return key, it is possible to use either the delete or backspace key to delete characters. To replace the contents of other cells, move the cell cursor to the desired cell and re-enter the data.

Copying Cells

The same formula can often be used over and over again with only slight modifications. For example, with a grade worksheet, the teacher may want to average a row of cells for a student. The same formula may be used for each student. Rather than re-type the formula, it is quicker and easier to copy the formula and alter it if needed. The software permits users to copy one cell, a range of cells, and even an entire worksheet.

Inserting Cells

It is also possible to insert new rows and columns. When inserting rows or columns, most spreadsheets automatically adjust formulas and functions to accommodate the changes.

Absolute and Relative Cell Reference

When copying formulas or inserting or deleting columns and rows, it is important to consider absolute versus relative cell reference. Copying a formula using absolute cell reference causes the formula to remain the same in both cells. In other words, absolute reference makes exact copies and does not change the calculation to fit a new location. For example, copying the function @ SUM(A1:A5) from cell A6 to cell B6 results in cell B6 displaying the sum of cells A1 to A5. This can be a problem if you wanted the sum of cells B1 to B5. Using a relative reference causes the function to change to fit the new column.

Recalculating

Some worksheets can get very large. They can have hundreds of formulas and functions. Each time new data is added to the worksheet, the spreadsheet program recalculates. For extremely large worksheets, recalculating all the formulas and functions for each new piece of data can slow down the user and become somewhat annoying.

Most spreadsheets allow you to control when recalculations will take place by offering a choice between automatic and manual recalculation. Manual recalculation will recalculate only when you issue a specific command. Automatic recalculation will recalculate after data entry in each cell. If a worksheet will require a great deal of recalculation, it would probably be faster to enter the new data for the entire worksheet, then recalculate manually.

In addition to the issue of when to recalculate, there is the issue of the order of recalculation. Suppose a formula in cell A1 refers to the contents of a formula in cell C12. Calculating A1 before C12 can cause inaccuracies. Many spreadsheets offer control over the order of calculation and recalculation by offering three approaches: column first, row first, and natural calculations.

Column first and row first determine order by location. However, neither of these options will solve the problem just described. Natural order examines each formula, and if a formula in another cell should be calculated first, natural calculation will calculate in the appropriate order. This is the most commonly used method of recalculation.

Sorting

Spreadsheets also offer the ability to sort rows and columns, either alphabetically or numerically. For example, it is possible to compile an alphabetical list of students. Next to the column identifying each student's name, another column identifying a test score can be created. A third column may list a quiz score. It is possible to sort the list of students by name, test score, or quiz score.

SPREADSHEET FILE MANAGEMENT

With spreadsheet software, as with other applications, saving data on a disk is important. It is not wise to wait to save a file after completing all work. If a power failure occurs, the computer fails, or a cup of coffee falls onto the keyboard before saving the file, all the work may be lost. To avoid problems, save frequently.

Spreadsheet software allows users to save files in a variety of formats. For example, it is possible to save a worksheet as a word processing file to copy the worksheet into a text document. Many word processors will not permit loading a worksheet directly into a text document. Therefore, using a format a word processor can read during the save procedure is important. After saving a worksheet as a word processing file, it is then possible to use the advanced text editing features of the word processor to edit and format text. Of course, after this conversion, one can no longer access spreadsheet functions (for example, to recalculate).

Some spreadsheets also allow you to import files created with other spreadsheet software, databases, or word processors. This feature can be very valuable, especially when using a variety of applications on a single big project.

Creating Templates

One useful feature of spreadsheet software is the capacity to use a basic pattern over and over. Such a pattern is called a **template**. Templates allow users to generate a worksheet design with labels, functions, formulas, and values. Usually, only the data is missing from a template. After creating a template, saving the worksheet on disk without any data makes the worksheet available for different data sets.

File names have an important role in the use of templates. After creating a template, it is important to give a template a generic name when saving. Using the template is as simple as recalling the generic file. Of course, after entering data one must save the new worksheet with a new name. Saving the new file under the generic template name will replace the template on the disk.

PRINTING

Spreadsheets usually offer a wide variety of printing options. The user generally has two choices for printing. The first is to use predefined print settings, known as print *defaults.* The second is to develop customized printing layouts.

Default print settings usually define margins, typeface, typestyle, typesize, locations of page breaks, headers, footers, and page numbering procedures. For many projects, these print defaults are appropriate. However, some projects require customized settings.

Custom print settings allow you to change any default setting. Some programs allow for landscape printing so more columns can be printed on one sheet. The more sophisticated the spreadsheet software and the more sophisticated the printer, the greater the ability to control the print format and settings.

An important piece of advice is never to print a worksheet before saving. Printing is one of the major sources of problems with all applications software. If the printer fails during the printing of a worksheet and the file has not been saved, the entire worksheet and several hours of work can easily be wasted. *Always* save the worksheet file on a disk before issuing a print command.

Teaching Tool

Club Accounting

Most school clubs must maintain a full accounting of income and expenses. Spreadsheets are the ideal tool for such accounting. Not only does using them help students accurately track budget information, it teaches students how accounting is done in almost any business. After all, many clubs are like small businesses.

GRAPHICS OPTIONS

While worksheets can provide a lot of information, it is easy to get lost in numbers and difficult to get an overall view of the data. That is, too much information may cause confusion. For this reason, many spreadsheets offer several graphics capabilities.

Spreadsheets can create graphic displays—line charts, bar graphs, pie charts, and other forms of graphs. It is easy to do, even for inexperienced users. For example, the process for creating bar graphs usually involves selecting a column or row of data for the horizontal axis, or x-axis, and another for the vertical axis, or y-axis, then choosing the bar graph option. The spreadsheet program will generate a bar graph to depict these data.

Spreadsheets offer users several features for enhancing the look of a graph. It is usually possible to enter labels for x- and y-axis descriptions, to enter headlines and captions, select different dot patterns, and create legends.

A graph can be displayed on a screen, sent to a printer, and saved on disk. Viewing can give a quick overview of the data, and sending the graph to a printer permits sharing it with others. Saving a graph as a file is useful not only for future reference, but makes the graph available for import into other programs. For example, a set of files saved on disk could easily be imported into a desktop publisher.

FIGURE 6-6
Some spreadsheets graphically display data.

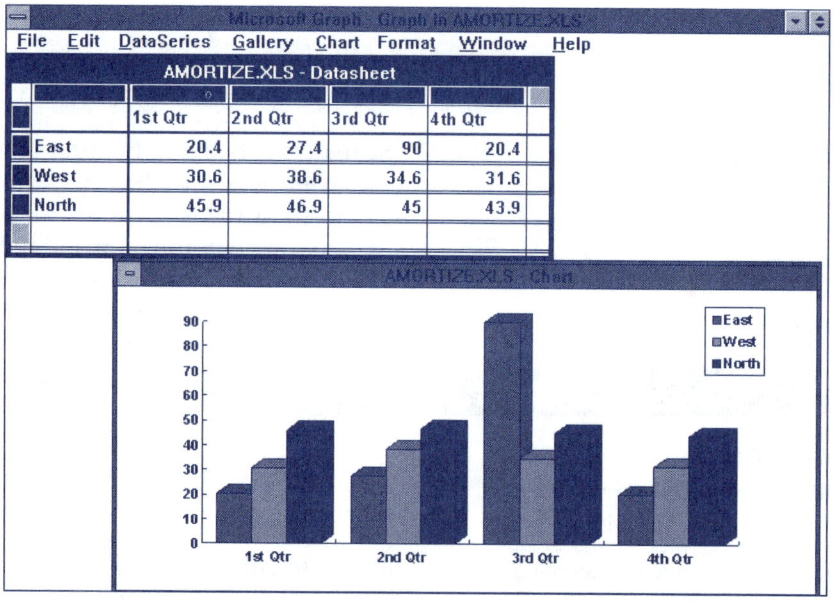

Summary

- Spreadsheet software is designed to support mathematical calculations on organized numerical information.
- Spreadsheet applications software uses worksheets to organize information.
- A worksheet is a series of cells—a giant grid.
- Cells contain words to serve as labels, numbers, and formulas to perform calculations.
- Worksheet cells are organized in columns and rows. Columns are generally identified by letter and rows by number.
- A cell address refers to one single cell (for example, B3).
- Several cells in sequence are called a range.
- There are three basic types of data: labels, values, and formulas.
- Labels are text entries that describe the content of other cells.
- Labels may contain numbers, but labels cannot be any part of mathematical operations.
- Values are the numbers that can be manipulated.
- Formulas are the means for mathematically manipulating the values in cells.
- The strength of a spreadsheet is in its use of formulas.

Fill-In Questions

Fill in the blank for each of the statements listed below.

1. Spreadsheets require information to be entered in ________________ locations.
2. Cells are organized into ________________ and ________________.
3. A reference to a group of several cells that identifies the first and last cell in the sequence is called a ________________.
4. There are three types of spreadsheet data: ________________, ________________, and ________________.
5. ________________ are never manipulated mathematically.
6. The real strength of a spreadsheet is its use of ________________.

Quiz

Answer the following questions.

1. What is the first step for placing data in a cell?
   a. press @ sign
   b. move the cell cursor to the desired cell
   c. press the Enter or Return key
   d. use the function option instead of a formula
2. Cell width is a spreadsheet constant and cannot be changed.
   a. true
   b. false
3. Which type of data does not allow for mathematical operations?
   a. value
   b. formula
   c. label
   d. function
4. Cells are organized into:
   a. columns and rows
   b. random linear arrangements
   c. memory allocation variables
   d. formulas and functions
5. What does a colon typically indicate in a spreadsheet?
   a. cell
   b. range of cells
   c. function
   d. formula
6. Which of the following is best suited for adding the contents of two hundred cells?
   a. value
   b. formula
   c. label
   d. function
7. Which of the following recalculating methods is most commonly used by spreadsheets?
   a. column first
   b. row first
   c. sequential recalculations
   d. natural recalculations
8. Which type of worksheet is used to create several similar spreadsheet files?
   a. natural
   b. directive
   c. template
   d. standard
9. Graphs generated by a spreadsheet program can be used only with that program.
   a. true
   b. false

Exercises and Applications

Follow the instructions for each exercise and application.

1. On a piece of paper, draw out a spreadsheet to calculate grades for a class. In one column, list all the assignments

required. In another column, make up grades already earned and leave space for grades that have not been completed. At the bottom, write down the calculation procedures needed to calculate the final grade.

2. Describe the advantages of using a template. Are there situations in which using a template is inappropriate? Be prepared to share your ideas.
3. Maintaining sports statistics can be time-consuming. Pick any sport and develop an outline for a spreadsheet to maintain the appropriate statistics. For example, what columns and rows are needed to keep statistics on the batting averages of baseball players or handicap scores of golfers?
4. Devise a spreadsheet to calculate your college expenses and income. Be sure to note the types of calculations needed and the locations of these calculations. In addition, create a line for totals. Does your income equal your payments? If not, what changes could you make to balance income and expenses?

7

ESSENTIALS OF GRAPHICS

LEARNING OBJECTIVES

Learning the material in this chapter will enable you to:

- describe the major types of graphics hardware
- distinguish among different types of display adapters
- discuss uses of scanners and other input devices
- identify major types of output devices for graphics software
- describe four major types of graphics software and their uses
- describe the difference between draw and paint software

CHAPTER OVERVIEW

For teachers and students with little artistic ability and training, the notion of creating a drawing, or even a simple sign, a pie chart, or a bar graph, can cause anxiety. With a microcomputer and graphics software, however, even the most artistically illiterate can create a variety of high-quality graphics. You need only supply a little imagination and a basic understanding of graphics software.

Graphics software performs many tasks that the unartistic may find difficult to do by hand. Drawing a circle takes a steady hand, but with graphics software, drawing a circle is as easy as selecting a command. Of course, just because graphics software makes many drawing tasks easier does not mean that it is only for non-artists. The professional artist will find tools to create, edit, and produce high-quality designs. A graphic artist can easily create a design with the various drawing tools, change colors with a simple click of the mouse, and even resize and rotate the orientation of a graphic with simple menu selections.

This chapter provides an overview of the capabilities common to graphics programs. Beginning with a discussion of the types of graphics, this chapter then discusses the fundamental process involved in controlling most graphics application. This chapter also describes the hardware used in creating visual displays and some software packages. Learning these concepts should make using graphics software a fun and rewarding experience.

GRAPHICS

Graphics is a generic term that describes visual output. This visual output can be a line drawing, photograph, picture, or almost any type of image. Graphics can also mean graphs or charts. In short, graphics is the generic term for output that is not primarily text.

The software used to create graphics comes in many different forms. Some software provides graphics capability though graphics is not the primary function of the software. For example, most spreadsheets have a graphics component. Other types of graphics software are dedicated exclusively to graphics production. In either case, the programs that generate graphics fall into three major categories: data-generated graphics, device-generated graphics, and user-generated graphics.

Data-generated graphics use numerical data to create graphics such as pie charts, bar graphs, and line charts. Software such as Lotus 1-2-3, Microsoft Excel, and Harvard Graphics create graphics from data. Lotus 1-2-3 and Microsoft Excel are spreadsheet programs that make a variety of graphics from numbers stored in columns and rows. For example, a spreadsheet may contain several rows reflecting different categories of household expenses. Columns may contain the amount budgeted for each category. The spreadsheet software can generate a pie chart to display how much each category requires from the total budget. Harvard Graphics allows the entry of data for the explicit purpose of creating graphics. These range from pie charts to three-dimensional images.

Device-generated graphics are the products of the combination of special hardware and software. Often, a special type of **graphics software** controls hardware to transfer images into a computer. Graphics created with a **scanner** belong in this group. A scanner is a hardware device that creates an electronic copy of a picture and sends that electronic copy to the computer. A scanner can reproduce a photograph on a computer monitor. When using a scanner, beware of copyright infringement if the material is to be reproduced. Check for copyright violation first!

The third major category is **user-generated graphics**. Certainly, users create *all* graphics in one way or another. However, user-generated graphics refers to art created with special draw and paint programs. MacPaint is a popular Macintosh program that allows people to create designs with several drawing and painting tools. **Computer-aided design (CAD)** software such as AutoCad is widely used by professional engineers to create detailed drafting designs.

Many graphics programs support two or all three major types of graphics. For example, PC Paintbrush is a popular drawing program available for IBM and IBM compatible computers. This software permits users to generate graphics via an assortment of drawing and painting tools. In addition, it supports the use of device-generated graphics. PC Paintbrush can control the way a scanner inputs data and allows you to change the image created with the scanner.

Teaching Tool

Student Faces

There are few things as exciting to students as when they can put their own personal touch to documents they create. Currently, there is graphics hardware and software that allows a video camera to connect directly to a computer. Through the video camera, students can record images and save them to disk as a graphics file. This file can then be used in other graphics programs and imported into word processing and desktop publishing software. With this tool, students can digitize their own picture and import it into their writing assignments.

For an art teacher teaching graphic arts, this tool can be very exciting. What better way to introduce the concepts of graphic control than to have students manipulate graphic images of themselves?

FIGURE 7-1
SuperPaint is a popular draw and paint program that provides several tools for freehand, creative drawing.

Teachers, Students, and Graphics

Graphics produced on computers are part of our everyday lives. For teachers and students, creating and using graphics to communicate can be as effective as creating and using text. Newspapers and magazines use pie charts, bar graphs, and other data-generated images created on computers. These images present information in a simple form. Posters, signs, and billboards often contain computer art, and so do newsletters, brochures, and advertisements. Computer graphics software helps create titles and special effects for both films and television. Some of the most popular Saturday morning cartoons are produced on computer, and fine art produced on computers is becoming an accepted genre.

Teachers use graphics software for a variety of visual displays. A history teacher may develop a time line depicting major historic events. A biology teacher may illustrate the parts of a frog. Displays can even be animated; a computer teacher may create a display that shows how information flows from an input device, through the CPU, to an output device. A science teacher, instead of using the chalkboard to draw a picture of a heat exchange system, can use graphics software to animate heat transfer. Other graphics capabilities help teachers create awards and certificates, signs and posters, and classroom newsletters.

Graphics are available to students for a variety of uses. One popular use is to incorporate graphics into term papers and other reports. A picture detailing environmental cycles can make a paper more interesting to read and convey information about environmental issues. In social science classes, bar graphs or pie charts are frequently incorporated into papers written to describe

FIGURE 7-2
Teachers often use programs like The Print Shop.

social trends. Students of geography often learn to use computer programs for creating maps. Engineering students spend time learning to use CAD software to design products or structures. Meteorology students often learn to use software to create weather maps and generate weather forecasts.

Among the first groups to recognize the value of computers in graphics were professional artists. Before graphics software developed the sophistication to be useful in commercial art, graphic artists in commercial art and advertising spent most of their time at drawing tables producing images by hand. Minor alterations required that the picture be re-drawn. Computers offered the advantages of ease of drawing, ease of editing, and ease of producing several versions of the same picture. For artists and art students, graphics software is becoming a popular medium.

GRAPHICS HARDWARE

Graphics software requires certain hardware. Not every computer can handle all graphics software. More than any other type of software, graphics software has very strict requirements for the type of computer, peripherals, system configuration, and supporting hardware. Supporting hardware is separated into three broad categories. First, graphics **display adapters** and monitors are required to display visual images. Second, devices that enter graphics data into the computer are necessary for some software. Third, printers and other output devices must support graphics software. How the computer uses these three types of hardware, and the level of sophistication of the hardware, directly affect the polish of the graphics produced.

Graphics Display Adapters and Monitors

Displaying graphics requires two elements. First, a graphics display adapter, sometimes called a **graphics adapter** or **graphics interface**, is the hardware that translates graphic images for the monitor. Second, the monitor displays the images created by the graphics adapter. Both are required; one will not work without the other. In many cases, the graphics adapter and monitor must match the requirements of the graphics software. In other words, some graphics software requires a certain graphics adapter and monitor.

One classification of graphics adapters determines if a display is monochrome (for example, black and white) or color. Within the classification of color graphic adapters, there are additional categories of color graphic adapters. Some graphics adapters generate 16-color displays. Other adapters generate 256-color displays. This classification of color graphic adapters also determines the caliber of the display. Images generated by graphic adapters are made up of dots, called **pixels**, organized in a minute grid. Both the number and the size of the pixels determine the **resolution** of the display—that is, the display's sharpness and clarity. Higher resolution means greater sharpness and clarity; the more pixels, the higher the resolution. For example, a graphics adapter that generates 300 by 200 pixels has a much lower resolution than an adapter that displays 640 by 480 pixels.

Just as there are different graphics adapters, there are different monitors. Some monitors are monochromatic, while others display color. Some monitors support only a low-resolution graphics adapter. Other monitors support several different resolutions. However, the key is that both the monitor and the display adapter must match. A monitor designed to display 300 by 200 pixels will only work with a matching graphics adapter. Anything not meshing will cause the monitor to remain blank or not work properly.

For computers with built-in graphics adapters and monitors, such as the Macintosh, how to combine the adapter and monitor is not an issue (unless the user adds an external monitor). In the MS-DOS family of computers, however, the issue of matching graphic adapters and monitors can be byzantine.

There are five major types of graphics adapters for MS-DOS computers. Each displays graphics in different resolutions. Table 7-1 contains the graphics type, the maximum number of colors it can display, and the level of resolution. Notice that as the level of resolution for each type of adapter increases, the number of possible colors it can display decreases.

Table 7-1 Graphics Display Adapters

Name	Resolution	Number of Colors
Hercules Graphics	750 by 348	Monochrome
Color Graphics Array (CGA)	640 by 200	2 of 16 colors
or	300 by 200	4 of 16 colors
Enhanced Color Graphics (EGA)	640 by 350	16 of 64 colors
Video Graphics Array (VGA)	640 by 480	16 of 256 colors
or	320 by 200	256 of 256 colors
Super VGA (SVGA)	800 by 600	256 of 256 colors
or	1024 by 768	16 of 256 colors

In addition to these five major types of adapters, there are others that have even greater resolution. Many of these additional graphics adapters support monitors that display more information than the traditional monitor. For example, some display at resolutions higher than 1024 by 768 to support a monitor that will display a full page of information at one time. These graphic adapters and monitors are typically used by graphic artists and other professionals and cost as much or more than an entire computer system.

There are as many different types of monitors as there are types of display adapters. There are monitors that support **Hercules Graphics, CGA** monitors, **EGA** monitors, **VGA** monitors, and **SVGA** monitors. Some specialized monitors support multiple adapters. These are called multi-frequency monitors because they automatically adjust to support a CGA, EGA, VGA, or SVGA graphics adapter.

Scanners and Other Input Devices

Several options are available for entering graphics information into the computer. Many computers support the use of a mouse as a drawing tool. Some computers can use specialized input devices. These specialized devices often provide greater precision than a mouse when entering data, or allow for different types of graphics to be entered into the computer.

One popular input device is a scanner. Scanners look like small copy machines and use a similar process. Scanners electronically reproduce an image, convert it to a digital format, and send the image to the scan software. Scanners differ in resolution as measured by **dots per inch (dpi)**. Some scanners read a picture at 75 dpi. Others can read the same picture at 300 dpi. The higher the dpi, the higher the resolution, and the greater the sharpness and clarity of the image.

Teaching Tool

Clip Art

For quickly and easily adding pizazz to a word processing or desktop publishing document, many teachers and students use clip art. Clip art is a set of finished graphics. Most clip art packages provide hundreds of graphics, covering almost any topic. From holiday designs, to award certificates, to automobiles, there is clip art available to illustrate almost any document's subject.

Another type of input device popular for graphics applications is a **graphics tablet**. Using a graphics tablet is similar to using a mouse. The tablet itself is marked with precise coordinates, which the mouse reads. One uses graphics tablets to draw to scale. Some highly specialized software comes with a special tablet that contains many of the symbols peculiar to drafting. These symbols can be entered along with the graphic drawing.

Laser Printers and Other Output Devices

If printed output is required, the quality of the printer is as important as the quality of input. A new company logo may be very appealing on a high-resolution computer screen, but printing the design on a low-resolution dot-matrix printer reduces the appeal dramatically. (Of course, dot-matrix printers differ in quality. Some dot-matrix printers, such as 9-pin printers, produce low-resolution and low-quality output. Other dot-matrix printers, especially 24-pin printers, produce a much higher quality graphic output.)

Laser printers provide high-quality output at a moderate price—well under $2,000. Laser printers can print graphics at higher levels of resolution than some monitors. A major disadvantage is that most laser printers print only black. Shades of gray and varying dot patterns simulate different colors. Color laser printers are available, but they are very expensive (often more than $10,000).

Most color printers are **ink-jet printers**, which spray paper with ink (rather than impact paper through a ribbon, as with dot-matrix printers) or use an ionization process similar to photocopying, as with laser printers. Ink-jet printers are usually less expensive than laser printers, and the resolution of many ink-jet printers matches that of laser printers. For line drawings, color **plotters** are a common output device. Plotters use ink pens to draw lines. Both the pens *and* the paper move. Typically, plotters draw all the lines of one color, move the paper back to the starting position, draw all the lines of the next color, and so on.

An output device becoming more and more common is the **film recorder**. Film recorders produce a photo negative from an image created on a computer screen. Typically, a film recorder takes a photograph of an image to produce a color negative suitable for reproduction. These devices are especially useful for creating color slide presentations, as well as for full-color printing.

GRAPHICS SOFTWARE

The best graphics hardware is, of course, of little value without high-quality software. Today, an assortment of graphics software for a broad array of applications is available. This section discusses the major types of software and their general applications.

Graphing Software

As mentioned earlier, graphics can be generated from data sets. Most graphing software falls in this category. For example, software such as Lotus 1-2-3 provides you with built-in graphing options, but other software may not. Too, programs that provide for graphing may have limited capabilities. Still other software allows users to create graphs from data generated by other applications programs. For example, Lotus 1-2-3 has some graphing capabilities, but other graphing software can take Lotus 1-2-3 data and offer a much broader selection of graphs with much more detail.

The range and types of graphics created with graphing programs differ from one package to another. As with all software, there are simple and inexpensive programs as well as sophisticated and expensive ones. The requirements of the user and his or her computer system will determine the quality of the software he or she buys.

Some popular graphics of data are bar graphs, line graphs, pie charts, flowcharts, histograms, and scatter plots. Some graphing programs, such as Freelance Plus from Lotus Development Corporation, have a library of graphic symbols. These programs may use pictures of people, rather than shaded areas, to represent population distributions. Some programs have maps of the United States that can be used to display sales and other types of information. Programs such as 3D-Graphics from Intex Solutions can produce three-dimensional images.

Most graphing programs also allow you to enter data and import it from other applications. These programs also allow you to edit imported data. However, the means of placing data into a graphing program, either by importing or directly entering

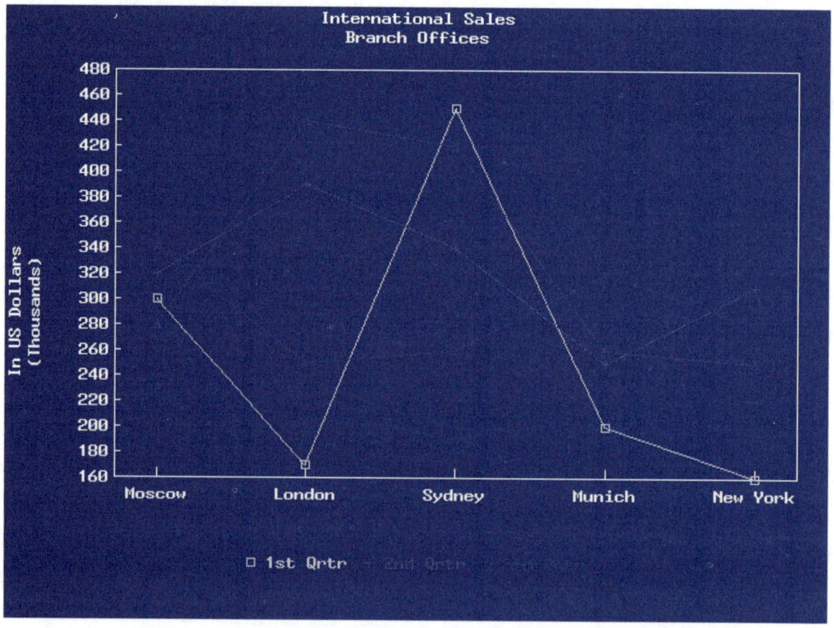

FIGURE 7-3
Lotus 1-2-3 makes it easy to chart spreadsheet data.

the data, must consider the type of data format supported by the graphing software. That is, entering and importing data is only possible when the data matches the requirements of the graphing software.

Paint and Draw Software

Programs that provide you with drawing and painting are called draw and paint software. Unlike data-generated graphing programs, this type of software is designed for freehand drawing and most closely resembles the creative tools of an artist. Electronic paintbrushes, color palettes, and dozens of other tools are typically available. In most cases, control over these tools is by mouse.

Draw and paint software are different. While both types perform many of the same tasks, their methods of creating, storing, and using graphics are different.

Draw software uses objects onscreen to create images, so this type is referred to as **object-oriented graphics**. With this type of software, selecting and using a tool creates an object. For example, selecting a line tool allows users to create a single line object. The picture produced with draw software is a combination of several distinct objects. An object can be a line, a rectangle, square, circle, or any other object created with the software tools. The key point with object-oriented graphics is independence. Each object in the total graphic image can be moved independently of other parts of the drawing.

The easiest way to understand object-oriented graphics is to think of a stick-figure drawing of a person. As an object-oriented graphic, the person is made up of a circle for the head and lines for

FIGURE 7-4
Draw and paint software provide a wide range of drawing tools.

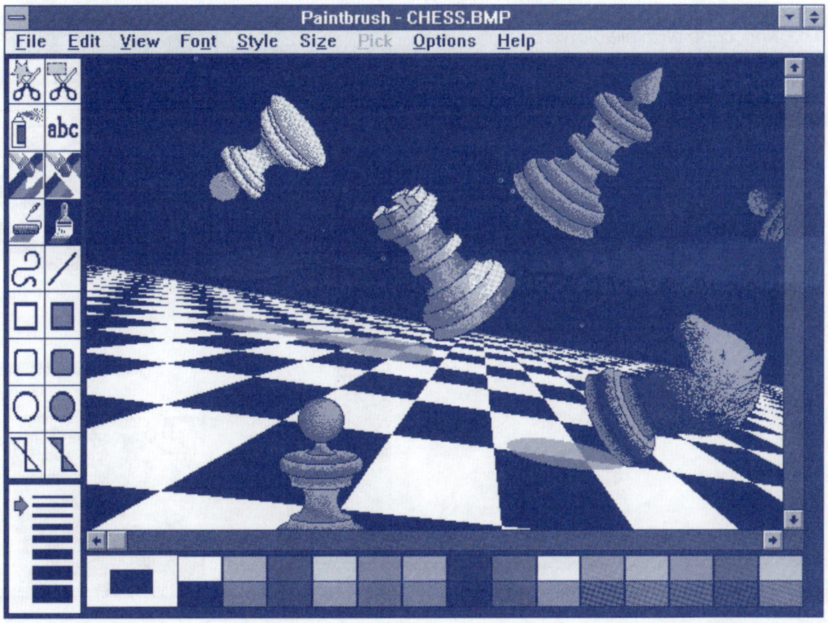

neck, body, arms and legs. Each object remains independent of all other objects. If you want to delete a body part, you can delete *only* the part you choose.

Paint software does not treat graphic images as a collection of independent objects. Rather, each time a tool is used to add to the graphic, the results become integrated into the total graphic. In other words, paint programs create graphics as a complete entity.

Graphics produced with paint software are called *bit-mapped graphics* because the image is generated by pixel. With bit-mapped graphics, the image of the stick person is a single entity rather than a collection of individual objects. Therefore, you cannot move or delete a limb in its entirely. You must do so by pixel.

Object-oriented graphics provide much simpler control than bit-mapped graphics. Object-oriented graphics use mathematical formulas to define independent images; these formulas make each object very exact and well-defined. Lines are smooth, crisp, and precise. Bit-mapped graphics do not always appear smooth because they are an integrated collection of dots. As a general rule, object-oriented graphics are preferable for line art and bit-mapped graphics for detailed pictures.

One of the major disadvantages of bit-mapped graphics is the amount of disk storage space required for each image. Bit-mapped graphics use much more disk space than object-oriented images; the size depends on the number of pixels in the image (some images may be larger than 1Meg). For a detailed photograph, the image file may require more storage space than is available on a floppy disk. Hard disk storage space may also become filled. Remove unwanted or unused bit-mapped graphics from the hard drive regularly.

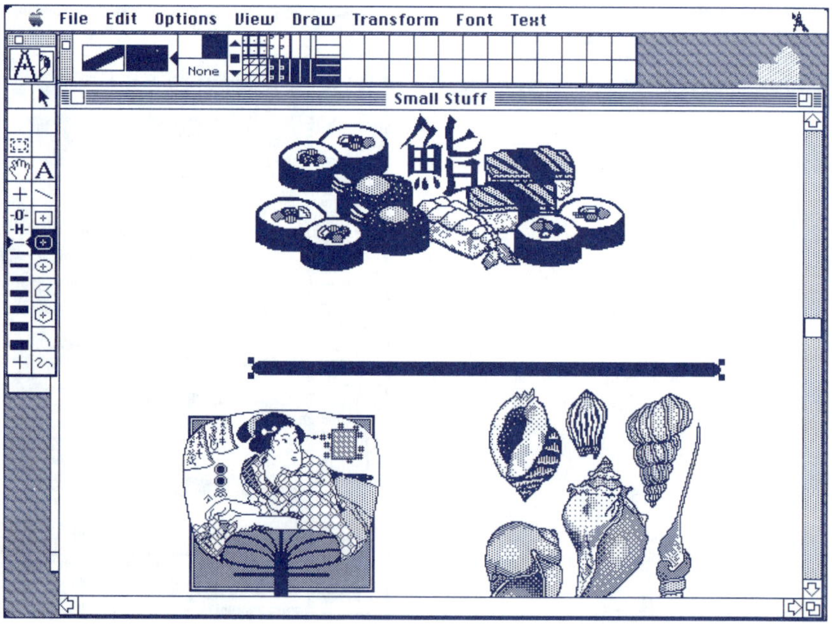

FIGURE 7-5
The fine control available with bit-mapped software permits the drawing of very detailed pictures.

Another disadvantage of bit-mapped images is the sometimes lengthy print time. A complex image may take as long as six hours to print.

Images produced with a scanner are bit-mapped graphics. The entire image is an entity, rather than a series of independent parts. Scanners use bit-mapped images, in part, because bit-mapped images allow for greater detail. In fact, scanners can input bit-mapped images with greater detail than many bit-mapped image programs allow. To help reduce the amount of space needed to store bit-mapped graphics, a special type of file format called *Tag Image File Format* (TIFF) is available in most bit-mapped software. TIFF files store bit-mapped images in less space than do the standard formats for paint programs. Because scanned images often consume large amounts of disk space, tighter file formats are important.

The table below shows some of the more popular draw and paint software packages.

Object-oriented

IBM	Corel Draw Micrografx Picture Publisher
Macintosh	Aldus Freehand Adobe Illustrator

Bit-mapped

IBM	PhotoFinish PC Paintbrush
Macintosh	Colorstudio Fullpaint

Presentation Graphics

The term *presentation graphics* refers to images that combine text and graphics for presenting information. For most uses, presentation graphics are produced in a sequence of computer generated images similar to a sequence of overhead transparencies and slides. The user displays the sequence on a monitor or creates slides and transparencies directly from the presentation graphics software. A user displaying the sequence on a monitor can control presentation order, rate, and detail.

Presentation graphics are increasingly popular, especially for businesses and schools. Imagine, for example, presenting information about a specific historical period to an elementary class. Instead of using hand-drawn or typed overhead transparencies, you could use presentation graphics software, which could include dissolving images, creating overlays, incorporating text and graphics, using images to display data, and other special visual effects. These help emphasize certain points and make presentations more appealing.

FIGURE 7-6
Presentation graphics software can incorporate text with graphics such as this to produce informational displays.

While presentation graphics cannot improve the quality of information, it can improve the quality of the presentation.

CAD Software

The number of drawing tools and the level of sophistication of most draw software is not well-suited for the precision drawing required by professional drafters, engineers, architects, and technical designers. For these users, computer-aided design (CAD) software is a popular choice.

Teaching Tool

School Calendars

The list of events in any school is constantly changing. One popular use of graphics software is to generate a weekly or monthly calendar for both teachers and students. For class, a teacher can keep a calendar of assignments' due dates, project work times, lesson schedules, and even who has specific duties on specific days. Calendars can be posted or given to each student, helping them prepare for upcoming events. School-wide calendars have the same uses.

Utility Graphics Software

Draw and paint programs are for general use and can create a wide range of images. However, this flexibility is sometimes overkill for users who need to create a limited and focused graphic. Utility software limits the control of draw and paint programs, allowing users to create only limited types of graphic.

One popular piece of utility software is The Print Shop. With The Print Shop, students and teachers can generate posters, signs, greeting cards, and letterheads by simply following a set of menus and prompts. The Print Shop provides a library for the selection of graphics and typefaces, the capability to enter text, and ease of printing. This program is appealing as much for its low price as for the types of graphics that it can create. Create A Calendar, also inexpensive, generates an assortment of calendars. This program

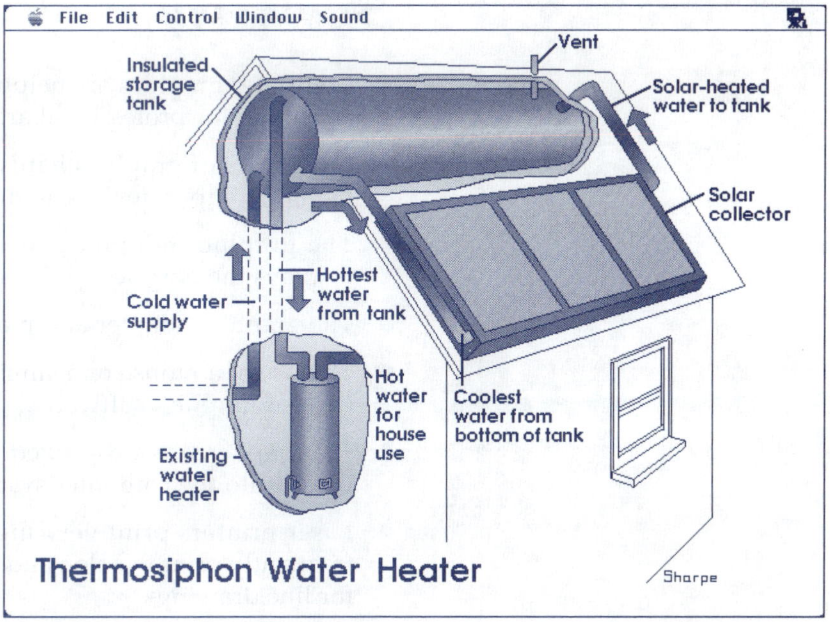

FIGURE 7-7
MacroMind Director gives users the ability to develop a complete presentation, including sound and animation.

uses many of the same simple procedures as The Print Shop. Certificate Maker, another popular utility graphics program, allows people to customize more than 100 predefined certificates, including athletic awards, humorous awards, and achievement awards. The Newsroom enables you to incorporate predefined pictures and text to produce simple, yet appealing, newsletters. Many schools and businesses use this program to create in-house newsletters.

FIGURE 7-8
These are a few of the popular graphic utility software packages.

Summary

- Computer graphics are helpful for those with little artistic ability as well as for professional artists.
- Categories of graphics hardware include graphics adapters and monitors, input devices, and printers and other output devices.
- The graphics adapter generates the display, and the monitor displays the output.
- The graphics adapter and monitor must match to work correctly.
- The use of a mouse or a similar input device is the main drawing tool for graphics software.
- Scanners create a digitized replica of an image and enter that image into the computer system.
- Laser printers print very high-quality graphics. Ink-jet printers frequently print in color, and plotters are common output devices for line drawings.
- Draw-type graphics are object-oriented. Each piece of an object-oriented graphic may be individually adjusted.
- Paint-type programs use bit-mapped graphics. A bit-mapped graphic is an integrated whole.
- Presentation graphics permit the creation of overhead transparencies, slides, and screen presentations. Both text and graphics combine to produce a visually appealing presentation.
- Graphic utility software permits users to easily create limited types of graphics.

Fill-In Questions

Fill in the blank for each of the statements listed below.

1. Graphics software falls into three major categories:
   ________________, ________________, and
   ________________.
2. ________________ is special hardware used to pass images into a computer.
3. Monitors and graphics adapters must ________________ to work effectively.

4. Five of the most common graphics adapters for MS-DOS computers are ________________, ________________, ________________, ________________, and ________________.

5. ________________ refers to the sharpness and clarity of the display.

6. ________________ printers have enhanced the usefulness of graphics software by providing high-quality output at a moderate price.

Quiz

Answer the following questions.

1. What is the most common type of graphic input device?
   a. scanner
   b. modem
   c. mouse
   d. graphics tablet

2. Which type of graphics adapter allows only monochromatic displays?
   a. CGA
   b. EGA
   c. VGA
   d. Hercules

3. Which type of software is typically used to create slides and transparencies?
   a. utility graphics
   b. paint programs
   c. presentation graphics
   d. object-oriented graphics

4. What unit of measure describes the resolution of a graphics adapter?
   a. pixels
   b. dots per inch
   c. resolution
   d. graphics display function (GDF)

5. Which type of device can create a photograph from an image created on a computer?
   a. scanner
   b. film recorder
   c. plotter
   d. laser printer

6. Which type of device is used to input photographs?
   a. scanner
   b. film recorder
   c. plotter
   d. laser printer

7. Paint programs use which type of graphics?
   a. object-oriented graphics
   b. bit-mapped graphics
   c. CAD-oriented graphics
   d. video array graphics

8. Draw programs use which type of graphics?
   a. object-oriented graphics b. bit-mapped graphics
   c. CAD-oriented graphics d. video array graphics

9. Which type of program is best for creating complex technical drawings?
   a. paint programs b. draw programs
   c. CAD software d. utility software

Exercises and Applications

Follow the instructions for each exercise and application.

1. Learning to use simple graphics software is an important part of learning to use a computer. Learn the basic elements of one draw or paint program and use it to draw a house. Experiment with as many of the drawing or painting tools as you wish. Have fun.

2. Computer-generated graphs, such as bar graphs and pie charts, are often used in newspapers, magazines, and other types of publications. Locate three computer-generated graphs and copy them to share with the rest of the class.

3. Utility graphics software is one of the easiest types of software to learn to use. Print Shop is one of the most popular utility graphics programs. If you have access to Print Shop, use it to create a sign. If Print Shop is not available, find another utility graphics program and create a different type of display to share with the class.

8

ESSENTIALS OF DATABASES

LEARNING OBJECTIVES

Learning the material in this chapter will enable you to:

- describe the major uses of databases in schools
- describe the three-level organization of a database
- describe the roles of database fields and records
- describe the major components of a database
- identify four data types
- identify the two methods of organizing data
- describe a data query
- describe Structured Query Language (SQL)

CHAPTER OVERVIEW

Maintaining school records was a major problem until the advent of database software. Just consider what it takes to keep track of student grades. Not only do teachers have to calculate grades, but those grades must be kept for years in cumulative folders. Before computers, school personnel began the process of updating cumulative records by locating and pulling each file from banks of file cabinets. The next step involved writing entries into the file—for each course grade, for attendance, for disciplinary information, and so on. The last step was to return the file to its proper location in the file cabinet and hope the data entry, as well as the filing, were accurate.

The first step in manual data storage—finding a file—is the first potential source of difficulty. Finding correctly-placed paper files takes time, but the amount of time and energy it takes to find a misplaced file is extraordinary. No matter how hard people try to be accurate, misplacing information and files with manual data storage is common.

Suppose a principal needed a list of all students who participated in extra-curricular activities or a list of all student addresses. Without using a computer, each file must be pulled from the file cabinet and carefully examined. The sought-after data had to be recorded in a new paper file. Usually, this meant using pencil and paper. After locating and recording data from a paper file, the file must be returned to the file cabinet—again, in the correct location.

Manual data collection and examination are time-consuming and prone to a high degree of error. Today, rather than searching through piles of paper to locate a file or to find specific data in several files, we have database software to perform these tasks very efficiently. Instead of storing data in paper files, database software stores data electronically on a disk. Instead of requiring an army of people to search through a file cabinet for one or more files, database software makes it easy to search through all files almost instantaneously. Instead of having to scan an entire file for specific data, database software will do it for you.

As do the chapters on word processors and spreadsheets, this chapter provides the basic knowledge needed to begin to use database software. It begins with an overview of the uses and users of database software and why this software is important. This chapter discusses procedures common to creating a structure to store data and methods for searching, locating, then reporting data within a database structure. A discussion of the major types of database organizations is also available, along with some useful methods for using databases.

DATABASE

In its simplest form, database software makes it possible for computers to store and retrieve large sets of data. In some ways, all computer applications are types of database software. Certainly, a word processor stores documents as data and a spreadsheet stores worksheets as data. But neither of these types of programs is database software.

For software to be true database software, it must have a quick and easy means of storing, recalling, sorting, and reporting on a wide range of data. Unlike wordprocessors, which only store text, or spreadsheets, which store mostly numbers, database software stores almost any type of data. This includes grades, address lists, extra-curricular activities, student medical information, or almost anything. It also offers several different ways to recall data. Word processors and spreadsheets can only recall one set of data—a document or a worksheet. Database software can recall as much or as little data as users need, in almost any type, form, or category.

What distinguishes database software from other types of software is the method for storing and recalling data. Database software stores data in individual locations within a file. The file is called a *database,* and locations of information within a database are known as *fields.* For example, a college's database of student information may contain a social security field, a name field, a grade

FIGURE 8-1
Database software works very well for maintaining student records.

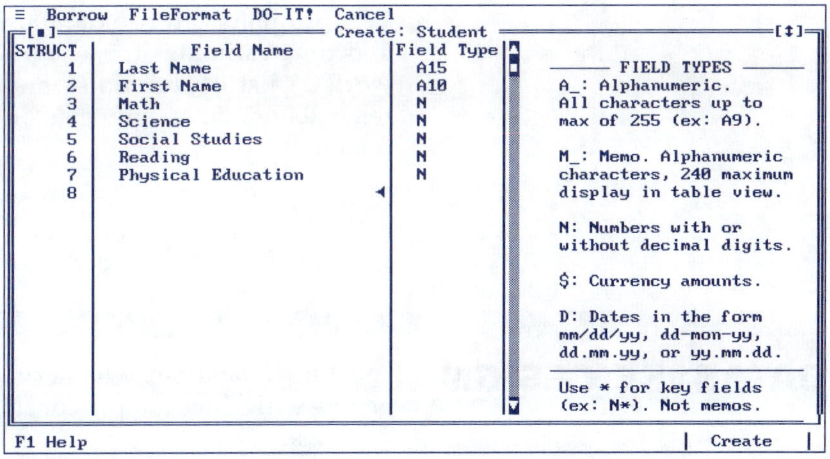

field, a telephone number field, and so on. By using fields to store data, the database software can locate individual pieces of information.

Database software is also differentiated by its ability to link groups of data stored in fields. These related groups of fields are known as a *record*. To understand the difference between a field and a record, think of the college's student database. Each student has his or her own record. That record contains several fields: the student's first and last names, major, and GPA. The record is specific to each student, but the field is common to all records.

Because of the organizational structure of fields and records, data entered into fields are available for recall in a variety of classifications. Suppose a registrar wishes to compile a list of all the math majors who have earned a GPA of 4.0. Database software can search every student record for those two parameters. From this search, the database software can collect appropriate records and produce a report. You can search records for any number of parameters. That is, the report may include student names, addresses, social security numbers, and information from many other fields.

Teaching Tool

Happy Birthday

School-wide databases can be used for much more than attendance and grade reporting. School databases usually maintain birth date information on each child; it is very easy to link the database to the other software that can produce birthday cards. While this may not be the most important use of database software, the goodwill is well worth the small amount of effort.

Teachers, Students, and Databases

Database software can be used in an almost endless number of ways. Here are a few of the most common.

One method of reducing paperwork for teachers and administrators is to centralize recordkeeping. Student grades are often part of a centralized database that can generate report cards, honor lists, detention notices, and many other reports. Student transcripts are part of a university database. Other databases used in schools may contain budgetary data, salary schedules, and personnel files. School administrators can retrieve data on all personnel earning a particular salary or all personnel with a specific educational degree.

Students can use databases to enter assignments, due dates, and time estimates for assignments to track and organize homework. A list of due dates and time estimates can help students remember to do assignments on time rather than waiting for the last minute.

DATABASE DESIGN

Creating a database, whether for personal use or for a large school, begins with three simple considerations—**data type, data size,** and **data use**. *Data type* specifies the kind of data included in the database. *Data size* specifies the amount of each data type. *Data use* determines the order for data input and the procedures for recalling data. Normally these decisions are made in a detailed planning process. (Once constructed in the computer, a database can of course be changed, but this task can be laborious; it's best to plan the best preliminary organization one is able to plan.)

Planning is the most important activity for successfully creating a useable database. Planning involves organizing data to account for data type, data size, and data use. As you will see throughout the rest of this chapter, organizational planning focuses on the design of files, records, and fields.

Files, Records, and Fields

Database software organizes data on three levels. The highest and most general level is the database file. A *file* is the total collection of data in a database. *Records* are collections of data related to a single entity, such as a person or a place. For example, a database file of student records normally contains one record for each student. All records in a file have individual names for identification.

Just as files are made up of records, records are made up of fields. A *field* is the location to enter and store one set of data. Fields are identified by field name. For student records, each record normally contains several fields. However, while data within fields are different from record to record, each record has the same *set* of fields. For example, a student record database may have a field titled Math Grade. This field appears in every record within the database file. However, the actual grade (data) placed in a field varies from record to record. This arrangement, having each record use the same fields, is known as the *database structure.*

Naming is a very important aspect for files, records, and fields because names identify groups of similar information. File names specify the collection of related records. Record names (often identified by numbers) specify the collection of related data stored in fields. Finally, each field within a record is named to identify the specific type of data.

The structure of the database determines the type and amount of data to store in each record. To picture a database structure, look at the following table for math students.

Table 8-1 Sample Database of Math Students

Rcrd #	Student Name	Student ID	Section	Pts	Pass	Date
0001	Smith, R.J.	123-45-6789	01	145	.T.	02/17/88
0002	Jones, S.B.	123-46-9876	02	140	.T.	02/17/88
0003	Vonk, J.A.	987-65-4321	01	100	.F.	02/17/88
0004	Erickson, F.	879-65-4321	02	90	.F.	02/17/88
0005	Bert, C.B.	987-56-4678	01	136	.T.	05/12/90
0006	Ernie, G.F.	456-76-3456	02	104	.F.	05/12/90
0007	Piglet, F.G.	234-76-9087	01	123	.F.	05/12/90

Table 8-1 identifies a single database file made up of seven individual records. Each record contains six fields—Student Name, Student ID, Section, Pts, Pass, and Date. Remember, all records use the same fields and field names. The only difference is the actual data stored in each field.

Data Types

For most databases, the four most common types of data are alphanumeric, numeric, logical, and date. Alphanumeric data includes letters, numbers, or any other type of symbol. It is similar to label data in spreadsheets. Alphanumeric data is descriptive.

Numeric data, on the other hand, are made up solely of numbers that can be manipulated mathematically. The computer determines whether numbers are alphanumeric or numeric based on the type of field in which the numbers are located. Numeric data in an alphanumeric field cannot be added, subtracted, or subjected to any mathematical operation. If the numbers are in a numeric field, then these numbers are available for mathematical operations. For example, a numeric field—that is, a field containing numeric data—may have attendance data. The user can add all the numeric data to determine how many days one or all students missed.

Logical data is *dichotomous,* meaning that this data may only be used in one of two states. Typically, this type of data is for yes/no or true/false operations. An example of logical data for student records is for sports participation. Either a student played on the football team or not. There is no middle ground.

A date field allows the entry of dates for making comparisons based on the occurrence of an event. With this type of data, for

FIGURE 8-2
Database structures, like this one in dBase IV, require a data type specification for each field.

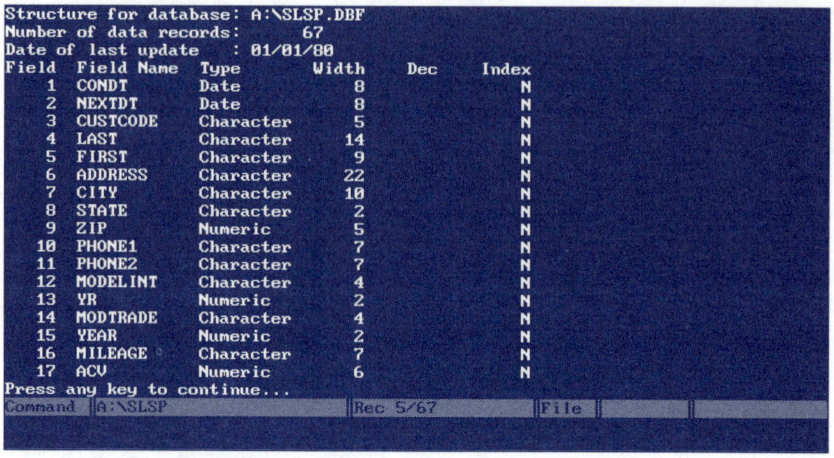

Structure for database: A:\SLSP.DBF
Number of data records: 67
Date of last update : 01/01/80

Field	Field Name	Type	Width	Dec	Index
1	CONDT	Date	8		N
2	NEXTDT	Date	8		N
3	CUSTCODE	Character	5		N
4	LAST	Character	14		N
5	FIRST	Character	9		N
6	ADDRESS	Character	22		N
7	CITY	Character	10		N
8	STATE	Character	2		N
9	ZIP	Numeric	5		N
10	PHONE1	Character	7		N
11	PHONE2	Character	7		N
12	MODELINT	Character	4		N
13	YR	Numeric	2		N
14	MODTRADE	Character	4		N
15	YEAR	Numeric	2		N
16	MILEAGE	Character	7		N
17	ACV	Numeric	6		N

Press any key to continue...
Command ‖A:\SLSP ‖Rec 5/67 ‖File ‖

example, it is possible to list students enrolled in Algebra I after 09/09/89. The software compares the specified date to all date fields in all records within the database.

Database Planning

Good planning leads to good database design and construction. Poor planning leads to a poor database. For example, a field titled Name would normally contain both first and last name data. However, if you wanted to sort the database by the last name of each student, the field Name could not be organized for this type of sorting. It would be much better to have two different fields—Last Name and First Name. With this organization, the user could sort on the last name of each student. If one of the goals of the database designer is to report on grade point averages for all students, then a field of numeric data called Points makes vastly more sense than an alphanumeric field called Grade.

Database designers must try to include fields for all necessary data. While it is possible to add fields to a completed database structure, doing so requires users to modify the data in all existing records. It is much easier have a complete and correct structure from the beginning so all data can be entered only once.

Because the basic building blocks for a database include fields, records, files, and the four different data types, these receive the greatest attention in planning a database. Normally the process begins by creating a column describing all the data to be included in the database. This is not a list of field names, but rather a description of the data.

In a good database plan, a second column contains actual field names for each description. The more precise the field name, the easier it is to know what kind of data to enter. Depending on the software, there may be limitations to field names. For example, some database software does not allow spaces in field names. Others may limit the length of the name. No matter what the limitation, the more descriptive the field name, the better.

Teaching Tool

Report Cards

For teachers, generating report cards can be a time-consuming, arduous task. Think of all of the calculations that must be made each time a teacher needs a report of student performance. Database software linked to spreadsheet software provides an ideal solution to generating report cards. While many teachers use spreadsheets to calculate grades for their entire class, importing that information into a database allows the computer to compile all the information and generate report cards on each student.

The third column should indicate the data type. This is a crucial consideration, because the data type controls access and use of the data. For example, an alphanumeric field will accept any letter, number, or symbol, but it will not permit calculations even if numbers are in this type of field. Generally, if the data is ever to be manipulated mathematically or if a numeric expression will be the criteria for sorting data, use a numeric field. Normally, we do not add or subtract ZIP code numbers, and it is common to think of these as alphanumeric. But ZIP codes should be in a numeric field because it is common to sort records based on ZIP codes. For example, searching for ZIP codes less than 49050 and greater than 49000 is easy with numeric data.

The final column in the database plan should be the data size. With most database software, data size specifies the number of characters permitted in each field. The upper limit is absolute; therefore, part of database planning is to determine the maximum number of characters for each field. For example, an address field with a data size of 15 characters will not accept more than 15 characters. Addresses longer than 15 characters must be abbreviated to fit in the data size.

Table 8-2 Planning a Database Structure

Description	Field Name	Type	Size
Entry date	DATE	D	8
Title	TITLE	A	3
First name	FIRST_NAME	A	10
Last name	LAST_NAME	A	20
Company name	COMPANY	A	20
Mailing address 1	ADDRESS1	A	20
Mailing address 2	ADDRESS2	A	20
City	CITY	A	25
State	ST	A	2
ZIP code	ZIP	N	5
Purchase date	PDATE	D	8
Purchase amount	AMOUNT	N	10
Mailing list	MAIL	L	1

If you've planned your database structure well, constructing it on the computer will be simple, and your database will be simple to use as well.

MODIFYING A DATABASE

After creating the database, if the planning was sound, then filling fields with data is the next step. However, if the planning was poor, or if new requirements come up, the database structure may need some modification. It is usually easier to change a database structure before entering any data into any record. However, that is not always possible. Many times you only discover the shortcomings of the database after entering large amounts of data.

If it is not possible to restructure before entering data, then it is best to make changes as early in the data entry process as possible. The more data entered, the more difficult it is to avoid having to re-enter large sets of data. The process of changing a database should correspond as closely as possible to the process of creating an initial database structure. Again, the most important aspect is planning. It is a good idea to change the original, paper plan before making the actual changes in the computer database structure. If additional fields are needed, add them to the original plan first. If fields are found to be superfluous, simply cross them off the plan. Remember, the database plan should completely detail the design of the database.

The key to restructuring a database is to think of two distinct structures—the original or existing structure and the new structure based on the changes. This is key because data in the original database transfers to the new structure based on field names. If the field names do not change, data converts easily. For example, adding a new field allows the database to convert any existing data to the new field. However, problems occur when renaming a field. For example, changing the field NAME to LAST_NAME may cause any data in the original NAME to disappear. Fortunately, most database software allows users to specify that data from one field transfer to another field.

Another issue in modifying a database structure is data size. Enlarging the size usually does not pose a problem, since any data in the original field will transfer and fit into the new size. However, reducing the size can cause some data to truncate. The database simply chops off any characters beyond the new, smaller size limit.

Changing the data type can also pose a problem, especially if the conversion is from alphanumeric to numeric. Letters will not normally transfer. Therefore, extreme caution should be taken when changing the data type.

If you plan and construct a database, then find you haven't planned well, take heart. You will find later databases, with practice, easier to plan.

INDEXING AND SORTING

In most cases, records are entered in a database randomly. In other words, users do not organize all the information alphabetically, then enter the alphabetized data. However, output from a database

Teaching Tool

Community Database

Elementary students studying neighborhoods and communities can find database software a most valuable tool. Students can design a simple database to store information about their communities. This community database might include businesses found within the community, neighborhood centers, and even student's homes. When students want a report of community businesses, the database serves as a useful tool.

is usually required to be organized. For example, an alphabetical list of students is generally more useful than a random list. There are two methods most database software uses to organize records—indexing and sorting.

Indexing is a temporary method of organizing records within a database. Just as an index in a book identifies a reference for each entry, a database index identifies the location of a specific record. In fact, the index is a separate file linked to the database file. In effect, the index temporarily reorders records according to the index criteria. For example, an index on last name temporarily alphabetizes records by last name. By using an index, you can enter data in any order and have the data print according to the order specified by the index. The index uses a pointer to identify a specific record within the database file.

It is possible to index a file based on any data field. Of course, alphabetic indexing on alphanumeric data is very common. However, numeric data such as ZIP code or date data or the order of entry, also make very useful indexes. Since indexing does not permanently change the order of records within the database, it is very common to create and use several different indexes for the same set of records. It is also possible to index on multiple fields. For example, one index may organize data by school, then by class, then alphabetically within a class. In this case a single index uses three different fields as the basis of the index.

Sorting permanently changes the order of records within a database file. While the initial results of a sort seem to be the same as the results of an index, sorting changes the actual arrangement and order of each record in the database. Sorting is done only when permanent changes are required. For example, it may be advantageous to sort a database of students on Last Name, since many reports generated by the database are according to a student's last name.

As a general guide, sorting takes much longer than indexing. However, once a database is sorted, there is no need to use indexes. Indexing is normally much faster and provides greater flexibility. Therefore, most database users prefer indexing for organizational control.

DATA QUERIES

Locating data quickly is an important part of any database software. After all, if you cannot find the data you need, in the order you want, a database would not be of much value. Queries are requests to databases to locate specific records. For example, if you wanted to locate all students who have a grade point average above 3.00, you would query the database to accomplish this task.

Simple queries typically identify the contents of specific fields. For example, searching for students who have taken a specific course is one example of a simple query. However, queries can become very complex. For example, you can query the database

Teaching Tool

Library Data

Keeping track of who has what is an ongoing dilemma for some school librarians and media center directors. Not only is it difficult to maintain data on which students have which books, but which teachers are using which equipment. Libraries were among the first in schools to recognize the benefit of maintaining information in a database. With this information, it is very easy to generate a list of missing books, overdue books, full inventories, and book and material usage information. After all, if the database can generate reports about the equipment used most often, then it easier to order new equipment intelligently.

to return a list of students who have a grade point average above 3.00, have a varsity letter, play in the band, have taken Algebra, Trigonometry, and Calculus and have perfect attendance.

Structured Query Language (SQL)

The approaches database software use for queries can differ among software packages. The problem with differing command sets is the difficulty of using data stored by one database application software with data stored by another database program. It is also difficult to learn a new command set for different database programs. A common standard form for queries is called *Structured Query Language (SQL).* When a database uses SQL, it is possible to use the same querying process as with other software that uses SQL. Paradox, dBase, and Oracle all use SQL.

SQL is actually a series of commands. In fact, may users view SQL as a database programming language. Therefore, learning to use SQL involves learning a wide range of SQL expressions. For example, SELECT Last Name, First Name, Student ID, GPA FROM STUDLISTS is an SQL expression to select the fields listed from all records. Adding the expression WHERE HOMEROOM = "Rodgers" causes the search to look for only students in Ms. Rodgers homeroom. Users may add many different expressions to focus the query and produce the exact desired set of data. While it is beyond the limits of this book to detail SQL, most users who get serious about database software find learning SQL very important.

GENERATING REPORTS

Report generation is closely tied to the query process, because queries locate the data to produce the report. Many brands of database software use a report generator to locate and display information onscreen or on paper. Report generators also make it possible to produce output in a desirable form. Instead of producing just a list of data, report generators allow users to include titles, page numbers, perform calculations, and control the full appearance of the presentation of data. In other words, report generators make the data presentable.

The first step in defining a report is to determine what data to display. Most databases contain more information than needed for a single report. Therefore, users select only data that is useful for a single report. After selecting data, the next decision is to determine the order of presentation. Some database software arranges data in columns and rows in the order the user desires; others produce data in sets.

After determining the data and its order, the next step is to determine the page format. Page format controls the overall appearance of the page. One popular format is title control. Report generators allow users to insert a title page, or titles on every page, of a report. One may also include headers and footers to further identify the contents of the report. (Of course, page numbers make the report easier to follow.) Finally, column headings label the contents of data in columns.

Report generators do more than format and print a report. They can also produce new information from data. One typical control subtotals and totals numeric data. For example, a report generator can subtotal sales by State, then produce a final total for all sales across the country.

DATA ORGANIZATION

Database software can employ one or more of the six different types or methods for organizing data within a database. These include relational databases, hierarchical databases, network databases, flat-file databases, HyperCard, and free-form. While each of these is an independent type, there is some overlap. The key to understanding each of these is to look at how each organizes data.

Relational Databases

Relational databases allow you to manipulate or control more than one file at one time. What makes this multiple file control possible is the organizational technique employed by the database program. Relational databases organize data into tables called *relations.* Relations are subdivided into fields and rows. Fields represent the individual location of data, and rows represent records.

In schools, relational databases are very popular. Instead of keeping all student data in one giant database, several databases are used. For example, there may be a database for academic grades, another for attendance, another for extra-curricular activities, and so forth.

Relational databases are popular because the data within each of the separate files can be combined to produce a wide range of queries and reports. The table structure makes this all possible. When the table structure of one file has one or more of the same field attributes as another file, called a common field, the two files can link together. Common fields need not have the same name.

One of the major advantages of relational databases is that relationships do not need to be predefined. In other words, if there is a common field, new files can easily be created to share data with other files. Relational databases also offer the advantage of adding new fields to any file without having to convert or rearrange data links. Other types of database organizations require precise definitions for linking files (these are discussed later).

Relational databases also offer the advantage of allowing changes made to one record in one file to change a record automatically in another file. For example, suppose one file contains a student's name, ID number, and GPA. Another file contains that

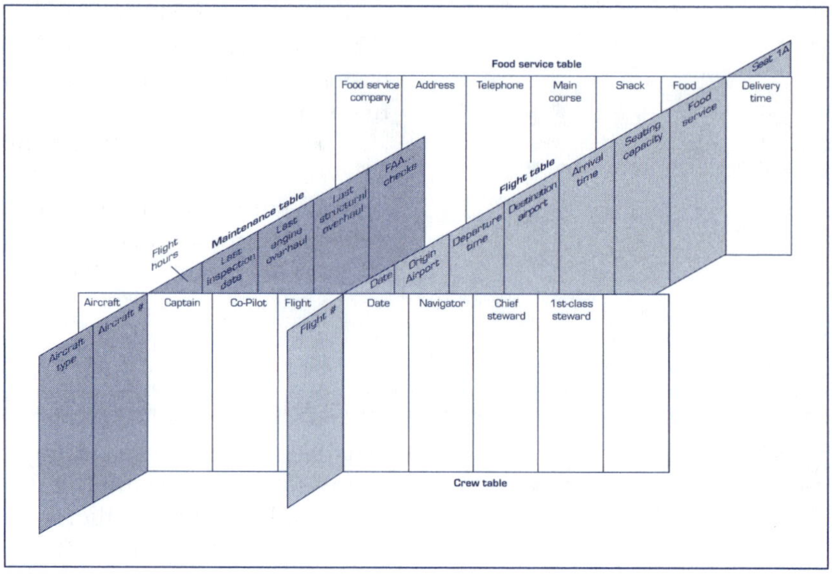

FIGURE 8-3
Relational databases use common fields to link two or more databases.

students's name, ID number, and math grades. Entering new math grades in the second database can cause the GPA in the first database to change.

Hierarchical Databases

A hierarchical database organizes data into a series, with the broadest grouping first followed by subgroups. In a family tree, each group of parents can branch down to several children. However, each child

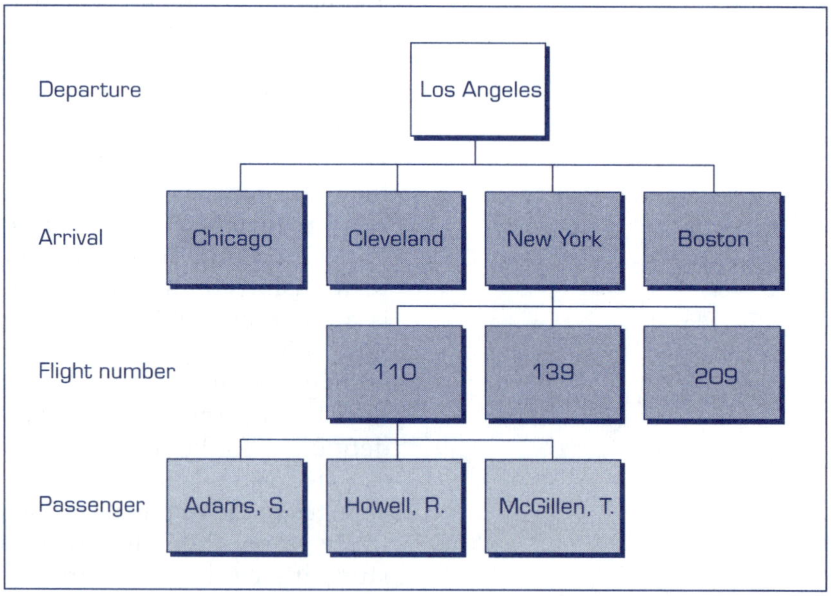

FIGURE 8-4
Hierarchical databases are characterized by single relationships from lower level records to higher level groups.

only links to one parent group. This is a prime example of a hierarchical structure.

Hierarchical databases were one of the initial data organizations developed with computers. Data accessed via a hierarchical database must be sequential. For example, accessing a student's record may require the database to move through university, college, and departmental data before accessing a specific student. By today's standards, this is cumbersome and has two distinct disadvantages. First, it is difficult to locate records in different areas, or sub-groups, of the database. In the example above, a search for a second student's record would again begin at the university level. This is an inefficient and time-consuming method for searching records in different groups. The second major disadvantage occurs when adding new fields. Hierarchical databases require a complete restructuring each time a new field is added—again, an inefficient and time-consuming process.

While accessing data from multiple groups and redefining an entire database can be time-consuming, once data is in place, searching for one specific record is very fast with a hierarchical database. The top-down organization helps the database eliminate the need for searching through all records. Instead, the database searches only specified groups for data.

Network Databases

Network databases are very similar to hierarchical databases. In fact, they work very much the same, with the addition that network databases can have more than one main group. The network database terms "member" and "owner" indicate this relationship. A record can be a member of more than one owner.

The major advantage of network databases over hierarchical databases is their access to multiple data sets. Data can be accessed from a variety of sources with speed and ease. However, network databases, as do hierarchical databases, require every relationship

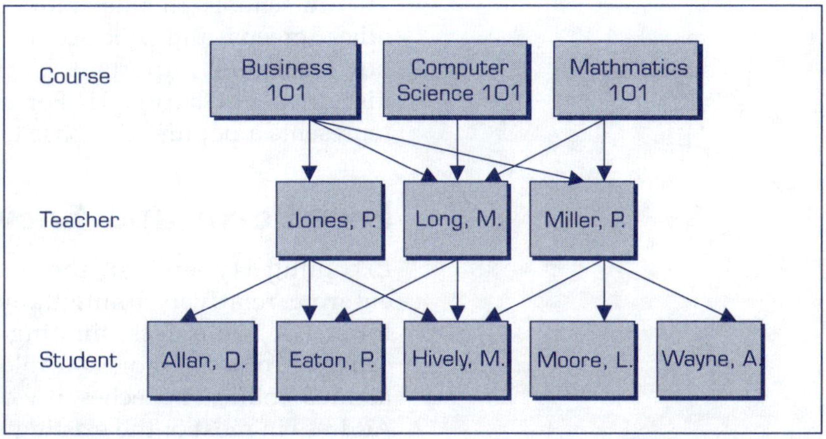

FIGURE 8-5
With network databases, lower level records can link to one or more higher level networks.

and link to be predefined. Adding any new field requires a complete redefinition of the database.

Flat-File Databases (File Managers)

Complex database structures such as relational databases, hierarchical databases, and network databases work very well for complicated data manipulation tasks. "Complexity" does not refer to how difficult it is to use the program, but refers to the fact that complex programs allow the user to perform complex functions. However, many teachers and students simply do not need many of these capabilities. They need an easy way to enter and sort data. Flat-file databases provide this ease.

The major difference of flat-file databases is that they are *single-relational*—they only work with one data file at a time. There is no linking to other data files, nor do flat-files allow multiple access or even advanced querying techniques.

There is a great deal of variation between flat-file programs. However, as a general rule, most flat-file databases do not permit much data merging with other types of application programs. For example, many flat-file databases have a predefined data size that cannot be altered for use in such programs as a word processor or spreadsheet. Some flat-file databases are very similar to spreadsheets in how they store and use data. Others allow records to be displayed individually, rather than in rows and columns.

HyperCard

HyperCard is a program that has revolutionized database use in education. Instead of focusing solely on data organization, HyperCard incorporates advanced graphic techniques to produce access to interactive data. In a nutshell, HyperCard provides a means for teachers and students to create individual screens of data, with both text and graphics. These screens are called *cards*. Users can link cards in any order to produce a stack. A HyperCard stack is roughly equivalent to a database.

In schools, this flexibility to create a screen, link the screen to other screens, and produce instructional data is very powerful. So powerful and important is HyperCard that it will be further discussed in Chapter 11. For now, just be aware that HyperCard represents a popular database tool in education.

Free-Form and Encyclopedia Databases

Excepting HyperCard, the databases discussed so far focus on entering relatively limited amounts of data in a very structured form. For some uses, limiting the amount of data one can enter causes problems. For example, if a teacher wants a database of famous political speeches, it would be hard to enter the Gettysburg Address in most of the existing types of databases. For this purpose,

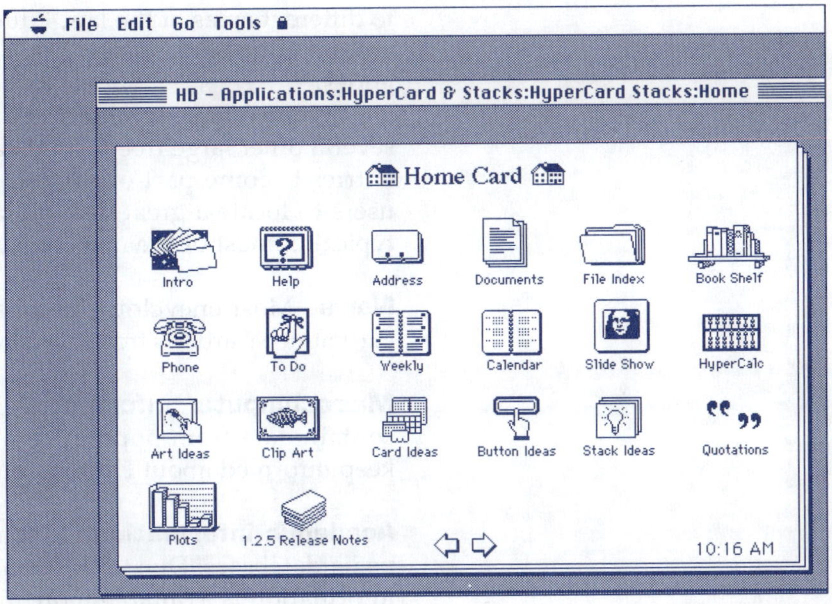

FIGURE 8-6
HyperCard incorporates text and graphics on a single screen. Each screen is a card, and a group of cards is stored and used in a stack.

there is a special type of database organization known as *free-form* or *encyclopedia databases*.

As its name implies, free-form databases allow users to enter large sets of text without having to specify data type or data size. Data in free-form databases is unstructured. The methods of entering and searching data are different from databases that rely on records. Data entry is normally accomplished by moving word processing files into the database. The search process in free-form databases uses a special *keyword* method (more on this later) instead of searching for data in specific fields.

The primary use of free-form databases is with on-line encyclopedias. Encyclopedia databases maintain large collections of highly detailed text organized around subject matter. For example, a law encyclopedia database may group free-form files according

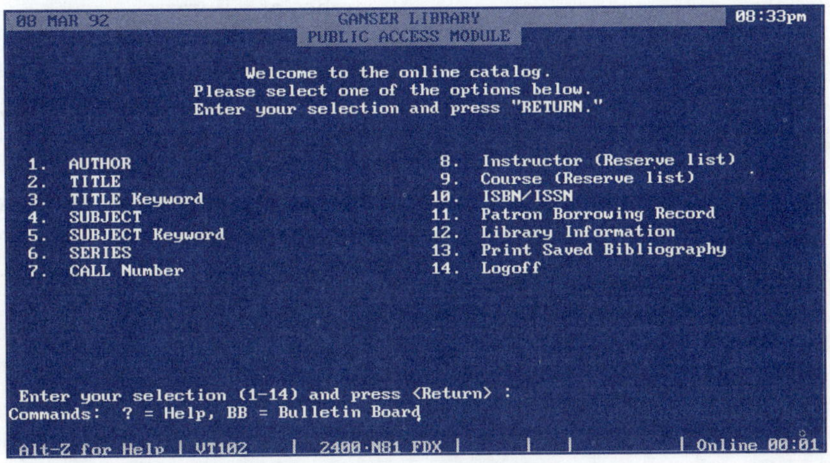

FIGURE 8-7
Many college and university libraries use free-form databases for storing entire library collections.

to different areas of the law. Education encyclopedia data may group around educational issues. This makes it possible to search by categories.

Quite often encyclopedia databases are collections of data from several other large free-form databases. Thus, encyclopedia database entries become part of several databases at one time. This allows users to locate a great deal of data. The following subject areas are typical in most of the major encyclopedia databases.

News Most encyclopedia databases have access to thousands of current news articles from news wire services and major newspapers.

Microcomputer information Some encyclopedia databases contain data from popular computing magazines. Subscribers can keep informed about current computing developments.

Academic information Research data are often part of encyclopedia databases. Due to the delays of publishing, the latest scientific information is available more quickly through a database. (It takes a long time for information to get into scholarly journals and traditional encyclopedias.)

Telephone numbers Some encyclopedia databases allow users to search through telephone directories across the nation for business telephone numbers.

Mail order catalogs Information from an assortment of mail order catalogs is available on many encyclopedia databases. Subscribers can purchase the catalog goods though electronic mail. That is, users can use their computer and modem to order specific items from a catalog.

Magazine articles Some encyclopedia databases have access to thousands of periodicals. Some focus on specialized areas, such as periodicals covering business, engineering, science, or medicine. Computer access to such data can reduce time-consuming literature searches at a library.

Career information Encyclopedia databases offering information on careers tips, writing resumes, applying for jobs, and interviewing techniques are frequently available.

Federal Government information Government publications on laws, regulations, legislative roll call votes, court decisions, and various speeches are available to help subscribers stay informed.

Medical information Information from medical journals is available on many databases.

The primary method of searching free-form databases is through keywords. In a keyword search, a user enters one or more words, and the software searches the text of all entries for matches. Keywords are important because they provide users with a great deal of flexibility. Suppose you want to retrieve an article with a specific title. Without keywords, if you had forgotten the exact title, you could not locate the article in the database. Keywords allow you to search for a single word in the title.

Keywords are also useful for searching large sets of text. For example, in addition to title fields, some databases contain abstracts of articles as a field. Keywords allow us to search fields for matches to the keyword. For example, suppose you wanted to search a list of articles in print in 1991. The word education could be a keyword. A list of articles containing the word *education* in the title or the abstract can be generated.

To make searches faster, easier, and to save storage space, encyclopedia databases present information in two formats: abstract form and bibliographic citation form.

Abstracts present articles or books in a very condensed form. In effect, they reduce an article or book to a fact-oriented summary. However, even abstracts can be lengthy and expensive to reproduce.

A **bibliographic citation** describes a book or article much more briefly and gives all of the information necessary to locate the book or article in a library. Bibliographic citations provide a cost-effective means of locating information.

Keywords are critical in locating data, but how do you choose the right keywords? The first step is to list words related to the topic. For example, baseball, American league, world series, Yankees, home runs. The next step is to organize the words into a hierarchy beginning with the most general and progressing to the most specific concepts. In this example, the most general appears first (baseball), and the most specific appears last (home runs). This organization of keywords will speed up the search of the database. Discard words that do not contribute much to the definition of the topic. A vague or misleading keyword will slow down the search of the database. If you added *sports* to this search, it would detract from the search effectiveness. The narrower the keyword, the faster the search; and the more precisely the keyword is related to the desired topic, the more satisfactory the results of the search. Spending a little extra effort in selecting keywords can make searching encyclopedia databases more efficient and rewarding.

DATABASES AND COMMUNICATION

Communications links between computers can make databases more useful in several ways. Through communications links, users at one location can access a computer and database at another location. For example, connecting a home computer to a database of airline flight schedules and prices helps locate both an airline carrier and an inexpensive flight. In this example, the user is

Teaching Tool

Teacher Recordkeeping

Teachers and administrators alike spend countless hours generating reports. State departments of education often require schools to submit attendance reports, test data, and financial reports, to name a few. Generating these reports from a database is much easier and usually more accurate than generating reports by hand.

For teachers who must update cumulative records for each child throughout the school year, a school-wide database can be most valuable. Instead of writing grades and attendance data into each student's cumulative record folder each reporting period, a good database can automatically update cumulative data as a teacher enters it.

only reading data from a database. Data from this database is not available to merge with a user's separate database.

However, computers can share and exchange data to expand databases. When data are exchanged, the receiving database expands the total data it contains and more people have access to the data. For example, a bank loan officer may have the bank's computer call a credit bureau's computer for information on an applicant. The credit bureau's database is shared with the bank's database, giving the loan officer access to this data. Similarly, a credit bureau's computer may communicate with a bank's database and ask for all data on the bank's credit customers. Data transferred to the credit bureau computer can easily be shared with other banks or credit organizations.

Databases also allow us to create new sets of information based on existing data. For example, a university database may contain the names of all students failing English and another database may list those failing math. From this data, we can create new data listing students failing *both* English and math. From this new list of data, we can go back to the original university database and search for commonalities to help determine why students are failing. New data of this sort are very important because they provide more information for decisionmakers.

Summary

- Database software stores and retrieves data.
- To be considered database software, it must provide users with a quick and easy means of storing, recalling, sorting, and reporting on a wide range of data.
- Creating a database begins with three simple considerations—. data type, data size, and data use.
- A file is the overall collection of data, made up of a series of records.
- Records store data according to a single specification.
- Records are made up of fields.
- Fields are specific locations for the entry and storage of one set of data.
- The arrangement and use of fields constitute the database structure.
- The four most common types of data are alphanumeric, numeric, logical, and date.
- Planning is critical to good database design and use.

- Queries search data files for specified records or field data.
- Structured Query Language (SQL) is a standard method of querying database files.
- Report generators control the creation and display of data reports.
- The six types of database organizations include relational, hierarchical, network, flat-file, HyperCard, and free-form.

Fill-In Questions

Fill in the blank for each of the statements listed below.

1. When data is entered in a database, it is placed in a ________________.
2. A set of related fields stored as a unit is called a ________________.
3. ________________ data includes any letter, number, symbol entered from the keyboard.
4. ________________ data is limited to numbers and does not allow letters or symbols.
5. ________________ data entries identify one of two alternatives—true or false, or yes or no.
6. A ________________ is a collection of records.

Quiz

Answer the following questions.

1. Databases can store several types of data.
   a. true b. false
2. To store ZIP codes in a database, we must identify a ZIP code:
   a. field b. file
   c. record d. index
3. A temporary sorting of data by ZIP code is:
   a. a sort b. search
   c. indexing d. inspection

4. A specific word used for searching fields is a:
   a. fieldword   b. keyword
   c. specificword   d. reportword
5. Types of data stored in a database include alphanumeric data, numeric data, logical data, and:
   a. numericalpha data   b. character data
   c. date   d. alphacharacter data
6. A database file is a collection of records, all made up of the same fields.
   a. true   b. false
7. Databases that allow more than one file at a time to be manipulated are:
   a. numeric databases   b. database generators
   c. relational databases   d. encyclopedia databases
8. Most databases must be run on large mainframe computers.
   a. true   b. false
9. The number of fields and the type of data entered into each field define the database:
   a. structure   b. report
   c. index   d. data type
10. Keywords used in searching an encyclopedia database should be organized from general to specific.
   a. true   b. false

Exercises and Applications

Follow the instructions for each exercise and application.

1. List five types of data that you have trouble keeping organized. Could database software help you organize this data? How? Be prepared to share your responses with the rest of the class.
2. When computers share data, more people have access to private information (for example, personal medical information). Consider the major drawbacks of computers sharing personal information with other computers. Should we be concerned about invasions of privacy?
3. Many libraries have access to encyclopedia databases. Visit a library and identify the types of databases available for student use. What types of data do these databases contain?
4. At the library, use a database to produce bibliographic citations on a topic of your choice. Be prepared to explain to the rest of the class the type of information found.

5. A set of index cards, all on a particular topic and each giving similar information, is a type of database. Each index card represents a record; the entire set of cards represents a file. Create an index card database by first defining a structure, writing the names of the fields on each card, then writing the data next to each field for each card. The contents of the database are up to you.

9

ESSENTIALS OF COMMUNICATIONS

LEARNING OBJECTIVES

Learning the material in this chapter will enable you to:

- describe the role of communications in education
- list the three major components of a telecommunication system
- discuss how telecommunication can expand access to data and information
- describe how telecommunication software and modems work together
- describe the major controls of telecommunications software
- describe the two major types of telecommunications
- describe byte length, stop bit, start bit, duplex, and parity
- describe the role of file transfer protocols
- identify information services
- discuss major elements of networks
- identify and differentiate among the major types of networks

CHAPTER OVERVIEW

Giving a computer user access to data stored on other computers changes the computer from a single machine with limited data storage to a machine with access to a world of information. Connecting a computer to a large national database permits access to news reports, financial data, scientific data, travel information, product specifications, legislative updates, and nearly any type of information you can imagine. Connecting a computer to other computers in a school encourages sharing and exchanging ideas and information, spreadsheet files, word processing documents, student records, and access to educational software.

Connecting computers is generally referred to as computer *communications.* When a computer connects to another computer, it is the communications system that transfers the data and information from one computer to the other. A communications system consists of both hardware and software. Most often the hardware consists of devices that send data over some form of communication line. For example, some communications systems use a device to connect computers through existing telephone lines—a modem. Other communications systems use direct wiring to link two or more computers. But lines, modems, and other hardware devices only work if software designed for communications is present. Therefore, computer communications requires both the hardware to send data and information and software to control the flow of information.

While there are many different variations of computer communications systems, two approaches are most common in schools—networking and telecommunications. Networking directly connects computers via specifically designated cables. Networking hardware makes the physical connection, and networking software controls the flow of data and information. Networks are usually confined to a small physical area such as an office or office building. The network provides access to data needed by several different users. Networking works well for sharing messages with others on the network.

Telecommunications uses existing phone lines for sending and receiving information over much greater distances than possible with a network. As with networks, software controls the flow of data and information. This software is called *telecommunication software.* A telecommunications user can send a letter electronically to another computer user across the country. This is known as *electronic mail,* or *e-mail.* User can create documents on a word processor, then sends them electronically almost anywhere in the world in a matter of seconds.

Computer communications has affected all our lives by making information easily available. For example, not too long ago it took days for a check to clear a bank. A check written on Wednesday would not come out of its account until the following Monday. After banks began to use computer communications to transfer funds from one bank to another, a check written on Wednesday could clear the same day.

For teachers, however, this speed brings the world directly into the classroom. With telecommunications, teachers can access instant news data, receive weather mapping data, even search millions of records, all in less time than it takes to locate a single book in a library.

This chapter focuses on computer communications. It examines the most common types of communications systems in schools, the types of software designed to control communications systems, and the impact of computer communication on users. Many of the most important computer advances are in the use and application of computer communications; understanding common systems should provide a sound basis for learning more.

COMPUTER COMMUNICATIONS

Telecommunications is a process by which computers communicate with each other via modems, telecommunications software, and existing telephone lines. The definition is simple, but the implications of telecommunications are far-reaching. Telecommunications allows teachers and students to share and exchange data with other computer users almost anywhere in the world.

The above definition of telecommunications begins with a device called a *modem* (*mo*dulator-*dem*odulator). A **modem** links the computer to telephone lines. The modem's major function is to convert computer-generated data into a form usable by telephone lines (this is the modulate function), then change the data on the other end to a computer-usable form (the demodulate function). Recall that computers process data in a digital format. That is, all data in a computer are represented by a series of separate signals, zeros and ones. These signals are called discrete signals because each piece is separated from every other piece. Telephone lines, however, transmit data in analog format, or continuous waves. Discrete signals cannot be sent on lines that require continuous waves. Modems convert digital signals to analog signals and back again.

Telecommunications software must be available in both computers. The basic functions of all telecommunications programs are similar, although the exact procedures differ among software packages. Some software is easy to use but does not offer a full range of controls. Other software offers a full range of controls but is more difficult to use. The considerations for selecting telecommunications software are the same as for all software; the software must do what is wanted as simply (and cheaply) as possible.

COMMUNICATIONS SOFTWARE

The major difference among telecommunications software packages is the balance between ease of use and capabilities. Generally, the more capabilities, the more complex the software, and the more difficult it is to use. The following sections should give you some idea of the considerations of telecommunications software.

FIGURE 9-1
Modems convert digital computer data to an analog signal and back again.

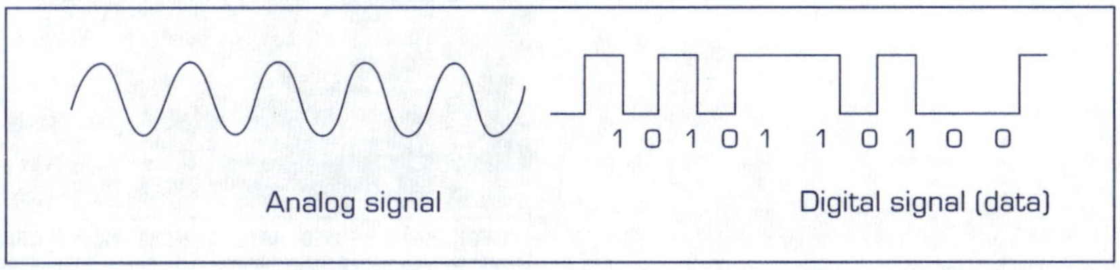

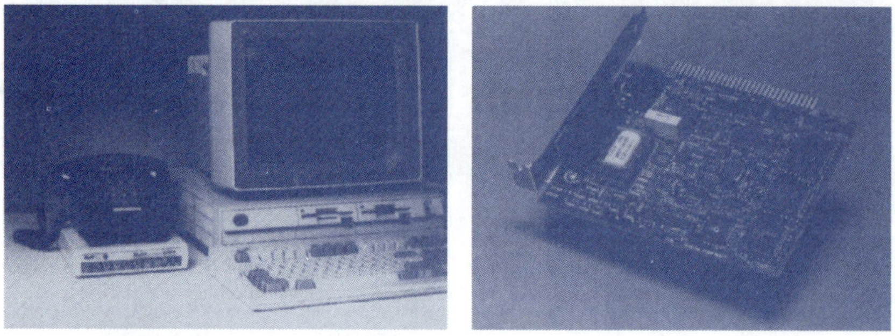

FIGURE 9-2
Modems come in a variety of forms, including those that reside on cards called internal modems, *and those that connect to a computer via cable called* external modems.

Baud Rate

Being able to control data transmission speed is important to all telecommunications software users. *Baud* is the unit of measure of speed— bits per second (bps) of data transmission and reception. For example, 2,400 baud modems operate at 2,400 bps, or 240 characters per second. The most common modems operate at 300, 1,200, 2,400, and 9,600 baud. The maximum speed of a modem is preset and cannot be increased by the user. However, users can control modems to transmit and receive data at slower speeds. For example, a 2,400 baud modem cannot operate at 4,800 baud, but it can be set by the software to operate at 1,200 or 300 baud.

Early modems used 300 baud or 30 characters per second, which is very slow by today's standard. The average person can read a page at about 45 characters per second. Think of how long it takes to read 100 pages of text; sending a 100-page file takes a very long time at 300 baud. A 4,800 baud modem will send the same 100 pages 16 times faster.

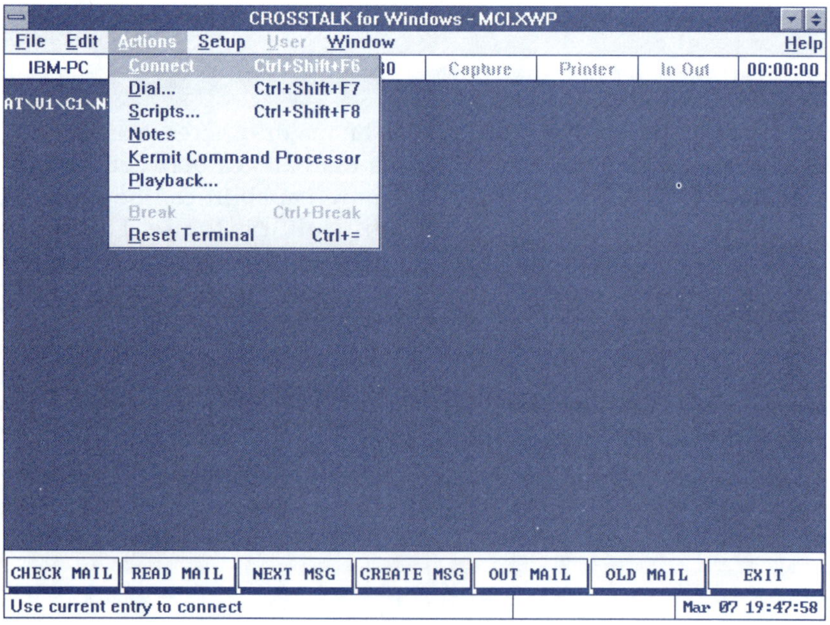

FIGURE 9-3
Telecommunications software controls the way the modem sends and receives data.

Teaching Tool

Play Chess

In most schools, you can find a few chess-playing students. Unfortunately, for those students finding others to play with is often a greater challenge than the game itself. Internet provides a means for a student to play chess with other players across the country and around the world.

Both the sending and receiving modem *must* operate at the same baud rate. Therefore, the telecommunications software must be set to match the baud rate of the connecting modem. If someone tries to send a document at 1,200 baud to a computer using a 300 baud modem, the data will not transfer. In this case, the person with the 1,200 baud modem must set the baud rate at 300 before transferring data.

Selecting Data Patterns

Before sending data, microcomputer users must also agree on the pattern for sending the data. The two patterns are known as *asynchronous* and *synchronous* communications. In **asynchronous** communications, data is sent one byte at a time. A **start bit** indicates the beginning of each byte and a **stop bit** indicates the end. Asynchronous is the more popular pattern for communications. **Synchronous** communication does not use start and stop bits and does not send data in a series of bytes. Rather, synchronous communication sends information in a long string of bits. Synchronous communication is generally used by businesses or organizations that must transmit very large sets of data.

Most modems used with microcomputers use asynchronous communications for two reasons. First, telephone lines have a lot of static and interference called *noise.* Asynchronous communications software sends one byte of data, then confirms that the byte received was actually the byte sent. Asynchronous transmission is much more tolerant of noise because of this approach. Second, asynchronous communications software allows people to read the information being transmitted. Two computer users can type messages back and forth.

The major problem with asynchronous communications is the slow speed. Synchronous transmissions quickly send data in large groups called *blocks.* However, these blocks are not readable until the completion of the entire transmission.

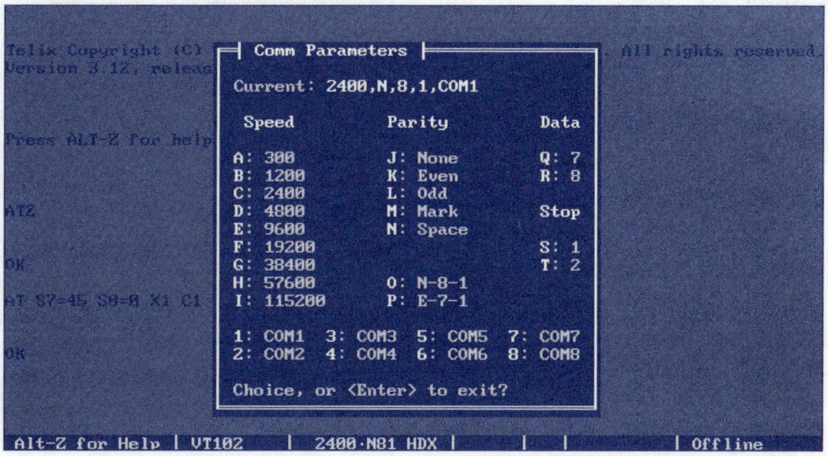

FIGURE 9-4
Telecommunications software controls the speed at which the modem will send and receive data.

With asynchronous communications, users of both the sending and receiving computers must agree on three additional software settings before successful communication can occur. First, each user must determine how many bits make up a byte, called the byte length, word length, or character length. Seven- and eight-bit byte lengths are most common. Second, each user must specify how many stop bits. Stop bits mark that a byte has been sent. Third, parity, or error-checking mechanism, must be established. If a data service or the modem at the receiving end of a call specifies 2,400 baud with eight-bit byte length, one stop bit, and no parity, the sending telecommunications software must be set the same. In computer jargon, *8N1* represents eight-bit byte length, no parity, and one stop bit. This information is usually provided by a service or is agreed on between computer users.

Setting Duplex

Duplex refers to the process or mode of sending data over telephone lines. With microcomputers there are two duplex settings—full- and half-duplex. A modem sends a character, or a block of data, to another modem, then the receiving modem sends a signal back to verify the transfer. For half-duplex, data sends in only one direction. As with other settings, the telecommunications software of both the sending and receiving computers must use compatible duplex settings.

One indicator of the duplex setting is the screen display. If double characters (such as *xx* for *x*), or no characters, appear on the screen, the duplex settings are not compatible. Users must change the duplex setting in the telecommunications software to eliminate double characters or to see characters onscreen.

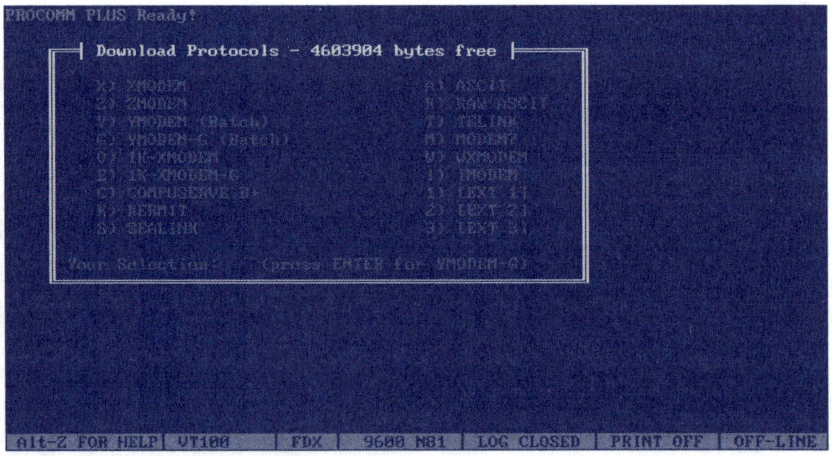

FIGURE 9-5
Telecommunications software, such as ProComm, provides several different file transfer protocols.

File Transfer Protocol

Most telecommunications software supports a variety of procedures for sending entire data files with asynchronous communications. This is called a **file transfer protocol** because it determines the method for sending and receiving files. In short, a file transfer protocol is a procedure for sending error-free data from one computer to another.

There are a variety of protocols for transferring files between computers. No matter what the settings of the sending and receiving computers, both must use the same protocol. Some communications programs provide their own unique file transfer protocols. Using file transfer protocols begins by *agreeing on* a file transfer protocol. Typically, the sending computer reads a file from disk and sends it to a modem. The receiving computer receives the file through the modem and sends it to be saved on a disk. The received file is exactly the same as the file originated by the other computer.

File transfers are only one method of receiving data. It is possible to capture non-file data as it is received. A capture buffer makes this possible. A capture buffer is simply the area of computer memory where the telecommunications software stores incoming data. Most telecommunications software can turn on a capture buffer to capture all information sent. This is a useful feature for receiving data from a variety of sources.

Teaching Tool

Internet

Probably the fastest-growing and most useful method of communicating with others and accessing a wide range of resources is through Internet. Internet is a system connecting computers in the U.S. and internationally. Most college campuses are connected to Internet. If you access Internet on one campus, you can access any other college's computers connected to Internet. For example, if you want to leave electronic mail for a student at the University of Michigan, you can do so through Internet. If you want to access the Alcoholism Research Database at Dartmouth, you can. If you want to check the latest research from Tsukuba Science City, Japan, it's possible. Not only are colleges connected, but so are businesses, and governmental organizations. Through Internet, you can access information on almost any topic.

Setting Terminal Emulation

Using a modem to access a mainframe requires that the connecting microcomputer behave like one of the mainframe's terminals. Computer terminals are different from microcomputers. One difference is the structure and use of keys on the keyboard. For example, most terminals have a *clear* key. Most microcomputers do not. For a microcomputer to act like terminal, keys must be redefined to match the terminal requirements.

Most telecommunications software provides several terminal options. This is necessary because different mainframes use different terminals to access data. For example, it is common for information services to require the use of VT102. If a VT102 terminal is required, the telecommunications software must allow the connected computer to operate as a VT102. Usually, VT102 terminal emulation causes several keys on the keyboard to be assigned new meanings.

Controlling Dialing and Using Packed-Switching Services

Telecommunications software also tells the modem whom to dial and when. Different software packages perform this task in different ways. Some provide autodialing; others require manual dialing.

FIGURE 9-6
Some mainframes support a wide range of terminal options, leaving it up to the user to select the most appropriate emulation.

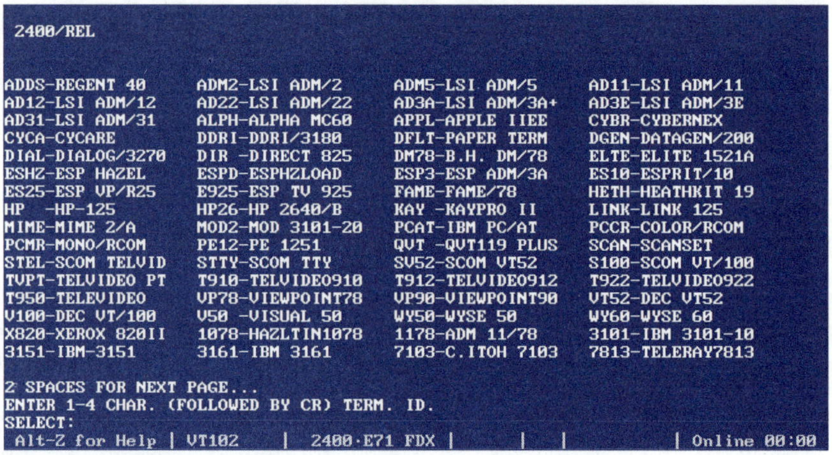

One of the major problems of telecommunication is the cost of long-distance charges. Anytime you call long-distance, whether voice or data, there is a toll charge. Instead of paying a long-distance carrier, packed-switching services provide long-distance access at greatly reduced prices. Packed-switching allows multiple computer users to share the same phone lines, thereby reducing individual costs. For example, a daytime call cross-country may cost $10 to $15 with standard long-distance toll charges, but as little as $2 per hour with Tymnet and Telenet (two popular packed-switching services).

INFORMATION SERVICES

With a computer, a modem, and the correct software, teachers and students can take advantage of several information services. This is similar to the use of the encyclopedia data bases, discussed in the previous chapter. That is, you need a computer, a modem, and telecommunications software to access information; however, the type of information available is different. A variety of information service companies offer access to news wire services, employment services, stock market sales, product trends, economic forecasting, and consumer product ratings, to name a few. Subscribers to these information services may interact with others interested in trading products and services, go catalog shopping, or use financial management software to purchase stocks and bonds. Other information service companies allow you to make travel plans or hotel and airline reservations, arrange to rent a condominium, or trade vacation houses.

Virtually anyone with a computer and modem can subscribe to, or become a member of, these information service organizations. The following sections provide an overview of a few of the many features available on popular information services.

The Source

One information service widely used by business is The Source. Subscribers to The Source have access to huge database files for financial and investment services. It also provides market analysis. A business education or economics teacher may find that access to The Source can provide current information unavailable in textbooks or other teaching materials.

Dow Jones News Service

Another business-oriented service is the Dow Jones News Service (DJNS). Although DJNS has expanded to include a wider variety of information, it is still primarily a business service used by the business community.

CompuServe

CompuServe is one of the most popular information services. While it provides business data, it also provides access to encyclopedia databases, travel, weather, games, entertainment, forums, geographic data, and hotel guide databases, and many other data sets. This is a very popular service for leaving and receiving electronic mail. For students, CompuServe offers the opportunity to have electronic pen pals or even have access to the latest news wire service reports. Think about teaching current events—there is no more current news information than can be found on wire reports. CompuServe offers easy access for both teachers and students.

Prodigy

Prodigy is a relatively new service provided by IBM and Sears. Subscribers to Prodigy can book their own seats on airlines, purchase tickets when there are discount opportunities, and make hotel reservations. In addition, Prodigy subscribers can shop electronically from major stores and catalogs, track stocks through the DJNS, play games, and access an encyclopedia, the Weekly Reader, and Consumer Reports abstracts. News and weather information from the Associated Press and USA Today is also available. A popular option in Prodigy is a home banking service. Subscribers can pay bills without writing checks, transfer funds, and check their account balances with their home computer.

Prodigy is different from other services in several ways. First, users have unlimited access without time charges. There is simply a monthly fee. Prodigy is also family-oriented and has a great deal of information written for use by very young students.

Teaching Tool

Electronic Pen Pals

With Internet, students can correspond with other students. As long as both students have access to Internet, the process is very easy. Students simply type a letter on a word processor and upload the file to any other user. In fact, it is possible to send the same file to hundreds of other users at the same time.

Teachers, Students, and Telecommunications

The benefits of telecommunications extend beyond the use of information services. Suppose a student in New York City is working on a creative writing assignment and wishes to have input from a teacher, professor, or even an author in Kalamazoo. The student can send the manuscript as a file, via modem with a file transfer protocol, to Kalamazoo. Transmission occurs in a matter of seconds. After editing the manuscript and offering suggestions, the file can be returned from Kalamazoo back to New York again in a matter of seconds.

Students find telecommunications a convenient research tool. Instead of spending hours searching through paper indexes and abstracts, they can gain access to many bibliographic resources through telecommunications services such as Prodigy, Dialog, The Knowledge Index, and others. Beyond searching bibliographic resources, students can use telecommunications to access a university computer to send files, generate statistical analysis, work on programming assignments, and almost anything from home instead of traveling to a crowded computer lab.

Teachers find telecommunications a valuable instructional tool because it provides students access to large university libraries and national databases. Teachers can also bring current events, instructional resources, and remedial and enrichment material into the classroom. No longer are teachers and students limited to the information available in one school building. Telecommunications allows teachers and students access to the world.

Local sports organizations, such as swim clubs or gymnastics clubs, use telecommunications to report record performances of individual members, register athletes, or share software with other,

FIGURE 9-7
Computer communications combined with video make it easy to originate a classroom presentation in one city for simultaneous presentation in several other cities. Commonly called teleconferencing, this process is fast becoming a useful form of educational communication.

Teaching Tool

Environmental Monitoring

The Global Laboratory is a telecommunications project designed to stimulate student participation in environmental research. Students from across the country and around the world monitor local environmental conditions and track environmental changes. Students monitor temperature, precipitation, air pollution, oxygen and acidity levels, and a number of other environmental factors. From their observations, students maintain data on weekly readings and use telecommunications software to send local data to the Global Laboratory for world-wide data analysis. Not only are U.S. students participating, but so are students in Mexico, Russia, and many other countries. To learn more, check with EcoNet on the Internet telecommunications network.

similar organizations in distant locations. Newspaper reporters use telecommunications to file reports of events occurring in distant cities. Phoning in a story used to mean reading an article over the phone to someone sitting at a typewriter; today, phoning in a story is as simple as using a modem.

One very special and popular type of telecommunications software is known as a **bulletin board**. Bulletin board software allows users to phone in via modem and post messages to other users of the same bulletin board. Many people use bulletin boards to share ideas and resources with others of similar interests, on subjects ranging from computer use and software applications to archaeology.

For the most part, bulletin boards are set up by a local user to provide a forum for ideas. However, message-sharing capabilities are only part of the use of bulletin board software. These bulletin boards maintain a large selection of shareware (software that is available at little or no cost) that users can download, or copy, to their own computer.

Although bulletin boards are very popular among modem users, they have created some problems. Over the past few years a few less-than-ethical computer users have created destructive programs that destroy data. These programs, called viruses, are attached to other programs, so they are hard to detect. The problem with viruses is that they spread from user to user. For example, one person could download an infected file from a bulletin board to a floppy disk. If that person uses that disk on a different computer, that computer becomes infected. The cycle continues, infecting every computer that has used an infected disk. The primary method of spreading viruses is through bulletin boards, so be careful when using one! It is a good idea to use virus-detecting software; it limits the risk of infection.

NETWORKING

This chapter has focused on telecommunications, but telecommunications has several limitations. First, telecommunications requires telephone lines. Not all locations have or need such lines. In a school, there is not much need to have a phone line available to communicate with the computer in the school office. In some schools, making one file available to a lot of different users *at the same time* is very important; this cannot be done with telecommunications. Also, even with high-speed modems, telecommunications is still rather slow. In a school, having instant access to data from several different computers is most important. Fortunately, another kind of communication tool is available to people who need to communicate with other computer users in the same location—networking.

Networking is the term used when two or more computers are physically connected. When computers are attached to a network,

FIGURE 9-8
Workstations enable users to access programs and data on a host computer.

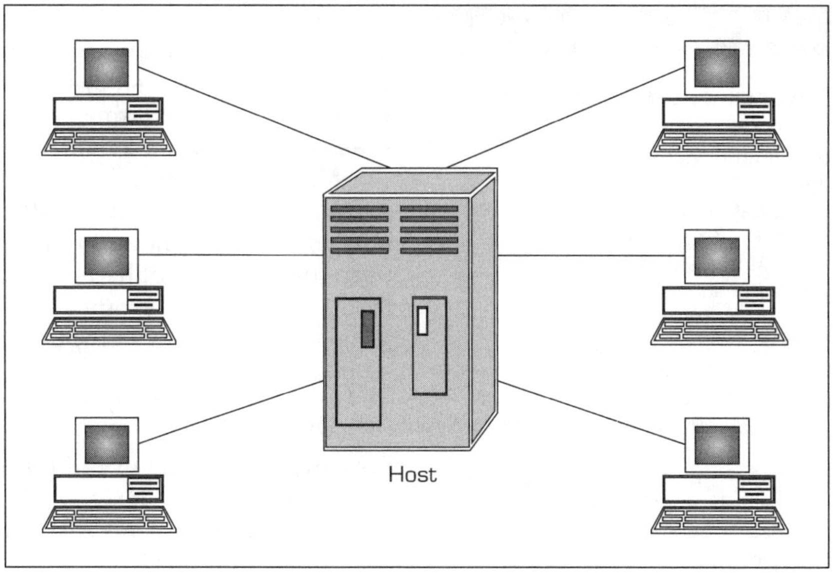

those computers can share files or operate the same programs. In short, they can act in the same way. While telecommunications lets users send and receive files, networking lets users share the same data and program files. Networking makes it possible for one computer to house all the applications software for all computers in a school.

Networks are made up of two types of computers—host and workstations. The host, or file server, is the main or central computer that houses all files that control the network and all files used by every other computer on the network. Workstations are the computers connected to the host or file server. The host provides the control, while the workstations provide access.

For most school networks, the necessity of using passwords is a critical feature. Passwords limit access to all or part of the network. In most cases, passwords limit access to the host. A password can be assigned access to some or all programs and data. A school may provide a password to students that limits access to a particular group of software, while providing a password allowing additional access to teachers.

Using a network offers several advantages over using a stand-alone computer. First, because networks centralize all information in the host computer, users can log on from any workstation. They are not restricted to a particular computer. Second, the network allows users to share files and programs. Several users can access a database or word processor at the same time. Several users can also share data files in this way. For example, if several teachers need access to a database containing student grades, the network allows them this access. These users can enter and review information at the same time.

Teaching Tool

Computer Fax

For teachers and administrators, sending a letter is not simply sending one typed page to one individual. In many cases, copies of the letter must be forwarded to the school office, the central office, the parents, the school psychologist, the counselor, the department chair, and the list goes on. One easy solution is to submit one letter using a computer fax. With a computer fax, it is possible to automatically send copies to all necessary individuals. For example, a discipline letter sent home could be automatically faxed through the computer to all required individuals at the same time.

A third advantage is printer sharing. All workstations on a network can access and use any printer connected to a network. If a network has both a high-speed dot-matrix printer and a laser printer, a user can choose which printer to use. Because printers are not used all the time by all computers, networking provides a cost-effective means of printer access.

A fourth advantage of a network is security. Networks control the flow of information to individual users and workstations. Security codes and passwords may be used to protect various files. Networks can also list individuals who have used particular files.

The advantages of networking are making it more and more popular. However, networks do have some limitations. The major disadvantage occurs if the host computer malfunctions. With the host disabled, all workstations are useless. Teachers who rely on the network can have real problems if the host fails—the lesson is over.

LANS AND WANS

Two types of networks are commonly used with microcomputers. The first is the Local Area Network (LAN). LANs link computers in close proximity. Typically, LANs operate in the same building. WANs, or Wide Area Networks, allow for the connection of computers across great distances. School districts often use WANs to connect computers in one building to computers in other buildings. This can be done even if the school buildings are in different cities.

Computers on a network are connected by a special cable that carries only digitally-formatted network information. Remember, telephone lines use analog signals, making data transmission relatively slow. Cables connected directly between computers that use digital signals make high-speed transmission possible. Both LAN and WAN networks require these dedicated cables. Connecting all computers in a school district is very expensive, however. Therefore, many WANs use existing telephone lines.

FACSIMILE TRANSMISSION

No discussion of telecommunications would be complete without a discussion of facsimile (fax) machines. A fax reads information on a page and sends that information to another fax via telephone lines. Businesses now fax information from one location to another as regularly as they use the postal service.

Fax machines are very similar to modems. The fax reads a page and turns that page into a file similar to a computer file. Once the page is in a file format, the fax machine sends the file over the phone lines. The fax machine also translates files received and prints the information on paper.

Summary

- Telecommunications is the process by which computers communicate with each other over existing telephone lines.
- Telecommunications requires telecommunications software and a modem.
- A modem (*mo*dulator—*dem*odulator) connects the computer and the telephone lines.
- A modem translates computer-generated data (digital signal) into a form usable by telephone lines (analog signal), then returns the data on the receiving end to a computer-usable form.
- The unit of measure for data transmission speed is baud.
- A host is the controlling computer of a network.
- Workstations connect to a network host.
- Networking makes it possible for one computer to house all the applications software for all computers.

Fill-In Questions

Fill in the blank for each of the statements listed below.

1. Telecommunications is the process by which computers communicate with each other using ________________ , ________________ , and ________________ .
2. Telecommunications gives computers the ability to ________________ data.
3. A ________________ transmits and receives computer information through telephone lines.
4. Computer-generated data is in a ________________ format, while telephone lines use an ________________ format.
5. A ________________ is a number of computers that are connected.
6. The ________________ computer generally maintains all of the files and programs used by all computers connected on the network.

Quiz

Answer the following questions.

1. Which type of signal is used to carry information over telephone lines?
   a. analog b. digital
   c. baud d. duplex

2. Which type of data pattern sends one character at a time?
   a. synchronous b. asynchronous
   c. multisynchronous d. nonsynchronous

3. Which term indicates the speed of data transmission?
   a. bit b. baud
   c. byte d. asynchronous

4. Which term is associated with the way files transfer from one location to another?
   a. protocol b. multiplex
   c. asynchronous d. baud

5. Which of the following is not required for telecommunications?
   a. modem b. telephone line
   c. communication software d. printer

6. Both the sending computer and the receiving computer must use the same baud rate to communicate.
   a. true b. false

7. To make telecommunications work, connected computers must first agree on the number of bits per byte, the parity, and the stop bit.
   a. true b. false

8. The maximum speed of a modem can be increased by the user and software.
   a. true b. false

9. The type of communication used by large businesses or organizations to transmit very large data sets is:
   a. synchronous communication b. asynchronous communication
   c. baudular communication d. multisynchronous communication

10. An area of computer memory where the telecommunications software stores incoming data is called a:
    a. packed switch b. VT102
    c. capture buffer d. terminal emulation

Exercises and Applications

Follow the instructions for each exercise and application.

1. Form a small group to explore the cost and benefits of several information services (for example, CompuServe or Prodigy). Each member of the group should find out about the types of services and data available from an information service. The group should be prepared to present the different features and costs of various services.

2. Many information services provide free, limited trial access. Contact one or more of the information services to find out if a trial password is available. If so, take some time to examine as many of the services as possible. Detail the types of information available from these services and some individuals who might use them. Be sure to find out the telecommunications software settings before trying to contact these services via modem.

3. Many local bulletin boards provide users with the opportunity to share ideas and information for little or no fee. If such a bulletin board exists in your area, contact the bulletin board and determine the type of information available.

ESSENTIALS OF MULTIMEDIA AND VIRTUAL REALITY

LEARNING OBJECTIVES

Learning the material in this chapter will enable you to:

- define multimedia and virtual reality
- identify educational applications for multimedia and virtual reality
- describe laser videodisc technology
- identify the major types of laser videodiscs
- identify several applications of video disc technology in the classroom
- describe CD-ROM
- identify several educational applications of CD-ROM
- describe the tools of image processing
- separate the science from the fiction of virtual reality
- describe the potential uses of virtual reality for educators
- identify the levels of virtual reality.

CHAPTER OVERVIEW

When computers were introduced into schools, they were heralded by some educators as the learning machines of the future. Computers were seen as the panacea for educational ills. Many educators were quick to point out the potentials of technology in the delivery of instruction. They pointed to the ability of CAI to individualize instruction, to excite students, and to bring an abundance of instructional material to the classroom. In fact, many educators were so excited by the computer's possibilities that they even predicted that in ten years teachers would be replaced by computers, or at least would be teaching partners with computers.

That vision has yet to be reified. It has been well over ten years since the introduction of computers in schools; with few exceptions, computers have not replaced teachers, nor have computers risen to the level of teaching partners. At best, they are tools used by teachers to enhance their own teaching. However, educators who predicted a technological revolution in education may yet see that time come.

Within the past few years there have been two dominant changes in computers and their use in schools. First, the hardware has changed. Ten years ago, a $3,000 computer took several minutes to display a photograph onscreen. Today, a $1,500 computer can not only display a photograph onscreen nearly instantaneously, it can also display full motion video. Ten years ago, having ten megabytes of storage capacity was considered overkill. Today, it is common to find storage devices having several gigabytes. (A gigabyte is one billion bytes.) In short, the speed at which computers now operate, along with the ability to store billions of pieces of information, give computers the power needed to realize a technological change.

Still, faster hardware is not enough. For computers to help realize the vision of so many requires a new kind of software. A much more complex, much more detailed, yet easier-to-use software is necessary. More than ever, there is a need for software that can access information not only in written form, but also as real-time video and audio. There is a need for software that enables students to immerse themselves in the technology, rather than be passive observers.

Multimedia and virtual reality are the teaching tools that truly have the potential to change the teaching and learning processes. Both play equally important roles. The next two chapters are designed to present you with the essentials of these new teaching technologies.

MULTIMEDIA

What is **multimedia**? The answer, in large part, depends on who you ask. Multimedia is a new term that has different meanings to different people. If you ask a media specialist, he or she might answer, "multimedia is an instructional system incorporating two or more media sources." If you ask a computer programmer, multimedia might be described as "an integration of audio and visual resources with computer technology." A training specialist might describe "a means of instructional delivery in which students control the form and content of presentation." Others may define multimedia as multisensory instruction. In fact, you could just about come up with your own definition. Multimedia is so new that its very definition has not yet finalized.

Accept for now that multimedia is a mode of instructional delivery encompassing the traditional role of computer control and delivery based on a multisensory and multimedium strategy. It is an integrated approach in which multiple forms of media are fit together to form a systematic presentation. Its multisensory

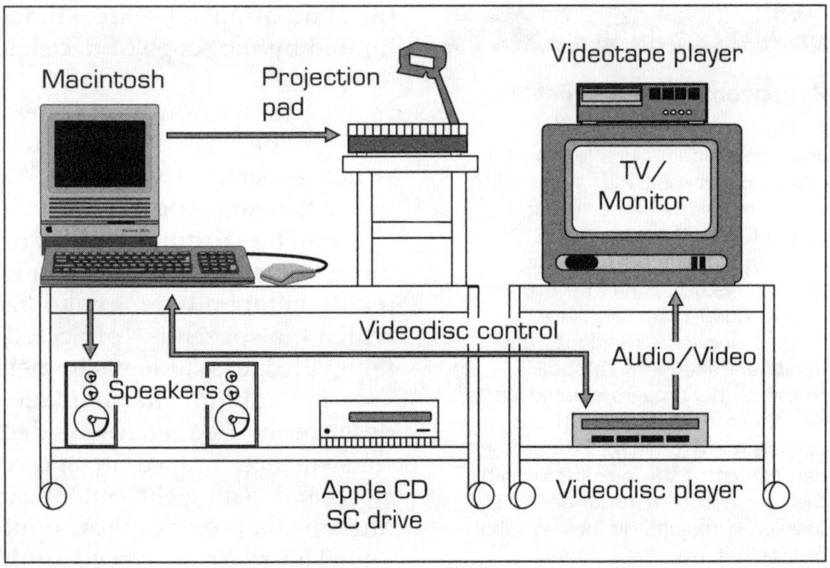

FIGURE 10-1
The computer is only one part of a multimedia teaching system.

approach is designed to involve learners and immerse them fully into the learning process.

To more fully understand multimedia, consider the following example. Imagine that you are to teach a unit on the Civil War. One method of teaching, of course, is to begin your instruction with a lecture on events immediately preceding the Civil War. A lecture might cover the issues of slavery and state's rights, and information on the cotton industry. You might lecture about major battles, the atrocities of war, Lincoln's Gettysburg Address, and the lives of Grant and Lee. Most of us can imagine such a lecture. In fact, at one point or another, most of us have listened to such a lecture.

The problems associated with a lecture approach are many. While most of us did actually learn something from all the lectures we have attended, the lecture method requires passive learning. Students sit, listen, take notes, then take a test.

Current computer instruction takes a somewhat different tack. Depending on the software, a student may be presented with a timetable of events relating to the Civil War. Based on this timetable, students can select an event, then receive instruction on that event. For example, a student may select the Gettysburg Address, see onscreen a picture of Abraham Lincoln, and read a copy of the speech. The software may even have some audio capability; the student can listen to excerpts of the speech. Finally, the software may provide a student-controlled quiz.

Some simulation software asks students to respond to different situations encountered by General Lee. Other software may map different battlefields and the major strategies employed by each general.

While good instructional software offers a great deal to students, there is still the problem of passive learning. With the tutorial example, students read or listen, then take a test. With

Teaching Tool

Researching Local History

At high schools around the country, students are leaving the classroom armed with hand-held scanners, video cameras, and computers. Their goal is to develop a multimedia production of local history. Students are able to use video cameras while interviewing local residents and hand-held scanners to copy historical documents. Based on just these two sources (there can be many others), students can return to the classroom with their research material and develop a multimedia presentation of local history. As a class assignment, students in small groups can work on different historical aspects of the community. By combining the work of all students in the class, a detailed history presentation is not only possible, but a very valuable learning tool.

the simulation software, students learn more actively but are still limited by the scope of decisions and consequences in the software design.

Consider now a multimedia approach to the same topic. The software begins with a timetable that allows student control over which aspects of the Civil War to examine. If a student selects the Gettysburg Address, instead of reading the speech onscreen, she can watch real-time video of an actor portraying Lincoln. There is more to a speech than reading the words or listening to someone recite them; body language, facial expressions, and the screen on which the speech is "projected" all play a role. By including real-time video, the student's immersion into the event is much greater.

In a multimedia simulation, instead of having words onscreen describe consequences of decisions, the video can make those consequences immediate and concrete. Imagine making battle decisions and seeing the outcome, both in tactical and human terms. Multimedia provides these opportunities.

The most advanced multimedia systems are referred to as virtual reality. With virtual reality, the world is presented in three dimensions rather than the two dimensions of a computer monitor. Virtual reality is true instructional immersion. Instead of reading about White House architecture, or listening to a lecture on that subject, it is possible to follow computer-generated plans of the White House, or even control full-motion video as you "walk through" the White House (more on virtual reality later in this chapter).

MULTIMEDIA TOOLS

As stated, what makes multimedia work is the interplay of hardware and software. Since hardware is necessary to multimedia presentations, are must understand the capabilities and limitations of the multimedia's various devices. The following is a listing of those devices.

Laser Videodiscs

Movies are actually a sequence of still photographs. It is called *film* because a motion picture uses photographic film as the medium to record events. Each film is made up of several thousand frames; each frame is an individual photograph. Of course, a projector passes light through each moving frame to project it on a screen. Understanding film is important to understanding the concept of full motion video.

The phrase *full-motion video* means a sequence of frames. A movie is a full motion video, because the sequence of frames causes the illusion of motion. A videotape uses much the same process. Each frame is recorded magnetically on a tape. It too is considered full-motion video.

Full-motion video works well on both tape and film. However, problems come up when trying to generate full-motion video on a computer screen. A computer deals with digital information only. Tape and film are in an analog form. For a computer to control a video image, it must first be digitized. A single frame converted to digital information can take more than two megabytes. If the computer hard disk has a 100 Meg capacity, it would still take only a few frames or pictures to fill the entire disk.

Standard magnetic storage devices (hard and floppy disks) for digitized information are not very practical. What does work well is a technology generally referred to as laser video discs (commonly called video discs). Video discs use a technology in which a laser burns small holes into disc. As each hole is "drilled," it exposes a reflective surface. The presence or absence of a hole represents a bit. As the disc spins within a laser disc player, it passes over a light beam. Because the "holes" are so small, laser discs can store billions of pieces of information. Translated to frames, a laser disc can store about 54,000 frames on each side of a disc that is exactly the same size as a $33\frac{1}{3}$ rpm phonograph record. This is about 30 minutes of video for each side of a laser disc. Some video discs, known as *extended play discs,* double the capacity to 108,000 per side, or one hour of video per side. These are often used to store full-length motion pictures.

There are several major advantages, and a few drawbacks, to storing video information on a laser disc. The major drawback to using laser discs is permanence—once a laser disc is recorded, it may not be changed. This is why laser discs are used for video, but rarely for computer data. Magnetic hard and floppy disks work

FIGURE 10-2
Laser video discs are the same size as old LPs but store large amounts of video data. Some can store as much as one hour of video per side. The smaller disc is a CD-ROM. As the technology changes, the applications of CD-ROM for video are increasing.

Teaching Tool

Video History

ABC News Interactive offers teachers video discs on important historical events. Their video disc *Communism and the Cold War* provides social studies teachers a visual resource to help teachers focus on this period. Teachers using the disk are able to show specific segments, discuss important events, and even have students project and revise outcomes.

better for these uses. Also, laser discs store information in a format different from the digital signal used by computers.

Some of the advantages are that video discs can store considerably more data than even magnetic hard drives. Video discs also are able to number each frame of a film independently, so it is possible to go to any point on the video disc and retrieve either a single frame or a portion of the video. For example, a video disc on the Civil War may have several different video segments, each segment directly accessed by a computer program. This makes it possible to select the video segment on the Gettysburg Address from a laser disc.

The ability of a laser disc to label each frame and access any desired frame or frames makes laser discs interactive. Videotapes and film are linear—you start at one end and go to the other end. It is difficult to move from spot to spot with any speed or precision. With laser discs, moving to a desired location is as easy as specifying a frame address. Combining the controls of computer software with laser disc technology offers great interactive opportunities. The interactive nature of laser discs allows users direct control over accessing portions of video data. There are four levels of control common to laser disc technology.

Level-one Level-one laser discs are those over which the user has limited control. About all a user can do is scan forward or back on a disc to locate a particular frame. With level-one laser discs, a student may be able to use features similar to a VCR's, such as slow motion or stop frame. With level-one laser discs, students control the presentation with a hand-held controller similar to a TV remote control. This level does not connect particularly well with computers and is not often directly used with computer software.

Level-two Level-two laser discs use a special laser disc player that contains a CPU similar to a microcomputer's and special level-two laser discs. With a level-two disc, information flows not only to a monitor, but also to a CPU inside the player for processing. This makes it possible to stop, start, and branch to different areas of the laser disc.

Schools do not often use level-two laser discs for a couple of reasons. First, they are expensive, and second, the programs and video on a level-two disc must be written for a specific level-two disc player. This means that the disc, player, and computer must all be closely integrated, which is much too specialized for general school use.

Level-three When a computer's CPU controls the laser disc player, there is level-three control. The laser disc player does not have its own CPU controlled by programs available on a laser video disc. In fact, level-three control uses the computer's CPU in the same manner as does a magnetic hard disk. Level-three control allows software to be written to control information access. In other words, a programmer can design CAI software to access different frames at different points in the software. For example, a programmer can develop a menu of famous speeches. When a student selects the Gettysburg Address, the program accesses the laser disc, plays the selected portion of video (the speech), then returns control back to the computer software.

Most level-three systems provide a tremendous amount of control over the presentation of video. In most cases, students can start and stop the video at will, use a bookmark to return to where they left off, and even review selected portions of a video. Because of this, level-three control is the most popular form of laser disc technology found in schools.

Level-four The most advanced systems use level-four laser disc technology. Level-four incorporates multiple laser discs and players. For all practical purposes, level-four has the same capabilities as does level-three, but the ability to link and use multiple discs at one time provides an added dimension. Level-four is most often used in flight simulators and other, military applications.

Applications of Laser Video Discs

Laser disc applications in schools are many and varied. However, the primary applications fall into two major categories—film-based and CAI-based.

Among the first to embrace laser disc technology were school film libraries. Laser discs are easier to store, higher quality, and more reliable than videotapes. The cost of a laser disc is about the same as a video tape. Considering that laser discs are durable (regardless of use frequency) and play at near-broadcast quality, the advantages of laser disc over video tape are significant.

Laser discs are also useful for storing large numbers of photographs or slides. Imagine having access to the 54,000 to 108,000 photographic slides available on each side of a video disc. Slides are all organized and directly accessible through frame numbers. A teacher could put a slide presentation together without ever having to organize slides in a tray or worry about damaging valuable photographs. Think of the applications in art appreciation or zoology.

CAI-based laser discs applications are almost endless. Bringing high-quality images and film into a self-paced, student-controlled lesson is very easy. Think of teaching a course on nuclear power. A laser disc could be used to animate the system at work. The program could then put students in control of the system and provide realistic feedback as the student operates the system.

CD-ROM

Compact Disc—Read Only Memory (CD-ROM) is a technology very similar to laser discs. It uses a laser to expose a reflective surface and a beam of light in a player to read the disc. The *CD* in CD-ROM refers to *compact disc,* because the discs used are the same size and type as those used for audio recordings. In fact, many CD-ROM players are the same as those used to play music. *ROM* designates the information on disc as permanent and unalterable.

CD-ROMs for computers were first developed to store large sets of text, such as the volumes of an encyclopedia. Depending on the method of storage, a single CD-ROM disc can store between 250,000 and 2.5 million pages of text.

The major difference between a CD-ROM and a laser disc, other than size, is how information is stored. CD-ROM uses the digital format directly readable by a computer. A laser disc uses a television analog signal, which requires conversion before being used by a computer. In usage, CD-ROM works best for text, and laser disc works best for video. In fact, a CD-ROM disc can store only about one minute of full-motion video, while a laser disc can store about one hour. CD-ROM, then, has the capacity to store graphic or video images (about 5,000 images), but not full video.

CD-I and DV-I Because multimedia incorporates graphics, video, audio, and text, there was a real need to offer an alternative to CD-ROM of the same small size and format. CD-I (Compact Disc-Interactive) and DV-I (Digital Video-Interactive) were developed to provide an expansion of the CD-ROM technology.

CD-I is a CD format developed by Phillips and Sony as a standard extension of CD-ROM for video, audio, text, and graphics. CD-I requires the use of a player containing its own microprocessor. This technology allows for full-motion video to be used on compact discs.

DV-I, owned by Intel, is another format for storing video on the standard CD-sized disc. In this format, up to about 72 minutes of video may be stored. Like CD-I, it requires a player containing a processor; however CD-I normally operates within a self-contained player. That is, it is not directly connected to a computer. There are special CD-I discs available to work with dedicated players—it is this technology that video games are moving toward. DV-I is usually connected to a computer but can also work with stand-alone players.

Teaching Tool

CD-ROM Books

For the next generation, the act of reading may be different than curling up in an easy chair and turning consecutive pages while your eyes scan a two-dimensional page. Books on CD-ROM not only make it possible for the printed word to appear onscreen, but also allow a wide range of photos, sounds, and even video to link directly to text. As students read sections of a "book," they can access illustrations, alter the plot, listen to recordings, and even see video segments. It is even possible to have the computer read the book out loud in several different languages. Reading can stir the imagination; reading on CD-ROM can stir the imagination in many new ways and help students explore worlds unavailable on a printed page.

Applications of CD-ROM, CD-I, and DV-I

As with laser video discs, the uses of CD-ROM technology are almost endless. The only limitations are the program developers' imaginations and how teachers use programs. Here are a few discs schools or teachers can purchase.

ERIC Information Systems

Books in Print Plus

Medline

Newsbank Electronic Index

Standard and Poor's

Oxford English Dictionary

The Bible Library

Grolier's New Electronic Encyclopedia

Compton's MultiMedia Encyclopedia

Geodis (U.S. Geologic Survey Maps)

Electronic World Atlas

SuperMap USA

The Electronic Map Cabinet

The Art Room (Clip Art Collection)

Image Processing

One of the most exciting tools in multimedia captures any image and imports it into a multimedia presentation. Doing so is called *image processing*. Typically, image processing involves the use of a video digitizer, image scanner, and still-video camera.

A *video digitizer* is a peripheral device that converts the image taken by a video camera or an image reproduced on a video disc player or videotape player to a direct, computer-usable format. In other words, with a video digitizer, you can use a video camera to produce a single video shot and import that image into the computer. For example, a video digitizer can put a child's picture right on a computer screen.

It is also possible to generate a video image onscreen from a videotape or a laser disc. For example, if you have a videotape of Mona Lisa, you can digitize the image from the tape and import it into your computer's memory. You can then modify the image any way you want using draw or paint programs. Imagine how much art students would enjoy improving on a painting by Picasso.

Image scanners allow photographs, line art, or virtually anything on paper to be digitized and placed into a computer. Image scanners work much like photocopiers; one places the paper on the scanner bed, and in a few moments, the image appears onscreen. Again, once the image is digitized, it may be modified using most draw or paint programs.

Still-video technology is the newest and, in many ways, one of the most exciting areas of photography. Instead of using film to record photographs, still-video cameras record an image onto a disk inside the camera. From there, the image can be placed into a

CPU and printed, altered with graphics software, and stored electronically.

One of the more popular methods of using still-video is with CD-ROM and CD-I technology. Kodak and other manufacturers are now producing systems to place photographs, including those generated with still-video, on CD. The CD then is able to play back the photographs on any television.

Uses of Image Processing

Again, the uses for this technology in education are almost endless. For teachers who want to take their own pictures for use in class, this technology can be very useful. Imagine a geography teacher who travels and takes photographs for use in class. Imagine an art teacher traveling to famous museums or a history teacher photographing all the battlefields of the Civil War. This technology allows teachers more control over multimedia than almost any other.

VIRTUAL REALITY

While multimedia technology, however infant, is already here, a newer technology may have a greater impact on teaching and learning. Virtual reality is a technology in which the learner is totally immersed in a learning environment. This immersion is based on visual, full and detailed audio, and tactile experiences—all in three dimensions.

Steve Aukstakalnis and David Blatner best defined virtual reality (*Silicon Mirage: The Art and Science of Virtual Reality* [Berkeley: PeachPit Press, 1992], 7). They write: "Virtual reality is a way for

FIGURE 10-3
With a simple interface card, it is easy to connect a video camera to a computer.

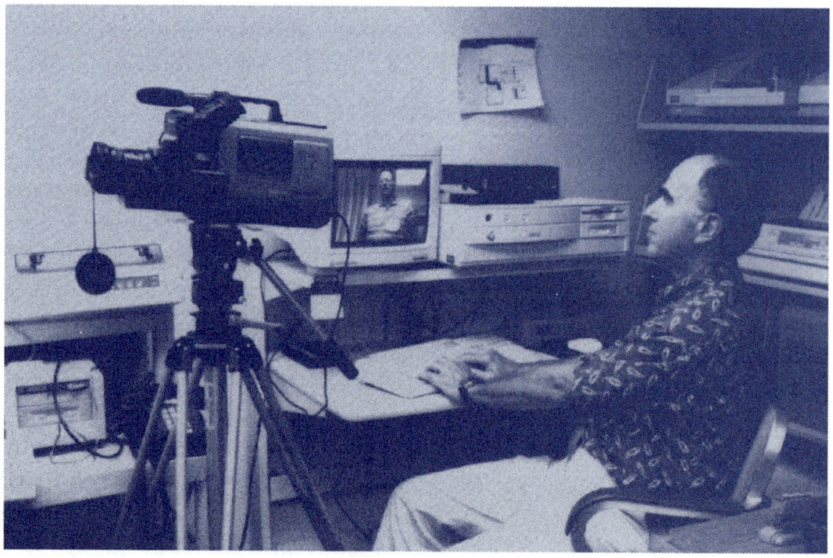

humans to visualize, manipulate, and interact with computers and extremely complex data." It is a conceptual leap away from how we normally interact with computers—through monitors and keyboards—to a system based on more "natural" controls. Using special gloves, goggles, headphones, and other devices to control an artificial environment, virtual reality places students *inside* events, rather than looking at events from the outside.

Virtual reality is no longer science fiction, though movies and books often fictionalize devices and software that link mind and machine. A perfect example is the Holodeck on *Star Trek: The Next Generation*. On the Holodeck, a person can fully interact with a computer-generated environment. One can see, hear, touch, taste, and smell. While the Holodeck is still science fiction, it does represent the direction and potential use of virtual reality.

Virtual reality is at present limited by the equipment required for it. This involves three basic devices—a viewer or goggles, headphones, and a glove. The first component of virtual reality is the goggles, the viewing device that blocks out all visual stimuli other than that presented by the computer. The goggles are more than a sophisticated monitor. The software written for them uses three-dimensional graphics techniques. The goggles also allow input through head movements. For example, if you look into a "room" through virtual reality goggles, you will see a full three-dimensional representation of a room. As you turn your head, the room will adjust to your new and changing perspective. If you move forward, the perspective changes again.

Headphones provide the audio source. Again, in order to represent reality, sound changes as you move closer or further away from a source.

The glove is what excites most people. The glove is linked to the goggles. As your hand moves, the glove and the image of your hand move. This enables you to reach out, point, and even touch and hold an object. For example, if your room contains a vase, you can reach out and pick up the vase. Within the goggles, you will see your hand move, grab, and pick up the object. In addition, you can turn the object and view the object from different angles.

While the science fiction movies show virtual reality in life-like forms, in actuality virtual reality uses modeling for representations of the real world. Instead of walking into a "real room," with virtual reality you walk into a model of the room. It is similar to looking at, and walking through, a blueprint of a room, rather than walking through a real room.

Aukstakalnis and Blatner identify three levels of virtual reality. The first is *passive*. In a passive model, the user is placed in the situation but has no control over it. For example, if you are placed in a room and the room spins to show all four walls, this is still considered passive, because you have no control over the sequence of events.

The second level is known as *exploratory*. At this level, the user can participate by controlling gross movements. Instead of only

Teaching Tool

Multimedia and the Hearing-Impaired

At the Burnaby South High School in Burnaby, British Columbia, the use of multimedia has become vital for both hearing and deaf children because multimedia provides information in a visual format. In the hallways are open-captioned monitors. Instead of making school announcements over a traditional speaker system, this school uses the monitors to visually present the information. Along with announcements, the open-captioned monitors are able to signal class changes (instead of using a bell) and use special visual cues for fire alarms.

seeing what happens next, as with the passive level, at the exploratory level the user has control over what appears next.

The third and most powerful level, and one that has been the vision of science fiction, is known as *interactive* virtual reality. The interactive level allows the user to interact with the environment, most often through the use of a glove or other special device. A student pilot may use this level to learn how to control an airplane. A glove is used to control the stick, activate various controls, and touch the environment in which the pilot is immersed.

While virtual reality offers the greatest promise for educators, it is a long way from becoming educational reality. While there has been significant progress over the last several years, most of the work is still at the developmental stage. There is also the issue of price. The computing power needed to control such a complex set of data is significant and costs much more than most schools are willing to invest. Nevertheless, there are remarkable systems available or soon to be available.

Still, we are a long way from using virtual reality as a common multimedia educational tool. Virtual reality will not soon be able to present realities indistinguishable from our own. In other words, the Holodeck is likely to remain on the Starship Enterprise for a while yet.

As with all technological development, virtual reality will have both benefits and drawbacks for education and society. Technology is neutral; the management of it and the uses it is put to are not. Whatever develops from the advances in virtual reality, as always we will have to work to ensure that the beneficial aspects of this technology become ascendant in our society.

Teaching Tools

ESL CD-ROM

Teaching English as a Second Language (ESL) is fast becoming an important part of many school districts. As the number of ESL students increases, so does the demand on local school districts. One of the most popular applications of CD-ROM technology supports the teaching of new language skills. The high storage capacity that is the trademark of CD-ROM makes it possible to include, on one disk, audio, text, video, visual displays, word lists, teaching and learning ideas, and much more. Think of the advantages for the student; as an image appears, students can listen to the word or phrase, type the word or phrase, and fully interact and control learning.

Summary

- Multimedia is a mode of instructional delivery that encompasses the traditional role of computer control and delivery based on a multisensory and multimedium strategy.
- In a multimedia simulation, instead of having words on the screen depict consequences of decisions, the use of video can make those consequences much more immediate and concrete.
- The most advanced systems of multimedia are referred to as virtual reality.
- The term *full-motion* video means that a collection of frames are placed in sequence.
- Video discs use a technology in which small holes are burned by a laser into a disc.

- A laser disc can store about 54,000 frames of video on each side of a disc that is exactly the same size as a 33⅓ rpm phonographic record.
- 54,000 frames translates to about 30 minutes of video for each side of a disc.
- CD-ROMs for computers were first developed to store large sets of text (250,000 to 2.5 million pages), such as volumes of an encyclopedia.
- CD-I is a CD format developed by Phillips and Sony as a standard extension of CD-ROM for video, audio, text, and graphics.
- DV-I, owned by Intel, is another format for storing full video on the standard CD-sized disc.
- Image processing involves the use of a video digitizer, image scanner, and still-video camera.
- The three levels of virtual reality are passive, exploratory, and interactive.

Fill-In Questions

Fill in the blank for each of the statements listed below.

1. Multimedia is a mode of instructional delivery that encompasses the traditional role of computer control and delivery based on a ________________ and ________________ strategy.
2. ________________ is an integrated approach to learning in which multiple forms of media fit together to form a systematic presentation.
3. With virtual reality, the world is presented in a ________________ form rather than in the two dimensions found on a computer monitor.
4. ________________ use a technology in which small holes are burned by a laser into disc.
5. The major disadvantage of using laser discs is that data storage is ________________ .
6. With ________________ laser discs, a student may be able to use features similar to a VCR's, such as slow motion or stop frame.
7. Schools do not often use ________________ laser discs.

Quiz

Answer the following questions.

1. Virtual reality attempts to provide students with which type of learning?
   a. passive
   b. immersion
   c. pro-active
   d. none of the above
2. What term indicates a series of frames in sequence?
   a. full-motion video
   b. interactive video
   c. linear video
   d. bi-linear video
3. About how many frames are stored on each side of a standard laser video disc?
   a. 1,000,000
   b. 500,000
   c. 108,000
   d. 54,000
4. Which type of disk stores information permanently?
   a. magnetic disk
   b. floppy disk
   c. laser video disk
   d. hard disk
5. Which level of laser video disc provides limited control?
   a. level-one
   b. level-two
   c. level-three
   d. level-four
6. Which level of laser video disc is most popular in schools?
   a. level-one
   b. level-two
   c. level-three
   d. level-four
7. Which type of disc is best for storing text based data?
   a. laser video disc
   b. CD-ROM
   c. CD-DV-I
   d. level-four LVD
8. Which of the following devices is best for importing a photograph into a RAM?
   a. laser video disc
   b. image scanner
   c. digitized MIDI
   d. CD-ROM
9. Which type of virtual reality offers the greatest immersion into an electronic event?
   a. passive
   b. exploratory
   c. interactive
   d. level-four immersion
10. Virtual reality is likely to offer mind control as a standard feature.
    a. true
    b. false

Exercises and Applications

Follow the instructions for each exercise and application.

1. Watch *Star Trek: The Next Generation* for a program that shows the Holodeck. List three facets of the Holodeck that provide a realistic look at virtual reality and three facets that are pure science fiction.
2. Are local schools using laser video discs and other multimedia tools? The answer is probably no, or at best in a limited way. Why are schools failing to implement multimedia technology? What obstacles do they face?
3. If you were given $3000, would you purchase any of the multimedia tools discussed in this chapter? Which would you choose and why?
4. Pick one subject area and develop a plan for integrating and implementing laser video disc technology. How can this technology be used to teach your discipline? What are the major drawbacks and concerns?
5. Imagine that the year is 2010 and virtual reality is now available. Write a news report depicting how virtual reality is being used to teach children. How has this technology changed the course of education?

11

ESSENTIALS OF HYPERMEDIA, AUTHORING, AND PROGRAMMING

LEARNING OBJECTIVES

Learning the material in this chapter will enable you to:

- explain why learning about programming is important to computer users
- define computer programming
- identify major high-level languages
- describe the purpose of applications generators, authoring systems, and hypertext
- describe the use of Hypermedia
- describe object-oriented programming
- begin to control the computer through the LOGO language

CHAPTER OVERVIEW

Multimedia and virtual reality are of very little use without appropriate software. For example, menu software that is designed only to access a portion of video on a laser disc does not always take full advantage of laser disc technology. Just as the hardware technology for multimedia has advanced considerably over the past few years, so has the technology of software development.

It was not too long ago that to use any computer, even microcomputers, you needed at least minimal programming knowledge. Little software was available to meet the needs of all users. Computer users had to spend countless hours creating programs or entering programs from books. Most of these programs were so simple by today's standards that they quickly lost their usefulness and appeal.

After the introduction of microcomputers, several programming languages used on mainframes were converted for microcomputer use. Not surprisingly, the capabilities of these programs were limited to the technology of the day. Programming languages such as BASIC, FORTRAN, and Pascal worked well with early microcomputers, but have several limitations for the complex software needed today.

Fortunately, the new standard for developing instructional programs doesn't rely on the cumbersome programming techniques of the past. The software development "languages" for today's educators are grouped into three categories—Hypermedia, program generators, and authoring languages.

This chapter introduces you to a few of the essential concepts related to developing instructional software. Beginning with an overview of programming, this chapter leads to a discussion of instructional software development using modern software development tools. The goal of this chapter is *not* to turn you into computer programmers; the goal is to provide you with a conceptual background, so that if you choose to develop some of your own educational software, you will have an adequate foundation.

A BRIEF BACKGROUND

For all practical purposes, people and computers cannot communicate directly. They do not speak the same language. Machines only speak or process information in a series of bits represented by zeros and ones. This is a very exact language not open to imprecision. On the other hand, people speak a language filled with ambiguity; the two are not compatible. What is needed is a common language that is both useful for people and easily understandable by computers. This is the role of a programming language: to provide a common ground for communication.

Programming is the art of writing computer-controlling instructions in a language comprehensible to people *and* computers. These instructions are known as *programs*. The act of creating a program is *programming*, and the language of common communication is a *programming language*.

There are many different programming languages, each designed to facilitate a certain type of program development. The term *high-level language* is associated with the major programming languages used to develop most computer programs. The following describes some of the common high-level languages.

BASIC

*B*eginners *A*ll-purpose *S*ymbolic *I*nstructional *C*ode (BASIC) was developed in the 1960s as a general-use language. **BASIC** uses a series of command statements, each beginning with a line number. The following lines are examples of a BASIC program.

```
100 PRINT "Please read the instructions before continuing."

110 LET Z = 10

120 INPUT "What is your name?"; NAME1$
```

The line numbers show the sequence of the program and the commands. PRINT, LET, and INPUT invoke specific actions. PRINT displays information following the command onscreen. LET assigns a numeric value to a variable; in the example, LET assigns the value 10 to the variable Z. INPUT displays information, then waits for the user to enter a response from keyboard.

Along with command statements, BASIC uses a variety of system commands to manipulate the program. For example, the system command RUN executes the program, and LIST displays all the program's lines of code.

BASIC has become very popular with microcomputer users because it is easy to learn and can produce a variety of different programs. It is very flexible, allowing users to develop almost any type of program. Paradoxically, this flexibility is also BASIC's major drawback. Many new programmers using BASIC do not write sensible, structured programs and BASIC is not idiot-proof. However, BASIC is still necessary to a programmer's repertoire.

Another drawback is that different computer families use slightly different versions of BASIC. That is, a BASIC program written for an IBM PC may not work on a Macintosh computer. For example, commands to access data may vary slightly. Finally, BASIC does not handle large sets of data efficiently. Commercial programmers rarely use it for large-scale programming projects. Other programming languages are better-suited. Nevertheless, BASIC remains popular for creating smaller programs with limited applications. This is especially true of newer versions such as Microsoft Quick BASIC and Microsoft Visual BASIC.

Pascal

Pascal is another general-use language (named for the famous French mathematician Blaise Pascal). Unlike BASIC, the strength of Pascal is that it provides an easy method for developing structured programs. There are no line numbers, only command statements. The following is a sample of a Pascal program.

```
VAR A: REAL;
    AMOUNT: REAL;
    B: INTEGER;
BEGIN
    AMOUNT:=0;
    FOR B:=1 TO 100 DO
    BEGIN
        READ(A)
        AMOUNT:=AMOUNT + A
    END;
    WRITELN("The Amount is ",AMOUNT)
END.
```

The sample program is based on a structure rather than the sequence of programming statements of BASIC. Because of this, Pascal has become a very popular language for general computer use and is popular as a tool for teaching techniques of structured programming. Pascal also works very well for creating graphic displays. Many games that use graphic displays are written in Pascal.

FORTRAN

For*mula* Tr*an*slator (**FORTRAN**) is a popular scientific and mathematical programming language developed in the 1950s. As with BASIC and Pascal, FORTRAN is considered a general-purpose language because the structure lends itself to supporting a variety of applications. FORTRAN combines optional line numbers (as does BASIC) and a structure similar to Pascal. However, unlike BASIC or Pascal, FORTRAN has very specific data format requirements. That is, each command, variable, or datum must be placed in a specific column location, or indented a certain number of spaces. If line numbers are used, they must be placed in the first five columns. Columns 7–72 contain the actual FORTRAN commands. Columns 73–80 are not used by the computer and are available for programmers to use for notes.

FORTRAN is common on minicomputers and mainframes, but it is not as popular with microcomputer users as are BASIC and Pascal. FORTRAN is used mostly by scientists and mathematicians. They use it on large sets of data not well-suited for most microcomputers. FORTRAN is used on mainframes because it can handle the large amount of data that other languages cannot.

COBOL

COBOL (*Co*mmon *B*usiness *O*riented *L*anguage), also developed in the 1950s, is popular for business applications. As with FORTRAN, COBOL requires each command and data line to be broken into several specific components. Because the structure of COBOL is intended to match business reporting systems, it is very rarely used in education.

C

One of the most popular programming languages for developing educational applications is **C**. Developed in the 1970s, C can control information flow from several peripherals. It is the language of choice for sophisticated software developers, including those who create computer games, database software, and operating systems. Unlike other languages, C is almost universal from one computer family to another.

All of these high-level languages require a great deal of study and expertise to use proficiently. In fact, these high-level languages are typically the purview of commercial software developers and people who program computers for a living. The languages are not particularly useful for teachers trying to develop software for their own students. High-level languages take too long for non-professionals to learn and use to develop a viable piece of software.

PROGRAMMING ALTERNATIVES

For educators, programming with high-level languages is not a realistic endeavor. Nevertheless, teachers can develop their own programs using special software tools designed to automate software development. These software development tools are called *applications generators* and *authoring languages*.

An **applications generator** is a type of software that condenses much of the detail of programming into a few simple commands. For example, an applications generator may provide a complete data-entry screen based on the user's specifications. An applications generator may also provide a complete reporting system, so users needn't program the control of output to different hardware devices. By virtue of a very simple command structure, applications generators are easy to learn and use.

Applications generators are a link between the way typical users think and how a computer program operates. This link, or interface, allows users to specify program operations without having to write program code. For example, an applications generator may list standard screen displays on which the user can base the program. Instead of requiring several hundred very precise lines of instructions, an applications generator asks the user to select a type of screen display, then writes the code to display that screen. Of course, applications generators create the code based on the user's input.

Several applications generators use a menu approach, in which the user selects features from a list of options. Often these options include the generation of menus and screen displays.

Authoring systems are similar to applications generators in that they create programs from a menu-based interface. A user can select a desired program command from a menu rather than having to type in one, or several hundred, lines of instructions to produce the same effect. They differ from applications generators in the types of programs they are adept at creating.

Authoring systems work particularly well for generating drill and practice and tutorial software. Depending on the kind of authoring language, the process works like using a draw or paint program. A user is given a working screen to develop a single display. For example, one screen may ask for the capital of Colorado and give four possible answers. In addition to the text, teachers may include a map of Colorado with a star indicating the capital. Authoring systems then help lay out answers onscreen; the user can create correct and incorrect answers and program the software to respond appropriately. Finally, authoring languages provide tools that enable the software user to move from one screen to another. Authoring systems using a graphical user interface have tools, such as arrow buttons, that link one screen display to another.

A more popular alternative to authoring systems and applications generators is a set of programming tools known as *object-oriented programming.* Object-oriented programming is a set of tools for developing software linked to some of the most popular graphical interfaces in use today (such as Windows). With object-oriented programming, the goal is to look at programming events as a whole. People think of an object such as a house, school, or magazine as the sum of its parts, rather than as a collection of independent pieces. In the same way, object-oriented programs look at events in totality. Each object, then, is treated as a complete entity connected to other entities by messages. Messages link objects in the environment to form full object-oriented programs. This makes objects seem more natural to users.

One of the big advantages to object-oriented programming is that each object is designed in a reusable format. Thus, objects can be used as modules; they can be "recycled" in different applications. For example, an object that sorts names in a mailing list can be used to sort names in a financial aid list. Users can design one object for a variety of users.

Another advantage of object-oriented programming is a process known as *inheritance.* This is the ability for one object to be the base for creating other objects with variations. With inheritance, users can take all the instructions and work done with one object, transport it to another object, then make minor changes to create a new object. Inheritance reduces the need to re-write new objects and saves time. Instead of having to write several thousand lines of code in a traditional high-level language, an object-oriented program could be developed by combining ten or fifteen existing objects. Even if changes are required, the time savings will still be significant. Some of the more popular object-oriented languages include C++, Smalltalk, Loops, and Objective-C.

HYPERMEDIA DEVELOPMENT TOOLS

For teachers, one of the newest and most exciting areas of program development is hypermedia. **Hypermedia** provides an easy-to-follow method to organize and access sets of text and graphics. In its simplest form, hypermedia is used to create a set of logically-organized screen displays. Each screen display is called a *card.* A series of cards is called a *stack.* Each card within the stack can display text or graphics different from the others. Most hypermedia software provides tools for creating a full range of text attributes, such as point size, typestyle, and typeface. In addition, graphics

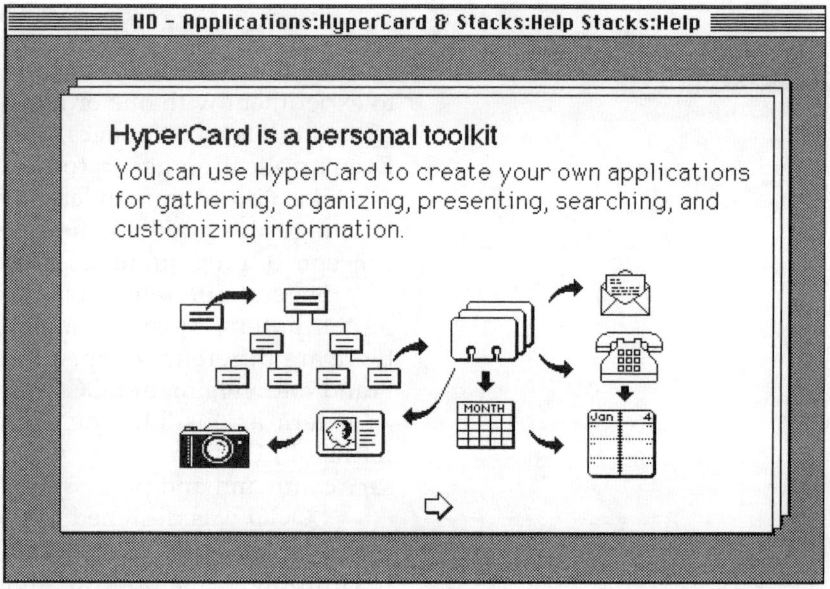

FIGURE 11-1
HyperCard is very popular among educators looking to develop organized curriculum presentations. Teachers are able to create a stack of information "cards," then link any card to any other card.

ranging from simple lines and boxes to complex graphic images are available for each card.

Hypermedia also provides an efficient method for moving from one card to another. The method uses a *button*—a location within a card that, when selected, shifts the display to another card. By linking different cards, the user develops a program without having to use a traditional programming language at all.

HyperCard for the Mac and IBM's Linkway are examples of hypermedia development tools. Both have a wide range of tools for creating screen displays and the other tools necessary to create a visual program. In both cases, the same types of screen-based programs can be programmed with traditional high-level languages; however, the number of lines of code needed to create a single screen display in BASIC, FORTRAN, Pascal, and others can be in the thousands of lines. With HyperCard and Linkway, the same screen can be generated in less than ten lines of code.

Hypertext is text that contains links to other text and graphics. It is possible to create hypertext with HyperCard and Linkway (hypermedia development tools). Hypermedia links the features of hypertext with the tools of multimedia. Programs such as HyperCard and Linkway provide a means to directly control laser disc players, CD-ROM, specialized audio systems, and imaging devices. Hypermedia is very appealing to teachers and students because of its ability to use video, music, sound effects, voice, and animation. Imagine a hypermedia stack of famous speeches. Music might be placed at the beginning of the stack, voices of presidents might be incorporated into various cards, and animation of a president delivering a speech might be included. Hypertext and hypermedia allow users to develop this type of sophisticated program.

Teaching Tool

Hypermanagement

One of the most useful methods of employing hypertext and hypermedia for teachers is with classroom and lesson management. Programs such as HyperCard and Linkway allow teachers to place their entire lesson plans into well-organized screen displays. From this, teachers can display critical points of their lesson, project outlines, even offer question-and-answer options. All this can be done onscreen, instead of using other devices such as overhead projectors.

LOGO

To fully understand the concepts of programming, it is a good idea to experiment with one or more programming languages. For many of the high-level languages, this translates into an extended exercise. Even application generators, authoring systems, and hypermedia can take a bit of time to learn. Fortunately, there is a programming language designed for new learners that enjoyably teaches the concepts of programming. This programming language is **LOGO**.

Several different versions of LOGO exist for different families of computers. Most use a similar command structure. However, there are differences depending on the computer you use and the brand and version of LOGO. The examples used in this section are as generic as possible; you should be able to use them with various forms of LOGO. You may want to check the manual for any necessary command and process modifications.

LOGO was designed in the early 1970s by Seymour Papert of the Massachusetts Institute of Technology to introduce students to computers in a non-threatening, fun way. It allows students to consider a problem and offer solutions to that problem. Using a graphic procedure, students are able to design from their own creativity and ingenuity. In creating such a tool, Papert hoped that children would be able to explore learning in whole new ways.

LOGO is a programming language. As with any programming language, learning begins with understanding the command structure. LOGO uses turtle graphics to execute commands which create graphic images. Through a series of commands, the user moves a turtle around the screen to create various designs. With imagination and an understanding of the commands, designs are unlimited. The following is a list of commands you will need to learn to begin to manipulate LOGO.

CLEARSCREEN: CLEARSCREEN places LOGO into the graphics or turtle graphics mode, leaving four lines at the bottom to enter information. In addition, CLEARSCREEN erases any previous design from the monitor and returns the turtle to the center of the screen or "home" position.

CLEARGRAPHICS: In some versions of LOGO, CLEARSCREEN is not a valid command. Instead the command CLEARGRAPHICS is used and has the same effect—to erase all lines and return the turtle to the home or starting position.

FORWARD: FORWARD commands the turtle to move forward the desired number of turtle units. For example, FORWARD 50 moves the turtle forward 50 turtle units.

BACK: BACK commands the turtle to move backward the desired number of turtle units. For example, BACK 50 moves the turtle backward 50 turtle units.

Teaching Tool

Re-purposing Video Discs

Authoring languages and hypermedia provide the software tools that enable teachers to easily develop customized lessons based on the video provided on a video disc. A biology teacher can use a video disc of images to generate a lesson for the class. A geography teacher can use a video disc of images taken across the U.S. to develop the equivalent of a customized slide presentation. In both of these examples, teachers can develop a series of question an answers to follow specific video segments. For example, a biology teacher may want to display a picture of a frog from the video disc. The authoring language can then be used to add questions and answers about each part of the frog. It may sound a bit complicated, but authoring languages an hypermedia make this process easy.

RIGHT: RIGHT commands the turtle to turn right the desired number of degrees (zero to 360). For example, RIGHT 180 turns the turtle 180° or completely around. RIGHT 90 will turn the turtle 90°. It is important to remember the turtle will turn the number of degrees right from its present position. For example, RIGHT 90 will turn the turtle right 90°. Another RIGHT 90 will turn the turtle another 90°. This will result in a 180° turn from its original position.

LEFT: LEFT turns the turtle left in the desired number of degrees. As with the RIGHT commands, LEFT will turn the turtle from its present position. For example, LEFT 90 will turn the turtle left 90°.

PENUP AND PENDOWN: PENUP instructs the turtle to lift up its pen. When the turtle is moved while the pen is up, the turtle will not draw; it will simply move. No drawing will occur until the command PENDOWN is given. For example, the string:

```
PENUP
FORWARD 50
PENDOWN
FORWARD 50
```

will lift the turtle's pen, move forward 50 turtle units without drawing, put the pen back down, and move 50 turtle units while drawing.

PENERASE: PENERASE allows the user to erase a line. After giving the command PENERASE, simply retrace the line already drawn. PENERASE will continue to erase lines until the PENDOWN command is given. For example,

```
FORWARD 50
PENERASE
BACK 50
PENDOWN
```

HIDETURTLE: HIDETURTLE makes the turtle invisible. However, the turtle can still draw while it is invisible. It is difficult to draw when the turtle is invisible, because the user cannot see the direction that the turtle is facing. When the turtle is drawing, it is a good idea not to hide the turtle. Hide the turtle only when the drawing or design is finished.

SHOWTURTLE: SHOWTURTLE is used to make the turtle visible again. For example, if the turtle is hidden, it can be seen again by entering the SHOWTURTLE command.

REPEAT: The REPEAT command allows you to repeat any series of LOGO commands a specified number of times. The format for this command is as follows:

```
REPEAT 60 [FD 5 RT 6]
```

The 60 after REPEAT designates how many times the commands contained within brackets will be executed. In this example, the REPEAT command creates a circle.

Many LOGO commands can be abbreviated. Abbreviations reduce typing and therefore reduce mistakes. Here are the abbreviations for the above commands.

CLEARSCREEN	CS
CLEARGRAPHICS	CG
FORWARD	FD
BACKWARD	BK
RIGHT	RT
LEFT	LT
PENUP	PU
PENDOWN	PD
PENERASE	PE
HIDETURTLE	HT
SHOWTURTLE	ST

Learning the commands that make up a programming language is only the beginning of programming. Real programming involves grouping several commands together to be sequentially executed. It is not enough to watch a turtle move with one command, then type another. Grouping all the commands to create an object then executing the group, creates the object all at once—*this* is programming.

In LOGO, the groups of commands are called *procedures*. In most versions of LOGO, one begins a procedure by typing the TO command, then the name you wish to use to identify the procedure. After entering TO and the procedure name, LOGO goes into an edit mode. In this mode, commands placed into the procedure are not immediately executed. The LOGO editor is used like a word processor; commands may be entered and edited using standard word processing techniques.

Any legal LOGO command may be placed within a procedure. There are many more commands than those discussed in this chapter. You may also include the execution of any other procedure. Consider the following examples: the first procedure draws a square, and the second uses a square to create a star.

```
TO SQUARE
FD 50 RT 90
FD 50 RT 90
FD 50 RT 90
FD 50 RT 90
FD 50 RT 90
END
```

```
TO STAR
REPEAT 72 [RT 5 SQUARE]
END
```

Note that each of the example procedures begins with TO, followed by the procedure name, and concludes with the END command.

The key to developing a procedure is to think like a computer. Computers think, or process information, only one step at a time. Information must be excruciatingly specific. A computer must have information that instructs it to do one specific task at a time, in a logical order. For example, in LOGO, a specific task is to FORWARD 50. This the computer can understand. However, a general statement like GOTO RIGHT CORNER will confuse the computer. Where, precisely, in the right corner is the turtle to go? All directions or commands must be specific. In addition, the computer cannot guess the command is if it is misspelled. For example, a person might understand FARWORD 50 to mean FORWARD 50, but the computer wouldn't. Correct spelling is very important for all work with a computer.

A computer thinks from the top down. That is, the computer follows and completes the first instruction, then completes the very next instruction, and so on. Again, the computer performs only one instruction at a time. On occasion, this progression may be altered if desired. Altering the top-down sequence is called *looping*.

Based on this brief introduction to LOGO, you should be able to begin experimenting with it. LOGO is best learned through experimentation. Ask your instructor if a manual of additional LOGO commands is available along with a guide for the basic process of entering, editing, and executing procedures.

Summary

- Learning about programming is important for those who desire to develop their own software.
- A computer program is a set of instructions designed to control a computer.
- Programming languages are a compromise between the language of computers and the language of people.
- Machine language is the native language of the computer and is based on a series of bits.
- Applications generators link how typical users think with how a computer program operates.
- Authoring systems are similar to applications generators, because they create programs from a menu-oriented interface.

- Hypertext provides an easy-to-follow method for organizing and accessing specific sets of text and graphics.
- With object-oriented programming, the goal is to look at programming events in totality. Messages link objects to form full object-oriented programs.
- LOGO educational programming language designed to teach programming fundamentals.

Fill-In Questions

Fill in the blank for each of the statements listed below.

1. A program is a ________________, written in a language that a computer can understand, designed to cause a computer to perform a series of specified tasks.
2. LOGO is sometimes called ________________ graphics.
3. ________________ is a high-level language commonly used for applications in mathematics, engineering, and science.
4. ________________ is the high-level language most often used in business programming.
5. ________________ is a type of software that builds much of the detail of programming into a few simple commands.

Quiz

Answer the following questions.

1. What is the language of the computer?
   a. machine language b. assembly language
   c. high-level language d. natural language
2. What type of language is most commonly used for programming?
   a. machine language b. assembly language
   c. high-level language d. natural language
3. In hypertext, a screen display is called a card. A series of cards is called a:
   a. pile b. deck
   c. stack d. group

4. The term used to describe linking the features of hypertext with the tools of multimedia is:
   a. linking b. linkway
   c. multitext d. hypermedia

5. Hypercard for the Macintosh and Linkway for IBM are examples of:
   a. hypertext b. turtle graphics
   c. hypermedia d. high-level languages

6. In most versions of LOGO, the process for beginning a procedure is to type the ______________ command.
   a. Line Number b. Procedure
   c. Repeat d. To

7. Which of the following is similar to applications generators in that they create programs from a menu-oriented interface?
   a. authoring system b. turtle graphics
   c. COBOL d. high-level language

8. Creating an object by joining data and instructions is called ______________ programming.
   a. object-oriented b. BASIC-authoring
   c. LOGO-procedures d. Graphic User Interface

Exercises and Applications

Follow the instructions for each exercise and application.

1. Develop a program to control a household robot. First, develop a specification sheet detailing your expectations for the robot. What tasks will the robot perform, and how will commands be issued? Are there other vital pieces of information about the expectations of the robot? Be as specific as possible. The outcome of this exercise will be used in several of the following exercises and applications.

2. Based on the expectations you developed in exercise 1, create a program design for one robot task. "Program design" means a general structure, not the specific commands. For example, the robot may have the goal of washing the dishes. What is the first step? Does it put dishes in the sink first, or fill the sink with water? What about the soap? What happens if the robot washes the dish, but it is not clean? How will dishes be dried? These are the types of considerations programmers examine when developing a program design. Be sure to include a sufficient level of detail in the program design.

3. Based on the program design in exercise 2, create a list of commands that can be used to represent one step in the program design. For example, washing one dish may include the commands GRAB DISH, GRAB CLOTH, DIP, MOVE CLOTH, RINSE, STACK. Make the commands as precise as possible.
4. The next step in developing a program is to write code for the program. Imagine that you are the robot. Go through each of the commands created in exercise 3 to determine if the program works correctly. If there are problems, correct them. It is possible to use this process to expand the program and to make several revisions.
5. Once the program is finished, write a one-page set of instructions for controlling the robot.

Appendix A

MACINTOSH ESSENTIALS

PURPOSE

If you have never used a Macintosh computer, this appendix is for you. It is designed to give you the fundamental knowledge needed to operate any Macintosh computer. While this appendix will not make you a Mac expert, it will start you in the right direction. As you progress through this appendix, be sure to practice. In fact, it is best to go through this appendix as you sit and experiment with a Macintosh computer.

THE MAC MOUSE

The one piece of hardware most closely associated with a Macintosh is a mouse. Virtually all Macintosh activities are controlled via mouse. Therefore, the first step in learning to use a Macintosh is learning to use a mouse—an easy task. On nearly every screen display there is an arrow (or some other specialized symbol) known as the *pointer.* Moving the mouse across a flat surface moves the pointer on the screen. The process for issuing a command or starting a program is to move the pointer onto the desired selection, then press the mouse button one or two times in rapid succession. Pressing the mouse button once is known as *clicking;* pressing it twice is known as *double-clicking.* That's it. That is all there is to controlling the computer with a mouse.

STARTING A MACINTOSH COMPUTER

Successfully starting a Macintosh varies with the type and model. However, all models require the operating system to reside on a disk. It must be the first program loaded into RAM. For computers with a hard disk, if the operating system is on the hard disk, turning on the computer automatically loads the operating system and puts the controlling program, Finder, into action. For those systems without a hard drive, a disk containing the operating system must be in a floppy disk drive before turning on the computer.

Most Macintosh II computers, the Macintosh Classic, Mac SE, and all other older models have one power switch that turns on both the computer and monitor. Because the monitor is part of the computer box, one power switch starts the entire computer system. However, peripherals such as external hard drives, graphics tablets, scanners, add-on monitors, or any other external devices may require using a separate power switch.

Guided Practice

1. Turn on your Mac.

   Check with your instructor for any specific requirements for the model of Macintosh computer you are using. You should notice the opening screen, shown in Figure A-1. This may differ slightly depending on how your computer is set up.

2. Move the mouse.

   Notice as the mouse moves on the table, so does the small arrow onscreen.

3. Move the pointer (the arrow controlled by the mouse) until it points at the small apple in the upper-left corner of the screen.

4. Press and hold down the mouse button.

   This produces a list of menu options. See Figure A-2.

5. Move the mouse pointer down the screen without releasing the mouse button. This is called *dragging*. Drag the mouse down until Chooser is highlighted.

6. Release the mouse button.

   This will activate the Chooser.

FIGURE A-1
The opening screen.

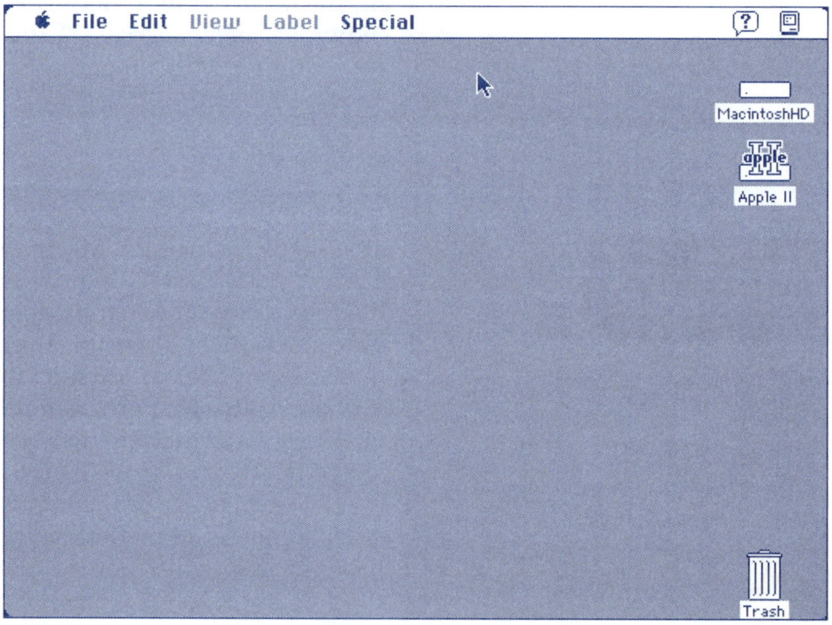

FIGURE A-2
The apple pull-down menu.

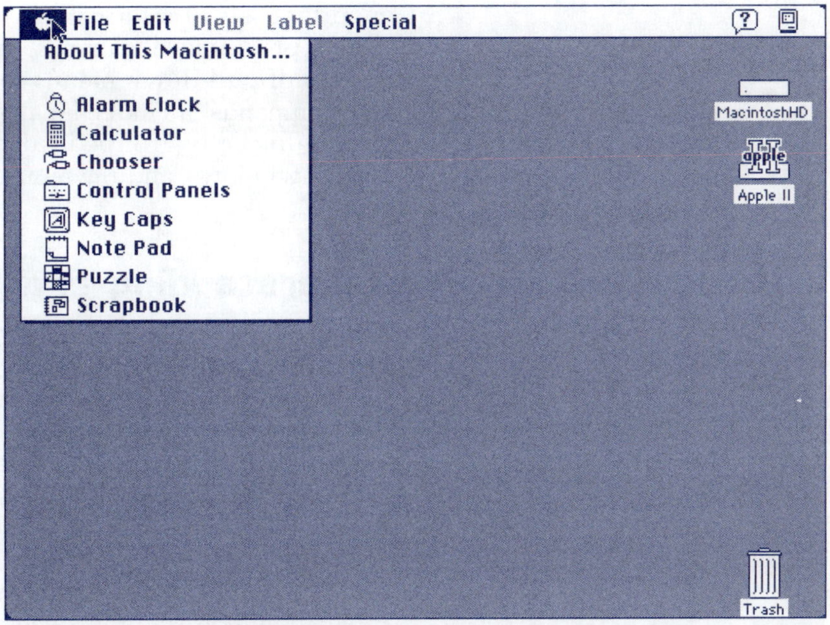

7. Move the pointer to the small open box in the upper left corner. This is the Close Box. Click the mouse button once and release.

   Notice this ends the Chooser.

USING FINDER

The operating system on all Macintosh computers is known as *System*. System controls the entire operation of the computer. There are several versions of System. Two of the most recent are System 6 and System 7. System 7 is an upgrade in operating system capabilities from System 6 and previous versions. There are now upgrades beyond the initial release of System 7. The important point with System is that it is not directly accessible. System uses a special, separate program to control the operating system. This special program is the Finder. For all practical purposes, then, it is the Finder that controls the Macintosh.

Finder is a graphical user interface, or GUI, that controls the flow of information. The GUI supporting Finder is primarily based on the use of a mouse and icons. Icons are small graphics or pictures that represent files, commands, programs, and groups of files. The mouse is the tool for selecting and activating these commands and programs.

When you start a Macintosh, a screen called the Macintosh *desktop*, (or simply desktop) appears. The desktop is the major controlling characteristic of Finder. In fact, the terms desktop and Finder are often used interchangeably. The desktop contains three important sets of information. First, it contains several icons representing programs, documents, disks, and folders. Second, it contains a series of pull-down menus to access several controlling options and commands in Finder. Finally, the desktop contains windows that display logically-grouped icons. Learning about icons, pull-down menus, windows, and the mouse is all that is needed to begin to use Finder.

Understanding and Selecting Icons

The first thing most users notice when starting Finder is the set of icons on the desktop. There are four types of icons—applications icons, document icons, disk icons, and folders.

Application icons show the software programs installed. Selecting an application icon activates, or starts, an application. For example, starting a word processing program from Finder is done by moving the pointer onto the word processor icon, then double-clicking the mouse button.

Document icons represent files typically created through an application. For example, generating a letter with a word processor and saving it causes Finder to create a document icon. Document icons link the document to the application used to create that document, so selecting or double-clicking on a document icon from the desktop causes the application to start. It also loads the document into the application. For example, double-clicking on a document icon created with WordPerfect for the Macintosh automatically starts WordPerfect *and* makes the document available for immediate editing.

FIGURE A-3
The Macintosh desktop.

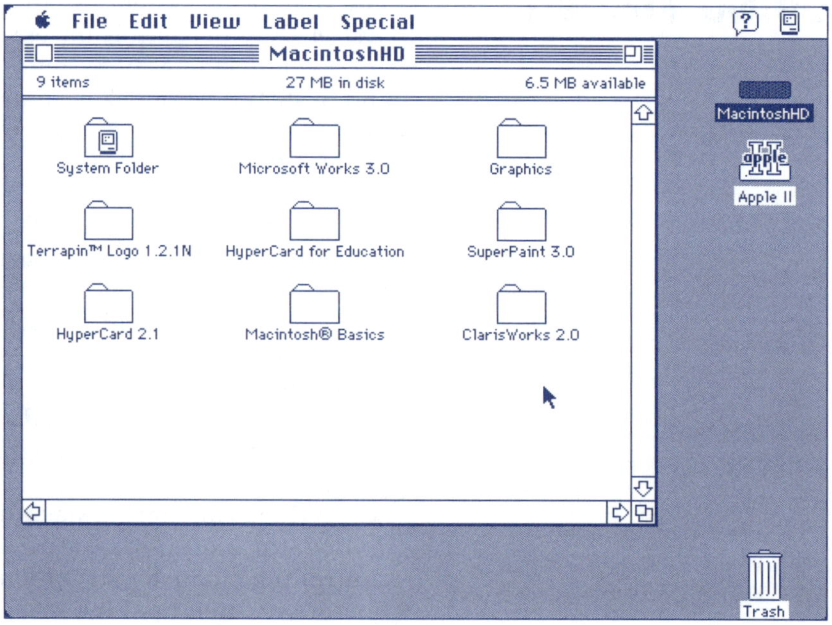

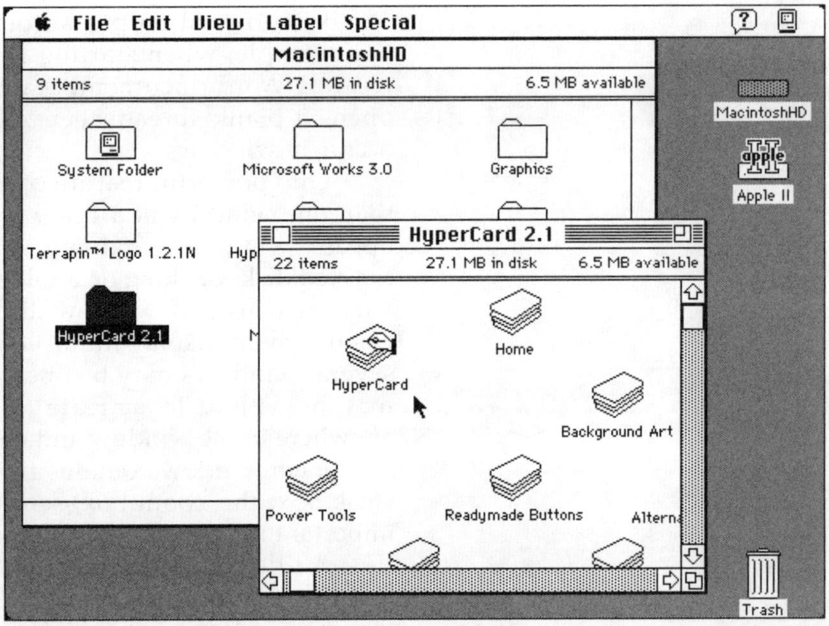

FIGURE A-4
The opened HyperCard folder.

Disk icons represent both hard disks and floppy disks. Inserting a floppy disk into a Macintosh disk drive causes a special disk icon (it looks like a floppy disk) to appear on the desktop. If a hard disk is internal to the computer or externally connected to the computer system, a special hard disk icon also appears on the desktop. Disk icons are important because they represent the locations of programs and documents. Opening or double-clicking on a disk icon displays all of the icons stored on that disk. The contents of the disk appear on the desktop in a special window (more on windows later).

Folder icons look like the file folders found in a file cabinet. They also serve a similar purpose—to store and organize information in a useful manner. A common practice is to group like documents in folders to make them easy to find. Since folders, like disks, contain several other icons, they are usually created to store related icons.

Another very special icon also appears on the desktop. This is the Trash Can icon. For now, just be aware that this special icon exists. This icon's use is in the section on deleting files.

UNDERSTANDING AND CONTROLLING WINDOWS

A window is a working location on the desktop. Double-clicking on a disk icon produces a window with all the icons on that disk. Double-clicking on a folder within a window opens another window with icons stored in that folder.

Windows also open automatically as part of many programs. For example, when starting Microsoft Word, a window opens to create a Word document. Starting Excel, a spreadsheet program, opens a blank spreadsheet. All work with applications software occurs in windows.

One powerful feature of Finder is its ability to display more than one window at a time. For example, clicking on a disk icon opens a window containing all files, programs, and folders on the selected disk. Clicking on a folder in an open window opens another window. This new window displays the contents of the folder. It is customary to display multiple windows at the same time. Though several windows may be open at any one time, only one window may be active. To activate an open window, move the pointer anywhere in the window and click the mouse button.

Each window contains five important parts—the title bar, the close box, the zoom box, scroll bars, and the size box. These are important in controlling the window. See Figure A-5.

A title bar containing the name of the window, the close box, and the size box appears at the top of every window. Lines show that the window is active. It is possible to move an active window to a new location on the desktop by moving the pointer onto the title bar, then dragging the window to a new location.

An active window often displays only a few of the icons in the window. There are three ways to see the remaining icons. The size box increases the size of the window; the zoom box displays a larger portion of the window; and scroll bars scroll through the window. Arrows in the scroll bars move the screen up, down, left, or right. For example, the left arrow moves the screen to the left.

FIGURE A-5
The Macintosh hard drive window.

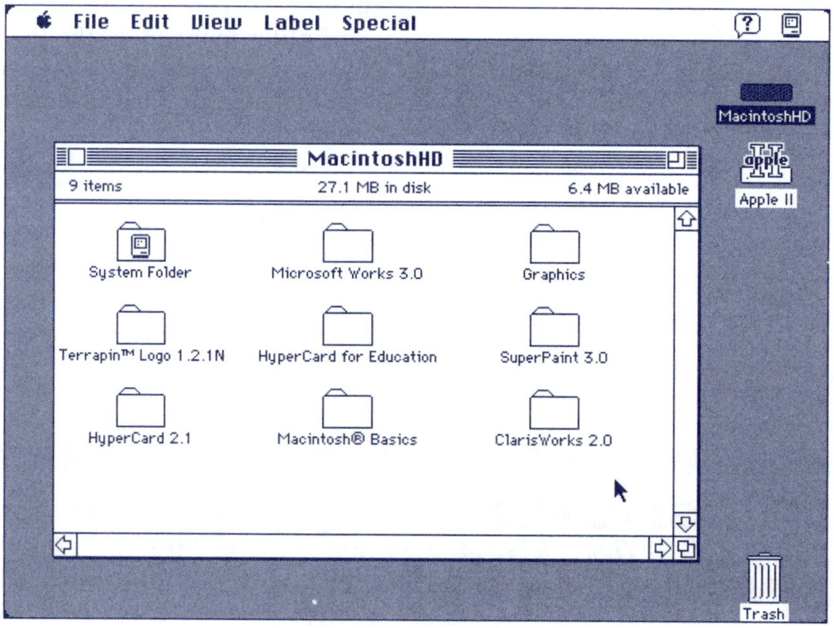

Scroll bars are available only if icons exist in the window but do not appear on the screen, that is, if there are too many icons to display in the window at one time, or if the window is too small to display all the icons. If all icons appear within the window, the scroll bars do not. If there are no icons below the window, but there are some to the left or right, only the horizontal scroll bar appears.

Viewing a large number of icons with the scroll bar can be time-consuming. Sometimes it is easier and more efficient to expand the size of the window. Dragging the size box down and to the right expands the active window. Dragging the size box up and to the left contracts the active window.

The size box is also useful for changing the size of one window to view the contents of another. When a window becomes active, it appears on top of other windows. To see inactive windows, it may be necessary to re-size the active window and drag the re-sized window to a new location.

The zoom box, located at the top right corner of the title bar, is especially useful for viewing windows containing several icons. Clicking on the zoom box causes the active window to fill the desktop. Clicking again reduces the window to its original size.

Clicking on the close box, located at the top left corner of a window, closes that window. If another window is open, it becomes active as soon as the first window closes.

Guided Practice

1. After you start the Macintosh, every desktop must contain at least one disk icon. In almost every case, you must open the disk icon to access folders, program icons, and document icons. Double-click on the disk icon on your desktop. This produces a window displaying the contents of the disk. See Figure A-6.
2. Find a software folder that resides on the disk you just opened. In this example, we'll use the ClarisWorks folder. Double-click on this icon.

   Notice that a second window appears on the desktop.
3. Inside the ClarisWorks window is the ClarisWorks program icon and two additional folders—Sample Files and the Tutorial Folder. Double-click on the Tutorial Folder. A third window appears. See Figure A-7.
4. Click on the close box to close the Tutorial Folder window.
5. In the lower-right corner of the ClarisWorks window is the size box. Click on the size box and hold down the mouse button.
6. Keeping the mouse button depressed, move the corner of the window down and to the right.
7. Release the mouse button.

   The size of the window changes, as shown in Figure A-8.

FIGURE A-6
Software applications folders.

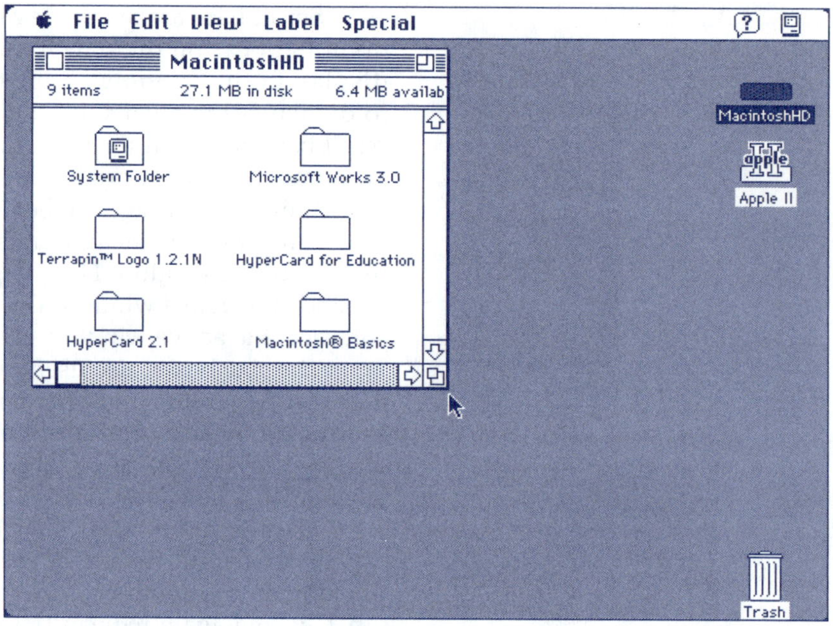

8. Click the mouse button on the title bar. Now drag the entire window to a new location, then release the mouse button.

   Notice that clicking on and dragging the title bar moves the entire window.

9. Click on and release the zoom box. This is located in the upper-right corner of the ClarisWorks window.

   Notice that the window zooms in or zooms out.

FIGURE A-7
The ClarisWorks 2.0 window and Tutorial folder.

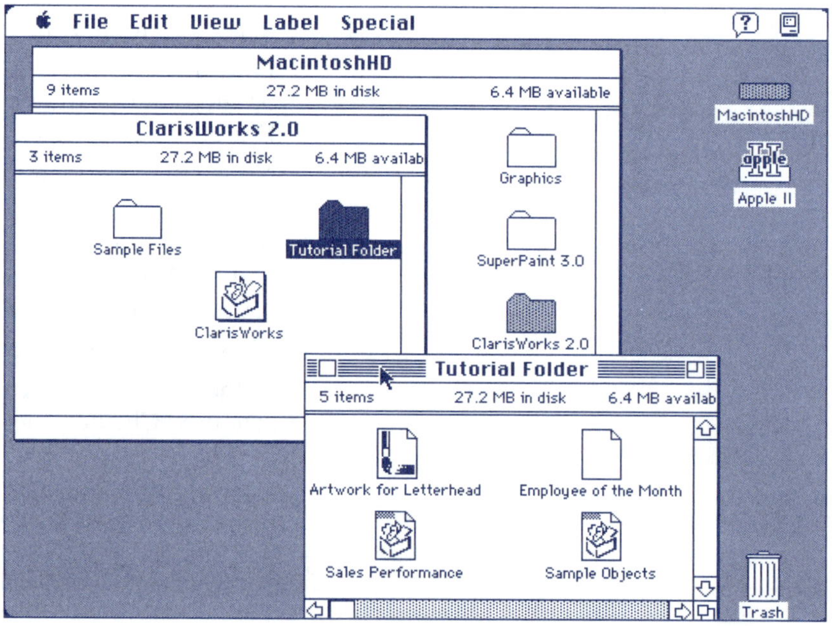

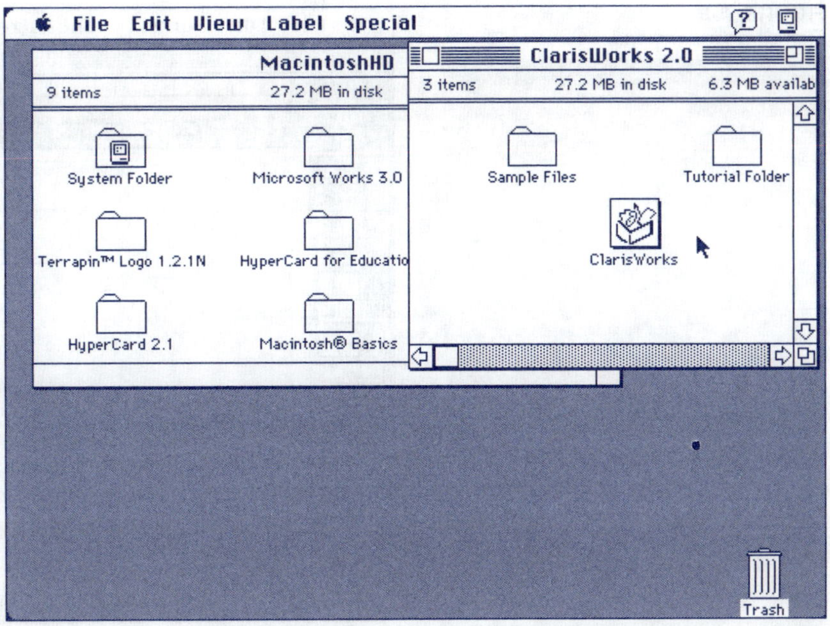

FIGURE A-8
Moving the ClarisWorks window.

10. Change the ClarisWorks window so that only one icon in the window is visible.
11. Practice using the scroll bars and scroll arrows to view different portions of the window.
12. Return the ClarisWorks window to a size at which all icons in the window are visible.
13. Double-click on the ClarisWorks icon.

    Instead of opening another window, double-clicking on a program icon launches the program. Click on OK and notice the opening screen, as shown in Figure A-9.
14. If you want to explore your application, go ahead. Otherwise exit the program and return to Finder. Next, click and hold the mouse button down on the word File. A series of menu options will appear. Keeping the mouse button depressed, drag and select Quit, then release the mouse button. See Figure A-10.
15. Open the Tutorial Folder in the ClarisWorks window.

    There are several document icons.
16. Double-click on the ABOUT Sample Files icon.

    Each time you click on a document icon, the program used to create the document is automatically launched and the document is available for editing. In this case, ClarisWorks is launched with the document ABOUT Sample Files ready for use. See Figure A-11.
17. Use the Quit option in the File menu to quit ClarisWorks.

FIGURE A-9
ClarisWorks launched.

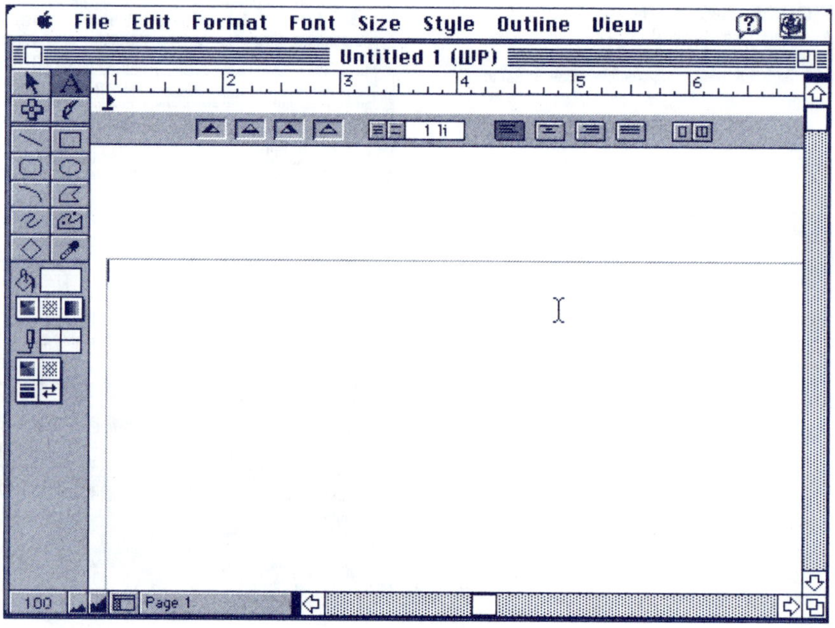

CONTROLLING ICONS

Using Finder to start programs and open documents is easy. Moving, renaming, copying, and deleting files is just as easy.

It is important to move icons to different folders to keep the organization of documents meaningful and efficient. The process for moving an icon is the same as for moving a window. Place the pointer on the desired icon, click and hold the mouse button, and

FIGURE A-10
Quitting ClarisWorks.

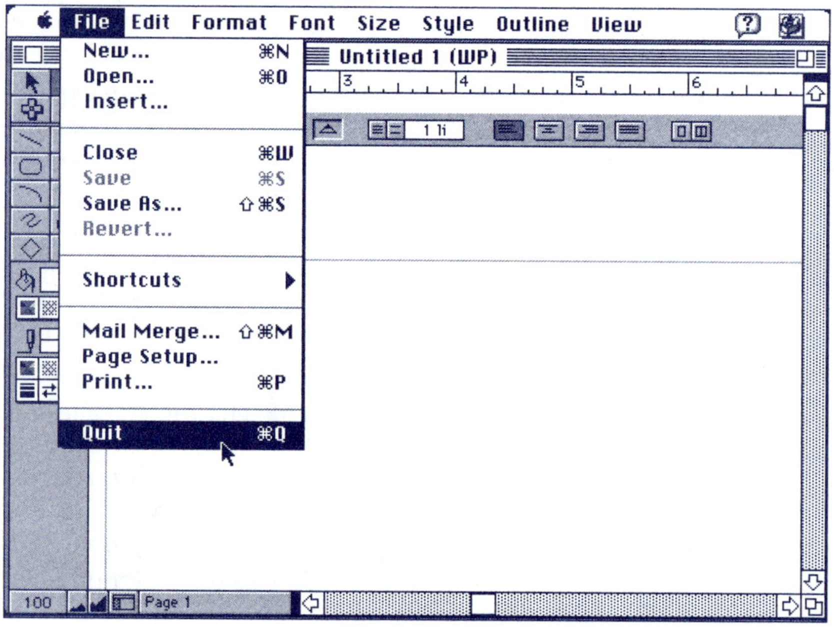

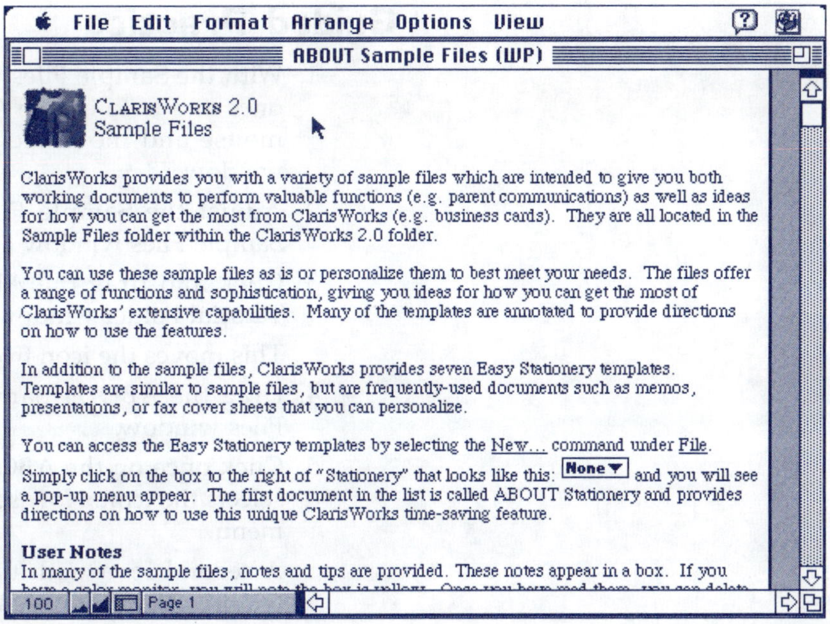

FIGURE A-11
An open Sample File.

drag the icon to a new location. It is important to click the mouse button only once. Clicking twice activates the icon.

The Trash Can is a very special icon because it is used to remove or delete an icon and the file or folder the icon represents from disk. Dragging an icon onto the Trash Can, then releasing the mouse button, places the icon or file into the Trash Can. When an icon moves into the Trash Can, the Trash Can expands. An icon in the Trash Can is not deleted, it is ready for deletion. Permanently deleting the icon occurs when the Trash Can is emptied. This is accomplished with the Empty Trash option in the Special menu.

You may copy icons or files from one disk to another disk by moving the icon within a window. Just drag the icon to a new disk window or icon and release the mouse button. Finder produces a message showing that the file is being copied to a new location. Copying icons or files on the same disk or in the same window requires the use of the Duplicate command in the File menu. First, click once on the desired icon, then move the mouse pointer onto the word File and click and hold the mouse button. This produces a list of options. With the mouse button still depressed, move the pointer onto the word Duplicate, then release the mouse button. An exact copy of the icon will appear in the window.

Beneath each icon is an icon name. To change the icon name, move the pointer directly onto the icon name, then click and release the mouse button. This causes a small flashing line, called the insertion point, to appear. Use the backspace key to delete the existing name. Typing a new name renames the icon. Moving the pointer away from the icon and clicking the mouse button ensures that the new name becomes part of the icon.

Guided Practice

1. With the Sample Files window open on the desktop, click once and hold on the ABOUT Sample Files icon. Drag the mouse and move the icon to a new location within the window.
2. Adjust the Sample Files window size so that both the Sample Files window and ClarisWorks window appear.
3. Click and drag the ABOUT Sample Files icon from the Tutorial Folder window to the ClarisWorks window.

   This moves the icon from one folder to another.
4. Drag the ABOUT Sample Files icon back to the Sample Files window.
5. Click once on the ABOUT Sample Files icon. This simply selects the icon. Now select the Duplicate option in the File menu.

   A second icon with the same name appears within the window. See Figure A-12.
6. Drag the Artwork for Letterhead copy icon out of the Tutorial Folder window directly onto the Trash icon located directly on the desktop. You can tell when you have placed the icon on the trash can—the Trash icon darkens. Now release the mouse button.

   Notice that the trash can enlarges. See Figure A-13.
7. The icon remains in the trash can until you select the Empty Trash option from the Special menu. Go ahead and make this selection.

FIGURE A-12
A copied file.

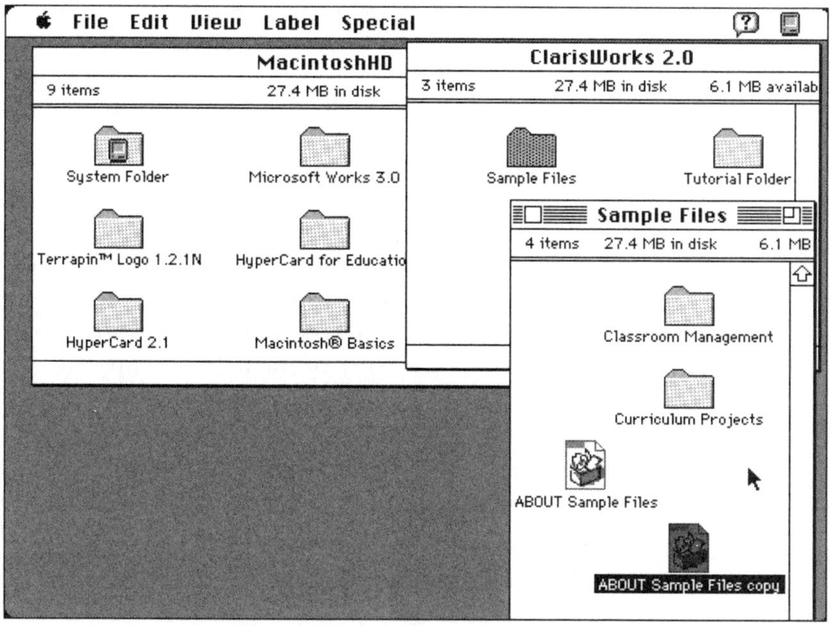

FIGURE A-13
Full Trash can.

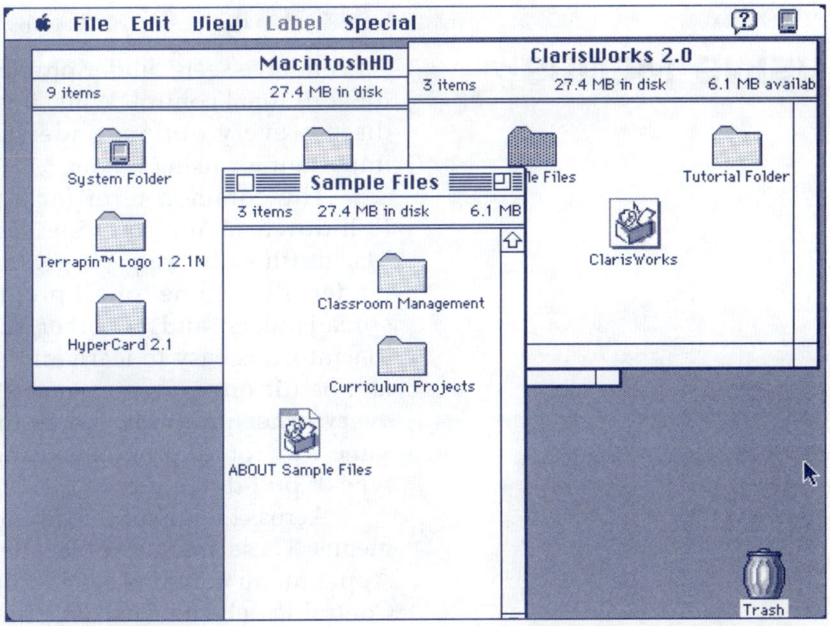

A message noting the number of items in the Trash appears, as shown in Figure A-14. This message is the last safeguard before permanently removing an icon from your computer. Click once on OK. The Trash icon will return to its empty size.

FIGURE A-14
The Trash Can warning message.

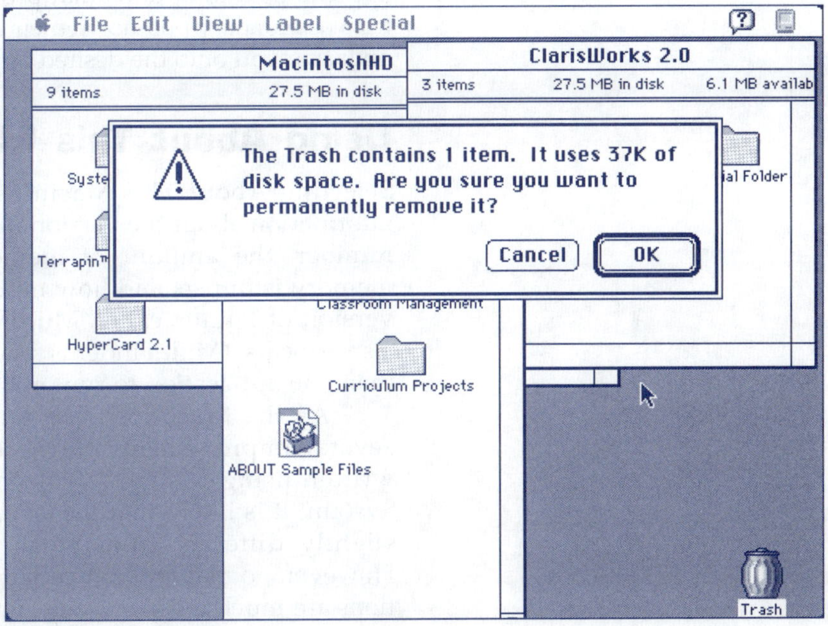

USING MENUS

As you have seen, Finder provides several menus and menu options for additional control. While it is beyond the scope of this chapter to discuss every option, understanding a few options is especially important for using Finder.

The common term for a menu in Finder is *pull-down menu.* Pull-down menus provide several important options for every Macintosh software package. In fact, the pull-down menu option in Finder is the same for all programs—word processors, databases, spreadsheets, and all other software. This is one reason why a Macintosh is easy to learn and use. After learning to use pull-down menus for one program, many of the commands are the same for every other program. For example, selecting Save is done in the same way for all programs using Finder and it is found in the same type of pull-down menu.

Across the top of the desktop is a list of all available pull-down menus. These are the Apple, File, Edit, View, and Special menus. The Apple menu contains several options, including About the Finder, Control Panel, and Chooser. The Special menu contains the following options: Clean Up Window, Empty Trash, Erase Disk, Set Startup, Restart, and Shut Down. Other menus contain additional options.

Selecting a menu option begins by activating the pull-down menu. Place the pointer on the desired menu name, then click and hold the mouse button. A list of all available options appears. Darker items are available for selection. Lighter, or shadowed, options are not currently available and cannot be selected. Select an available option by dragging the pointer onto the desired option, then releasing the mouse button.

Some options produce secondary menus. That is, placing the pointer on these options causes another menu to appear. A small arrow appears next to options that produce additional menus. Select items from a secondary pull-down menu by dragging the pointer down the secondary menu onto the desired option then releasing the mouse button.

Using About This Macintosh

Selecting About This Macintosh from the Apple menu provides information about the version number of Finder, the System version number, the amount of memory in the computer, how much memory is in use, and how much remains available. With a special version of Finder, called MultiFinder, a list of all active programs also appears. (MultiFinder is a version of Finder that allows for more than one application to run on the computer at the same time.)

As the Macintosh computer has evolved, there have been several improvements to the operating system. This book was written using System 7.1. If you are using a different version of System, it is likely that the screen shots appearing in this book are slightly different from what you may see on your computer. However, no matter what version of System you are using, the functions are much the same. See Figure A-15.

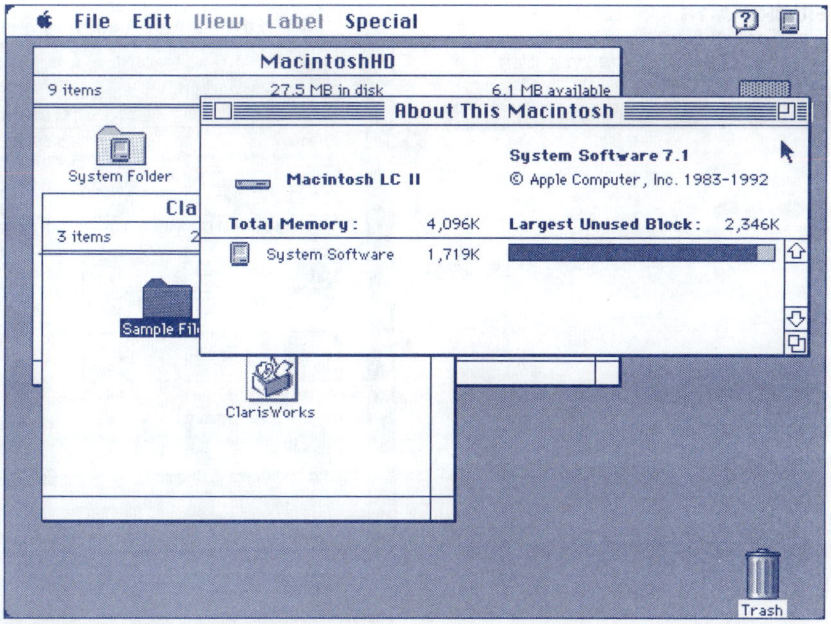

FIGURE A-15
System information under About This Macintosh.

Using the Control Panel

The Control Panel option in the Apple menu contains several controlling features; which appear depends on the type of Macintosh you are using. In general, the Control Panel controls the monitor, the keyboard, the mouse, and other settings.

To activate the Control Panel, select Control Panel from the Apple menu. This produces a list of icons. The first of these is the general icon. This icon controls the date, time, mouse speed, desktop background, and many other features. Changing these settings changes the overall operation of the Macintosh. See Figure A-16.

Guided Practice

Time to explore! The Control Panel determines how you interact with the Macintosh. The best way to learn about this is to explore the different options. Don't be afraid to double-click on any of these options to find out what is inside. However, make changes to Control Panel that are appropriate for the computer you are using. For example, if you are using a Mac with a black and white monitor, don't change the settings to color.

Using Chooser

Also in the Apple menu is the Chooser option. Chooser specifies the type of printer used with the Macintosh. This is important, because selecting a printer through the Chooser sets the printer for all software.

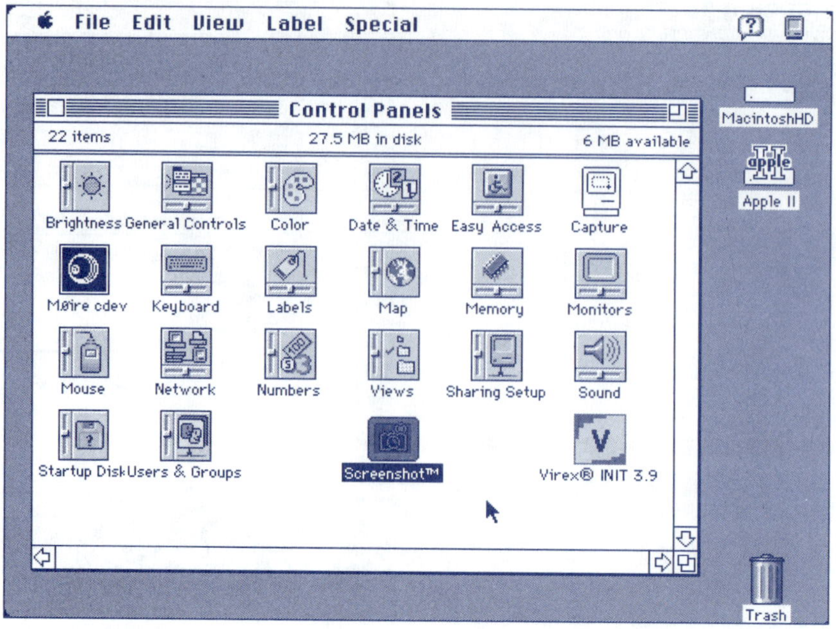

FIGURE A-16
The Control Panel icons, through which one controls the operation of the computer.

To select a printer in Chooser, click on the icon representing the correct printer. If the Macintosh is on a network, an appropriate zone must be specified. If multiple printers of the same type are available, the name of the printer must be selected. After selecting the necessary options for the printer, closing the Chooser window is done the same as closing any other window—click on the close box. See Figure A-17.

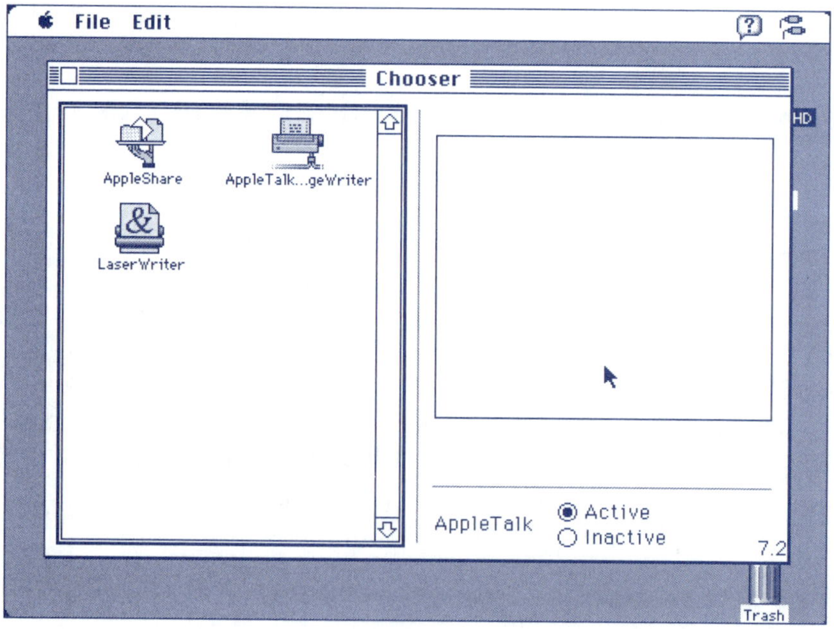

FIGURE A-17
The Chooser, from which one selects a printer.

Guided Practice

Unlike the Control Panels, changing options within the Chooser can have a powerful impact on your computer. For example, if you are using a computer in a lab, changing the Chooser may keep you from printing. Therefore, make changes to the Chooser only with the guidance of your instructor.

USING DIALOG BOXES

Another useful feature of the Finder is that most applications use the same basic design for accessing data and controlling menus. Virtually every program written to run on a Mac has the File menu. Some of the options within the menu may differ from program to program, but many are the same. Most programs on a Macintosh have the Save, Save As, and Open options.

Another standard feature is the use of special screens to help control software. These special screens are known as *dialog boxes*, as it is through them that users converse directly with the software. As with other features, the design and use of dialog boxes is standard from program to program.

A very important dialog box handles saving and retrieving files from disks. For example, after launching a word processing program and creating a new document, it is important to save the document to disk. Selecting Save As from the File menu produces the Save As dialog box.

Dialog boxes that manage the saving and retrieving of files always have three important features. The first is the disk and folder location of the file. The second is a file list. The third is a list of buttons. Above the list of files is the name of the disk or folder that produced the list. If the disk or folder name is not desired and a new name is preferred, clicking and holding produces a list of available disks and folders. If the desired name is still not present, clicking on the Drive button permits a new disk name to appear.

Loading or retrieving a file from the list of files begins by moving the pointer onto the desired file name, then clicking the mouse button. This selects the file. The Open button activates the selected file. Saving a file is much the same; however, rather than selecting a file name from a list, a small box is available to type a new file name. Usually, clicking on the Save button completes the task.

In dialog boxes that control the loading or saving of files, two important buttons are almost always present—Eject and Cancel. The Eject button causes a disk in the floppy drive to eject. This makes room to insert a new floppy disk. Cancel is available in most dialog boxes as a means for leaving the dialog box without executing any of the available selections. This is especially useful when the user selects a menu by accident and a dialog box appears.

For many other dialog boxes, the options available depend on the software being used. A word processor may produce a dialog box to determine text alignment, while a spreadsheet dialog box may contain options for setting numeric calculations. In these, as well as almost any other dialog box, both OK and Cancel buttons are available. Clicking once on OK means accepting all settings as they appear. Settings in dialog boxes are executed only after clicking on OK. Clicking on Cancel closes the dialog box without executing any changes.

Guided Practice

1. Dialog boxes are in programs used by Macintosh. The only way to practice using dialog boxes is to use a program, such as Microsoft Word. Launch any application available to you—word processors are generally the simplest to use—and experiment with it.
2. Another excellent way to learn to use a Macintosh is to use an on-line tutorial, such as Macintosh Basics, provided by Apple Computer, Inc. If you are still a bit unsure about using a Mac, take a few minutes to work through a tutorial. A bit of time invested now will return large dividends later.

SHUTTING DOWN

One final consideration. Although it is possible to turn off the Macintosh by simply shutting off the power switch, it is better to select Shut Down from the Special menu before turning off the power. Selecting this option performs a variety of tasks that ensure that the Macintosh is ready to be turned off. On some Macintosh computers, selecting Shut Down actually turns off the power. Therefore, as a general rule, be sure to use Shut Down before turning off the power.

Guided Practice

1. Select Shut Down from the Special Menu. See Figure A-18.

   A message appears indicating that it is now safe to turn off your Macintosh.
2. Turn off the power to both the computer and monitor. On some Macintosh computers, using Shut Down actually turns off the power for you.

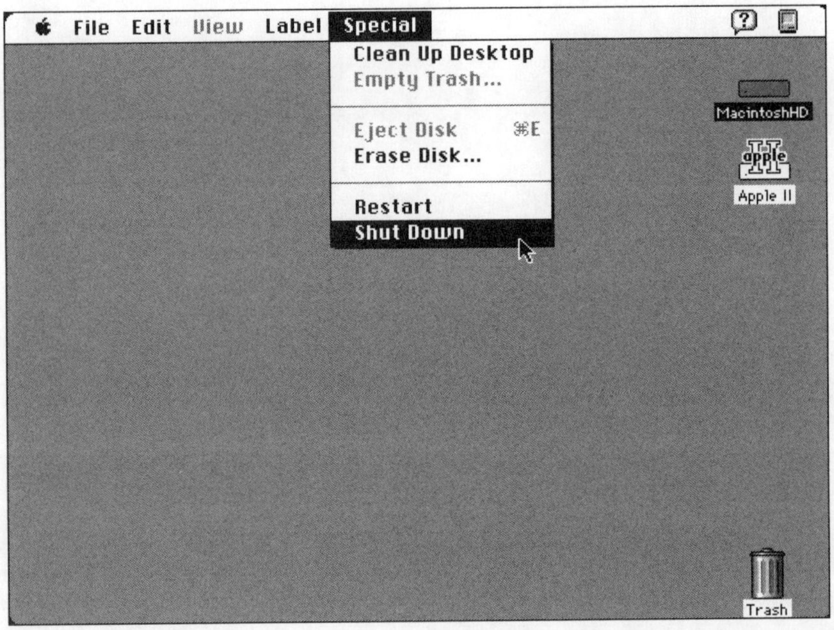

FIGURE A-18
Shutting down the computer.

Appendix B

MS-DOS ESSENTIALS

PURPOSE

This appendix is designed to provide you with the fundamental knowledge and skills for controlling and using an IBM or IBM compatible computer using the MS-DOS operating system. You will not be an expert at the end of this appendix. However, you should have enough information to make it possible for you to become an effective user of any computer using the MS-DOS operating system.

STARTING THE COMPUTER

Because the operating system is so important to computer operations, the operating system must be the first set of instructions loaded into RAM. When a computer is booted, the operating system must load into RAM before any other activity can take place. For most microcomputers, this loading of the operating system into RAM occurs as part of the boot process.

Turning on the power switch causes the CPU to search all disk drives for the operating system. If a disk containing the operating system is in the first floppy drive, the operating system loads into RAM and the computer system is ready to operate. However, if the operating system is not in the first drive, the CPU searches the second floppy drive, then searches the hard disk for the operating system. If an operating system is not available on any of these disk drives, a message saying the computer is not ready to operate appears on the screen. Most users keep the operating system on a hard disk to make the DOS loading process automatic. However, when first turning on the computer, all floppy disk drives must be empty for the operating system to load from the hard disk.

MS-DOS AND PC-DOS

Most microcomputers can use several different operating systems. The IBM and IBM compatible family of computers, for example, can use operating systems such as UNIX, ZENIX, OS/2, PC-DOS, and MS-DOS. However, of these operating systems, PC-DOS and MS-DOS remain the most widely used.

When IBM introduced the PC in 1981, Microsoft Corporation developed and sold IBM an operating system to control its line of personal computers. This system was known as PC-DOS (Personal Computer-DOS). Microsoft also developed its own version of PC-DOS and called it MS-DOS, for Microsoft-DOS. Since the same corporation initially developed both, PC-DOS and MS-DOS are, for all practical purposes, the same. PC-DOS is available for all IBM microcomputers. MS-DOS is available for IBM compatible microcomputers. Because they are so closely related, the term DOS has become synonymous with both the PC-DOS operating system and the MS-DOS operating system.

VERSIONS OF DOS

The original versions of DOS supported the 8088 and 8086 microprocessors and the peripherals common to these microcomputers. However, since DOS' beginning in 1981, it has undergone several revisions to keep up with advances in computer hardware. In 1981, only 5.25-inch disk drives were available, and that was all DOS needed to support. Today, it needs to support 3.5-inch disk drives as well as 5.25-inch drives.

Each new version of DOS has a number. The first release was DOS 1.0. Shortly thereafter, DOS 1.1 was released to fix a few bugs, or problems, in the original version. It also expanded the capability of the operating system. The first revision was minor and the new version number reflects this minor change. The first number of the DOS version indicates a major change. The number after the dot signifies a minor revision.

The most important change with different versions is probably upward compatibility. Programs written for use with one version will operate with more recent versions. For example, software written to use DOS 2.1 also works with versions 3.0, 3.1, 3.2, 3.3, 4.0, 4.1, and so on. On the other hand, applications written for a more recent version may not work with earlier versions—software written for DOS 5.0 may not work with DOS 1.1. Therefore, an important consideration in selecting and using applications software is to determine what version of DOS the software requires.

THE DOS PROMPT AND COMMAND STRUCTURE

To let users know that DOS is in RAM and ready to operate, a special symbol called the DOS prompt appears on the screen after the boot process. This prompt shows that DOS is ready and waiting for a command. Commands are either DOS commands or commands to execute a program. Because DOS uses typed words, or text, rather than a menu or a graphic icon to execute the command, it is known as a command-driven operating system.

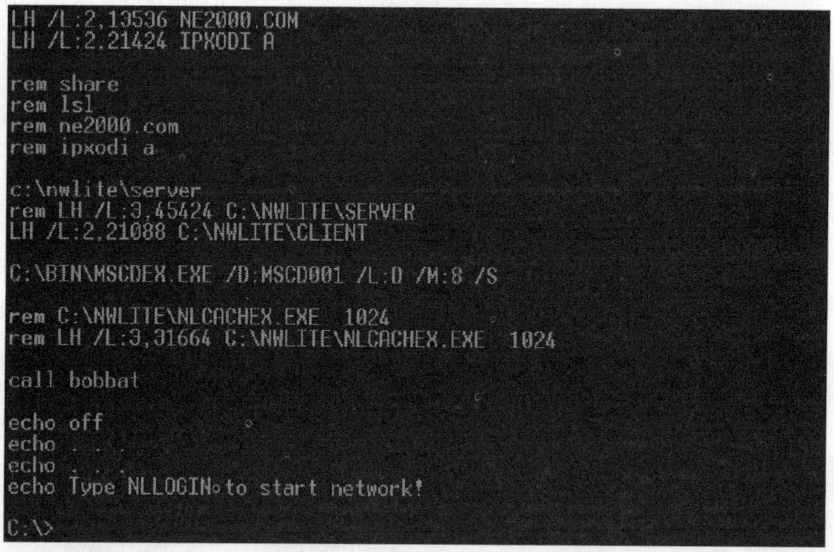

FIGURE B-1
The screen after booting the computer. The DOS prompt on this system is the C:\ > at the bottom of the screen.

The DOS prompt consists of at least two characters—a letter followed by a greater than sign. The letter signifies the active disk drive. All disk drives are identified by a letter. The first floppy drive is the A drive, the next floppy drive is the B drive, and normally the hard disk is the C drive. For systems with multiple hard drives, letters D and beyond are used. By using a letter, DOS indicates which drive is active. For example, a C prompt (C:\>) means that the C drive is active. Any command issued at the C:\> prompt will cause the computer to search the hard disk for the command.

The greater than sign (>) is a delimiter. It simply identifies the starting location for typing DOS commands and separates the drive letter from the command. If only a letter appeared, it would be easy to confuse the drive letter with a letter typed from the keyboard. The delimiter makes it easy to identify the drive letter. In fact, DOS allows for the use of other signs if desired.

It is easy to change the active drive. Type the new drive letter followed by a colon (:), then press Enter. The letter identifies the desired disk drive and the colon (:) tells the computer that the letter identifies a disk drive. If a computer has one hard drive and one floppy drive, for example, changing the prompt from A to C is done by typing C: and pressing Enter. The prompt should change to C>.

Learning to use DOS consists of learning to use and issue specific commands. There are two types of commands available. The first type is known as an internal command; internal commands are those which load automatically into the computer on each boot. They are available without specifying a disk drive. Since internal commands reside in RAM and in auxiliary memory (that is, on a disk), it is possible to issue internal commands from any DOS prompt with any drive active.

The second type of command is the external command. These are DOS programs located on the disk rather than in RAM. These programs must be loaded into memory individually—they do not load during the boot process. When issuing external commands, the first step is to be sure the DOS prompt shows the correct disk drive. Once the correct disk drive is active, the command is issued by typing the command name and pressing Enter. DOS will load the command into RAM and execute it.

UNDERSTANDING FILE NAMES

Because one of the purposes of DOS is to control files on a disk, working with files is one of its major functions. There are several rules for working with files. One important rule is that every file must have a unique file name that fits the requirements for names. All file names consist of two parts—the name and an extension. It is easy to remember if you think of a complete file name as having a first name (file name) and a last name (extension). For example, FORMAT.COM is a file on the DOS disk (an external command). *FORMAT* is the file name, and *.COM* is the extension.

File names may contain from one to eight characters, but no more than eight. Extensions may contain up to three characters, but are always preceded by a period. Only certain characters listed in Table B-1, may be used in file names and extensions.

Table B-1 Acceptable Characters for File names and Extensions

Letters	All
Numbers	All
Special Characters	' ^ { % } $ _ # - @) ! (~ &

FIGURE B-2
If you see this message, insert a disk containing programs or files into the disk drive and press Enter. If this message continues with a disk in the correct drive, it is possible the disk is damaged or the format is inappropraite for the computer. Try a new disk.

In addition, there are restrictions on file names and extensions. DOS reserves some names for internal applications. These names are listed in Table B-2.

Table B-2 Unacceptable File Names and Extensions

AUX	CLOCK$	COM1	COM2
COM3	COM4	CON	LPT1
LPT2	LPT3	NUL	PRN

The extension identifies the type of file. There are two basic types of files used in DOS — data files and program files. A program file is software that can be run by the computer. It is an executable program. Data files, on the other hand, only contain information used by program files. For example, a program file may require information about the type of printer connected to the computer. This information may be in a data file. While the computer cannot execute a data file, it must have the data file to do meaningful tasks.

To make it easy to separate program file names from data files, DOS uses special extensions to identify different types of executable files. Table B-3 outlines some of the common extensions used for program files.

Table B-3 Program File Extensions

.EXE	Execute files
.COM	Command or execute files
.BAT	Batch files
.SYS	Device drivers

The last, device drivers, control input and output devices.

File name extensions .EXE, .COM, and .BAT all indicate executable program files. For program files with these extensions, typing the file name and pressing Enter executes, or causes, the program to go into operation. A few files with the .SYS extension are also executable. However, these are rare. File names with other extensions are not executable. Typing a file name that is not executable causes DOS to display the message *Bad file name.*

While the extension for program files identifies executable programs, the extension for data files plays an equally important role. Usually, the extension in a data file name identifies the type of the data file. For example, the extension .TXT commonly represents a text file; .WP5 indicates a WordPerfect (a word processor) data file. While these are two common extensions, there are very few rules for using extensions with data files. The most important rule is that a program file name extension should not be used for data files. Using a program file name extension with a data file confuses DOS.

As you will see later, the importance of using meaningful extensions cannot be overemphasized. For example, if you are writing a letter, use a consistent extension such as .LET. If you are writing a memo, use a consistent extension such as .MEM. It is important to develop a method of naming files that will help you organize documents or data. That is, use extensions that are meaningful to you, and be consistent. If extensions are meaningful, manipulating files with the same extension can make using DOS quick and efficient.

THE DIR COMMAND

One widely used command is DIR, an internal command that refers to DIRectory. A directory is a list of all the files on the disk drive identified at the DOS prompt. For example, typing DIR at the A: prompt produces a list of all the files on the disk in the A drive. The format for the DIR command is DIR, followed by a specification of the types of files to include in the list. DOS uses the marker *[File Specs]* to indicate the types of files to include in the directory. This part of the command permits including a disk name or the names of specific types of files stored on the disk. For example, typing DIR C: next to the A: prompt produces a list of all files on the C: drive. Since no additional [File Specs] are included with the DIR C: command, all files will be listed in the directory.

Wildcards

File names and extensions play an important part in organizing information on disk. The [File Specs] of the DIR command takes advantage of this organizational structure. They allow us to specify exactly which files should appear in the directory.

One method of using [File Specs] is to specify the exact name of a file. For example, typing DIR A:COMMAND.COM will result in listing only one file, COMMAND.COM. The [File Specs] in this example is A:COMMAND.COM. After typing DIR A:COMMAND.COM, the computer will search the disk in the A drive for a file named COMMAND.COM. If it finds this file, it will display the name on the monitor.

A more powerful and flexible approach to using [File Specs] is incorporating wildcards. Wildcards substitute an asterisk (*) or a question mark (?) in place of specific characters. The asterisk replaces all characters for either the entire file name or the extension. For example, DIR A:*.* lists all files on the disk in A drive. DIR A:*.EXE lists all files on the disk in the A drive with an .EXE extension. DIR A:FIRST.* lists all files on the disk in the A drive named FIRST with any extension.

The question mark replaces specific characters within a file name or extension. For example, DIR A:CHAP????.TXT will list all file names on the A drive that begin with CHAP and use the .TXT extension. Four question marks are for any last four characters in the file name. DIR A: CHAP1.TX? lists all CHAP1 files that have .TX and any last character in the extension.

Wildcards are especially useful for limiting the number of files in a directory list. Using meaningful extensions with file names makes it easier to list efficient directories. Any command that allows [File Specs] can use wildcards.

DIRECTORIES

With recent versions of DOS (2.0 and higher), the term *directory* also refers to a section on a disk. That is, in addition to being a command, the term also refers to a place. Keep in mind that a disk is similar to a file cabinet, and files are similar to paper files in the file cabinet. The command DIR lists files in the filing cabinet. However, filing cabinets also have drawers. The term *directories* can also refer to specific drawers. Just as there are several drawers in a file cabinet, there may be several directories on a disk.

Three commands directly support the creation and use of directories—MD, CD, and RD: make directories with the MD command; change directories with the CD command; and remove or delete a directory with the RD command.

Learning to use directories begins by understanding two important terms—root directory and subdirectory. The root directory is the main, or upper-level, directory. All disks have only one root directory. The root directory is not given a name. A root directory is identified with the disk drive letter followed by a backslash (\). For example, A:\ refers to the root directory of the disk in the A drive. Thus, typing DIR at the A prompt produces a list of all files contained in this root directory. The results of the DIR A:\ command causes the words *Directory of A:* to appear at the top of the file list.

Contained within the root directory is the first level of subdirectories, commonly called *directories*. When displayed on a monitor, directories are listed in the root with a name followed by the characters <DIR>. At first glance, the characters <DIR> may look like an extension. However, it is not an extension but an indicator that the name is a directory name, not a file name. Directories are identified by both a root directory label and a subdirectory name. For example, A:\UTILITIES shows the directory UTILITIES in the root of the A:\drive.

Directories may contain other subdirectories. For example, the directory A:\UTILITIES\PROGRAM shows that the PROGRAM subdirectory is within the UTILITIES directory contained in the A:\ root directory.

The MD Command

The DOS command for creating directories is MD, for Make Directory. The command MKDIR has the same meaning as MD. The first step in making a directory is to specify the disk where the directory will reside. Once the DOS prompt is at the desired disk, typing the command MD, followed by a backslash (\), then followed by the desired name of the new directory, creates the directory. For example, typing MD\TEST from the A prompt creates a subdirectory called A:\TEST. To create directories within directories, type the root, then the first directory, followed by the second directory. For example, typing MD\TEST\ONE creates a subdirectory within the\TEST directory. It is not possible to create A:\TEST\ONE without first creating A:\TEST.

Directories created with MD behave like separate disks within a disk, with a few exceptions. Like separate disks, it is possible to store program and data files in separate directories on a single disk. However, not all disk commands can be used with directories. Most notably, directories are never formatted. The command FORMAT A:\TEST is not acceptable. Entire disks are formatted, not directories (formatting is discussed later).

The CD Command

The DOS command for activating a different directory is CD, for change directory. The command CHDIR has the same meaning. Changing directories makes a directory active in much the same manner as changing disk drives. For example, typing CD\TEST from the root directory C:\> changes the active directory to C:\TEST. Typing DIR with C:\TEST active produces a list of files only from the TEST directory, rather than from the root directory.

The RD Command

The DOS command RD removes, or erases, a directory. RMDIR has the same effect. For example, typing RD\TEST from the A prompt removes or erases the A:\TEST directory. RD\TEST\ONE removes the ONE directory from the TEST directory.

There are two important rules for using RD. First, the directory to be removed cannot be the active directory. If A:\TEST is active, typing RD\TEST will not remove it. Second, a directory must be empty before removing it from the disk. It is not possible to remove a directory that contains files or other subdirectories. Therefore, to remove an A:\TEST directory, all files and subdirectories in the

\TEST directory must be deleted or erased. The DOS prompt should indicate that the root directory is the active directory. Then you may use RD to remove the A:\TEST directory.

THE FORMAT COMMAND

All new floppy disks are blank so that they can be used in several different types of computers and several different types of disk drives; different computers use different strategies for storing programs and data. Different operating systems store information differently. Therefore, before using a disk to store information, it must first be prepared. This preparation is known as formatting.

Formatting a disk has three outcomes. First, formatting erases any data on the disk. This insures that the disk is clean and ready for preparation. (Always be sure that there is no data you wish to keep on a disk to be formatted.) Second, formatting divides the disk into sectors and tracks. These sectors and tracks create cells for storing information. The type of disk drive determines the number of sectors and tracks placed on a disk. In large part, it is the number of sectors and tracks that determine the capacity of the disk. Third, formatting places several important pieces of DOS information directly on the disk. This makes the disk accessible and functional.

Formatting a disk requires the use of the external DOS command FORMAT.COM. As with all external commands, the disk or directory that contains FORMAT.COM must be active. This may mean the DOS system disk, or simply DOS disk, must be in drive A: and the DOS prompt set to A>. However, for computers with a hard disk drive, the FORMAT.COM command is usually in the C:\DOS directory. Access this directory by typing CD\DOS to make the C:\DOS active. In either case, once the correct drive is active, the process of executing the FORMAT command is done by typing FORMAT followed by the drive letter of the disk to be formatted.

THE DISKCOPY COMMAND

Floppy disks are reliable, but only to a certain extent. As experienced computer users will testify, everyone damages disks and loses work. To avoid the sometimes catastrophic results of damaging a disk, DOS provides an important command for making duplicates of disks. This command is DISKCOPY, and it is an external command.

DISKCOPY takes an original, called the source disk, and creates an exact duplicate, called the target disk. At the DOS prompt, type DISKCOPY, followed by the drive letter of the original disk and the drive letter of the duplicate disk. For example, DISKCOPY A: B: copies the disk in drive A to the disk in drive B. DISKCOPY A: A: copies the disk in drive A, instructs the user to insert the duplicate disk, then copies the contents onto the duplicate disk. A word of caution: DISKCOPY formats the target disk before copying files onto the disk. All previous files stored on the target disk will be destroyed as part of this command.

THE COPY COMMAND

Another important feature of any operating system is the ability to copy selected files from one disk location to another. Use the internal COPY command to duplicate one or more files. Since the COPY command only deals with specific files, it does not format disks as DISKCOPY does. Therefore, COPY will only copy files from one formatted disk to another.

The COPY command consists of the word COPY, the original location of the file or files, and the desired destination and names for these files. The structure of the COPY command is COPY [Source File Specs] [Target File Specs]. For example, COPY A:FORMAT.COM B:INITIAL.COM copies the FORMAT.COM file from drive A to drive B and renames it INITIAL.COM. The file is the same; only the name is changed. Similarly, COPY A:FORMAT.COM B:FORMAT.COM copies the FORMAT.COM file from drive A to drive B and gives it the same name. In this instance, however, since both the source and destination copies have the same name, we need not include the file name for the destination copy. COPY A:FORMAT.COM B: produces the same results.

It is also possible to copy files from disks to directories, or from one directory to another directory. When copying files to a directory, the location and name of the directory must be in the [File Specs] part of the COPY command. For example, COPY A:\FORMAT.COM C:\DOS\UTIL\FORMAT.COM copies the FORMAT.COM file from the A drive to the \DOS\UTIL directory on drive C.

Rather than specifying one file name, it is possible to use wildcards in the [File Specs] with the COPY command. For example, COPY A:*.* B: copies all files from drive A to drive B. This is similar in effect to DISKCOPY, with one major exception. COPY does not format disks. Therefore, only formatted destination disks are acceptable when using this command. The copy command is frequently used when making backup copies; Table B-4 is a table of common copy commands.

Table B-4 COPY Command

Command	Use
COPY A:FORMAT.COM B:	Copies FORMAT.COM from A: to B:
COPY A:*.COM B:	Copies all .COM files from A: to B:
COPY A:CHAP1.* B:	Copies all CHAP1 files from A: to B:
COPY A:C*.* B:	Copies all files on A: that begin with C to B:
COPY A:CHAP????.TXT B:	Copies all files that begin with CHAP and have a .TXT extension
COPY A:*.TXT A:*.FJE	Copies all files on A: that end with .TXT to the same disk and changes the extension to .FJE

THE DEL COMMAND

Another important file control command is DEL, for DELete. DEL removes files from a disk or directory. Since DEL is an internal command, it is available from any active disk or directory.

The structure for the DEL command is DEL [File Specs]. To remove one or more files, use DEL followed by the [File Specs] of the file or files to be deleted. For example, the command DEL MOTHER.LET deletes MOTHER.LET from the active disk or directory. DOS does not usually provide safeguards against accidentally deleting files unless you are deleting all files on a disk or directory. Therefore, make sure the [File Specs] are accurate before issuing any DEL command.

DEL can delete files from any disk or directory by giving the location of the disk or directory in the [File Specs]. For example, typing DEL A:*.* with the C drive active deletes all files on the A drive. However, this can be dangerous. It is easy to forget to type the location and erase needed files. Suppose the C drive is active, and the user wishes to delete files on the A drive. If he forgets to type the location, and simply types DEL *.*, all files on the root directory of the C drive will be deleted. As a general rule, then, make sure the disk or directory that contains the file or files to be deleted is active, then use the DEL command.

THE RENAME COMMAND

Another useful internal command is RENAME. RENAME allows users to change the name of an existing file by specifying the original name (or source) and a new name (or target). If no drive or directory is specified, RENAME affects the active disk or directory. For example, the command RENAME A:\FORMAT.COM FMAT.COM, changes the name of the FORMAT.COM file on drive A to FMAT.COM.

Because [File Specs] offers the option of using wildcards, it is possible to rename all or part of several files on a disk. For example, RENAME A:*.TXT *.FJE changes the extension for all files on drive A from the .TXT extension to a .FJE extension. The format of the RENAME command is RENAME [Source File Specs] [Target File Specs].

The major limitation of RENAME is that only one file can have a given name. It is not possible to have two files with the same name on the same disk. This is important to remember, especially when using wildcards to change the names of several files. Be sure the target name is not in use before including it in the RENAME command.

USING DOS

The key to using DOS is to learn to use the commands. This brief overview discusses only a few of the most important commands and should help you get started. However, the only way to learn to use DOS effectively is to practice. Since it requires very accurate and precise commands, it is a good idea to practice creating directories, copying files, and using DISKCOPY with unimportant data and copying the data to a blank disk. Only use new disks when practicing the format command.

Appendix C

APPLE II ESSENTIALS

PURPOSE

Of the three major families of computers, the Apple II is a dying clan. Apple computer no longer makes this family of computers. So why learn about them? The Apple II family has been the computer of choice for schools for the past ten years or so. A lot of schools have, and still use, these computers. If you are to be truly literate about computers in schools, you must be able to operate an Apple II. If you hope to get a job in a school with a significant Apple II investment, you'd better know Apple II. This appendix should start you on the right track for developing a full understanding of this once-popular family of computers.

THE APPLE II WITH GS/OS

The Apple IIgs (the *gs* stands for *graphics* and *sound*), first introduced in 1986, was the first Apple computer to combine sophisticated color graphics with enhanced sound capabilities. Upon its release, it immediately appealed to educators because it doubled the amount of available memory over previous Apple II family computers and more than doubled the speed. Even more important, educators delighted at the enhanced graphic and sound capabilities to motivate students and enhance learning. No longer were teachers limited to the dull and superficial graphics found in educational software. The Apple IIgs made the computer as lively as a video game.

STARTING THE APPLE II

Provided with every Apple IIgs is a tutorial called "Your Tour of the Apple IIgs." The easiest way to begin to learn to use the Apple IIgs is to go through this tutorial.

The first step in starting the Apple IIgs is to insert a disk into the disk drive. Once a disk is in the drive, turn on the computer, then turn on the monitor to put the system into action. As soon as power to the computer is on, the disk drive light goes on as data from the disk is read into the computer. For programs such as "Your Tour of the Apple IIgs" and others, the last step is to wait until the program loads and executes. However, if the Apple IIgs

Program Launcher appears, be sure to read the section on GS/OS (GS/Operating System).

For computers with a hard disk drive, the process for starting the computer is almost the same as starting the computer from a floppy disk. Since hard disks contain the operating system, there is no need to insert a disk to start the computer.

Using GS/OS, the Finder, and the Program Launcher

There are three ways to start the Apple IIgs. If the software is in the disk drive when turning on the power switch, the application starts with the computer. There is no need to interact with the operating system when starting directly with an application.

The second approach is available when the computer screen displays the Program Launcher. The Program Launcher is an intermediary between the operating system and applications software. It makes starting a single program easy by providing a list of programs on a disk. Starting any program from the Program Launcher is as simple as moving the mouse cursor onto the desired program, clicking the mouse button to select the program, then clicking Open to start or launch the application.

The Program Launcher provides information about all files on a disk. At the top of the area displaying the list of files within the launcher (a window) is the name of the disk containing the listed files. You can view a list on another floppy disk by ejecting one floppy disk and inserting a new floppy, then placing the mouse pointer onto the word Disk and clicking the mouse button. The list of files is important. It is possible to display actual application program files, documents, and folders containing lists of other files. Clicking on an icon that looks like a folder produces a secondary list of files. Selecting any application program starts the desired software.

The third option when starting the Apple IIgs is to use a special controlling program called the Apple IIgs Finder. The Finder provides direct operating system control of GS/OS. It controls disks and disk drives, printers, and other peripherals in addition to starting applications software.

The major controlling feature of the Apple IIgs Finder is the desktop. The *desktop* is the interface in Finder that enables users to communicate with the operating system. It places everything needed to control the operating system on a single screen display. The desktop has three major facets—pull-down menus, icons, and windows.

Along the top of the desktop are the pull-down menus that provide access to several controlling options within Finder. These include the Apple, File, Edit, View, Disk, Special, and Color pull-down menus. Open these menus by moving the mouse pointer onto the desired menu name, then clicking and holding the mouse button. This produces a list of all options within the menu. Select any of the options by holding down the mouse button, move the mouse pointer onto the desired item, then release the mouse button.

Icons are graphic pictures or images that represent disks, files, application programs, or groups of files called *folders*. The Apple IIgs uses these icons to provide an easy method for controlling files. The first type of icon is a program icon. Program icons are directly accessible, that is, the user starts or launches a program from an icon by moving the mouse pointer onto the icon and clicking the mouse button two times in rapid succession (double-clicking).

File icons usually suggest the program's use. For example, a file created with a word processor may look like a piece of paper. File icons are also directly accessible, as they can be moved and copied to various locations within the desktop and to and from different disks.

Folder icons look like folders. Folders are storage locations for grouping similar files. For example, a single folder may contain all the program files of a word processor and the document files created using that word processor. Clicking on a folder provides access to the files within the folder. With the desktop, clicking on a folder opens a window. A window is a viewing tool to look inside a folder.

WORKING WITH WINDOWS

Activating, sometimes called double-clicking, either a disk icon or a folder icon causes Finder to open a *window.* Each window has lists of other files or other folders to activate additional windows.

Controlling a window is very easy. At the top of every window is a title bar containing the name of the window, the close box, and the zoom box. It also has lines that show the window is active. It is possible to move an active window to a new location on the desktop. Moving the pointer onto the title bar, clicking and holding down the mouse button, then moving the mouse causes the window to move to a new location.

It is common for an active window to display only a few of the icons in the window. There are three ways to see the remaining icons. These are to use the zoom box to increase the size of the window, to use the grow box to see a larger portion of the window, and to use the scroll bars to scroll the icons through the window. Arrows in the scroll bars move the window up, down, left, or right. Scroll bars are present only if icons are available in the window but do not appear on the screen.

Viewing many icons with the scroll bar can be time-consuming. Sometimes it is easier to expand the size of the window. Clicking on and dragging the grow box toward the bottom right of the window expands the active window. Dragging the grow box to the upper left contracts the active window.

The zoom box, at the top right corner of the title bar, is especially useful for viewing windows containing several icons.

Clicking on the zoom box causes the active window to fill the desktop. Clicking again reduces the window to its original size.

Clicking on the close box located in the top left corner of a window closes the active window. If another window is open, it becomes active as soon as the first window closes.

DELETING, MOVING, AND COPYING FILES

One special icon, the Trash Can, removes files or folders from disks. Dragging an icon onto the Trash Can and releasing the mouse button places the icon or file into the Trash Can. When an icon or file moves into the Trash Can, the Trash Can expands. An item in the Trash Can is not deleted, it is ready for deletion. Permanently deleting it occurs when the Trash Can is emptied. This is accomplished by selecting the Empty Trash option in the Special menu. If the Trash Can is not emptied, the Apple IIgs will do it automatically when turning off the machine.

Moving files from one location (folder) to another on the same disk is as easy as dragging the file to a new window. To copy icons or files from one disk to another, move the file or icon onto the new disk or folder icon. Just drag the icon to a new disk window and release the mouse button. Copying icons or files on the same disk or in the same window requires the use of the Duplicate command in the File menu. First, click once on the desired icon, then move the mouse pointer onto the word File and click and hold the mouse button. This produces a list of options. With the mouse button still depressed, move the pointer onto the word Duplicate, then release the mouse button. An exact copy of the icon will appear in the window.

USING THE CONTROL PANEL

The Apple IIgs provides a Control Panel accessory which allows users to set up the computer to meet their own requirements. With the Control Panel, it is possible to set the speed of the microprocessor, the speed of the mouse, the speed at which the cursor moves, the text, background, and border colors, and volume and tone settings. It also controls the use of available RAM, slot, and port settings.

Instructions that make up the Control Panel are in a very special part of memory that receives constant battery power. A battery inside the computer keeps the information settings from the Control Panel constantly active. However, if the battery should ever fail, all information stored from the Control Panel will disappear.

Holding down the open-apple key and the control key while pressing the excape (esc) key accesses the Control Panel. Open the Control Panel by pressing the up or down arrow to highlight the words *Control Panel,* then pressing Return to complete the selection.

It is also possible to use the Control Panel directly from Finder by selecting Control Panel Desk Accessory under the Apple pull-down menu.

The settings available in the Control Panel include Display, Sound, System Speed, Clock, Options, Slots, Printer Port, Modem Port, and RAM disk. While all of these are important, this book discusses only three of the most important settings.

One Control Panel option commonly used is the display, that is, the screen color, text color, and border color. To change any color, highlight the Display option, then press Return. This produces a list of display option settings. To change any setting, move the highlight bar with the up or down arrow key, then use the left and right arrow keys to change the setting. For example, to change the background color to dark grey, press the down arrow key until the cursor arrives at Background: highlights, then press the right arrow until the words *dark gray* appear. After completing one setting, change any other setting using the same procedure. When all settings are set as desired, press the Return key to save the settings and return to the Control Panel.

Many of the Control Panel options are self-evident. For example, Sound changes the volume and pitch, and Clock sets the current date and time. The Options menu controls the keyboard and mouse. There are a few settings that need a bit of explanation to get the most out of the Apple IIgs system.

One important setting is System Speed. The Apple IIgs offers two microprocessor speed settings—normal and fast. The normal setting causes the microprocessor to work at the same speed as older versions of Apple II computers. This is important when using software that requires the old speed. However, it is a good idea to leave the setting on fast, then change it to normal only when needed.

Another important setting is the RAM disk. The Apple IIgs allows the computer to take a part of available RAM and make it act like a floppy disk. RAM operates much faster than a floppy disk. For example, if a word processor uses a floppy disk drive to check words in a document against the words in an electronic dictionary, the process can take a long time. However, if the dictionary is in a RAM disk, accessing the electronic disk can be five or six times faster. The disadvantage with a RAM disk is that it is not possible to save files in RAM. Using a RAM disk is like any other use of RAM; the contents erase when the computer is turned off.

Setting the size of a RAM disk can be very important. If the size is too large, there many not be enough RAM left to operate a program. Setting the RAM disk size too small may prevent the loading of important files into the RAM disk. If the RAM disk settings are too large, an application will not load into the computer. For example, if the computer has a total of 512K of RAM, and half of that is used as a RAM disk, only 256K remains for application programs. If the application requires 512K, the RAM disk must be set to zero for the application software to work.

Another important setting is the Slot option. Slots are locations inside the computer that physically connect peripherals added to the computer system. As mentioned earlier, the Apple IIgs provides slots for seven different peripherals. Each slot is assigned a number, and each slot has a specific purpose. Remember, the Apple IIgs also provides ports for connecting peripherals. Ports are in the back of the computer; slots are inside the computer. The important issue with slots and ports is to determine if the peripheral device is connected to a slot or to a port. The setting in the Slots options must match the physical connection of the peripheral. For example, if a printer is connected to the port in the back of the computer, the Slot 1 setting in the Slots options must be Printer Port. If the printer is connected to a card plugged into Slot 1, the setting must be Your Card.

After making all selections and all settings for each option in the Control Panel, the Quit option is available. Selecting Quit causes the Control Panel to exit, and returns you to the original start menu. Selecting Quit again returns control to the original window.

Appendix D

MICROSOFT WINDOWS ESSENTIALS

PURPOSE

If you have access to Microsoft Windows (a shell program popular with MS-DOS), but never had a chance to use it, this appendix is for you. It's designed to provide you with the fundamental knowledge needed to control an MS-DOS computer using Microsoft Windows. While this appendix will not make you a Windows expert, it will start you in the right direction. As you progress through this appendix, be sure to practice. In fact, it is best to go through this appendix as you sit and experiment with Windows.

MICROSOFT WINDOWS

Learning to use any computer begins with understanding the set of controlling commands that directs the entire computer system. Within the IBM and IBM compatible family of computers, the dominant operating system is DOS (*D*isk *O*perating *S*ystem). There are two versions of DOS—MS-DOS (*M*icro*S*oft *DOS*) and PC-DOS (*P*ersonal *C*omputer-*DOS*). Both versions are very similar; the only major difference is the distributor. MS-DOS was developed by Microsoft for use with computers that operate much like IBM computers (known as IBM compatibles). PC-DOS is distributed by IBM, primarily for use with IBM-brand computers. Because both function the same, most users simply say "DOS" when referring to both MS- and PC-DOS.

DOS is a command-driven operating system. To use DOS, you must type specific and detailed commands, then press Enter. For example, if you want to copy a file from one location to another, you might type: COPY C:\WORLD\HISTORY\US\CIVIL.WAR E:\TRANSFER\CIVIL.TMP. If you want to execute a word processing program, you might type something like:

C: (Enter)

CD \WP\PROG (Enter)

C:\WP\PROG\WP (Enter)

It seems simple—type a command and press Enter. Unfortunately, if you are not familiar with DOS, these lines may as well be in a foreign language. Learning DOS commands and command structure can be one of the most frustrating experiences for new computer users. While DOS is very powerful, it has a long-standing reputation for being difficult to learn and difficult to use. For this reason, some software manufacturers have developed programs designed to make DOS easier. Instead of replacing DOS, these programs offer enhancements to simplify the learning process and, more importantly, to ease the process of controlling a DOS-based computer. Microsoft Windows (Windows for short) is just such a program.

Microsoft Windows is a graphical user interface (GUI) that automates many of the functions of DOS. Using icons (pictures), menus, and a mouse, Microsoft Windows creates an environment for controlling a computer without having to deal with DOS commands. Instead of learning to use DOS command structure, you need only learn to control the computer by pointing at objects on the screen and clicking a mouse button. In short, Microsoft Windows makes using a DOS-based computer much easier and more efficient.

Microsoft Windows looks very different than the nearly-empty DOS screen. At first, it may seem that learning to use Microsoft Windows' icons, menus, scroll bars, and other tools is more difficult than learning to use DOS. This is not the case. Learning to use Microsoft Windows is not very difficult. It does, however, require you to learn how Microsoft Windows accesses programs, what types of programs are written for Microsoft Windows, and how to use the various controls within Microsoft Windows. The goal of this appendix is to teach these things.

Microsoft Windows is a completely different environment than DOS. Because it is so different, and because it is so popular, many software manufacturers design programs written specifically to operate under the Microsoft Windows environment. Programs written for Windows will not work without Microsoft Windows operating and controlling the computer.

STARTING WINDOWS

In most cases, starting Microsoft Windows is as simple as turning on your computer. Most people install Microsoft Windows to execute every time they turn on the computer. There are some important issues related to installing Microsoft Windows; these are fully discussed in the Windows manual's installation procedures section.

Assuming that Microsoft Windows resides on your computer and is set to launch each time you turn on your computer, the first thing to do is start your computer. If you do not get a screen that looks something like Figure D-1, then Microsoft Windows is probably not installed or is not installed to execute when the computer is turned on. If this is the case, check with your instructor or follow the installation procedures provided with Microsoft Windows.

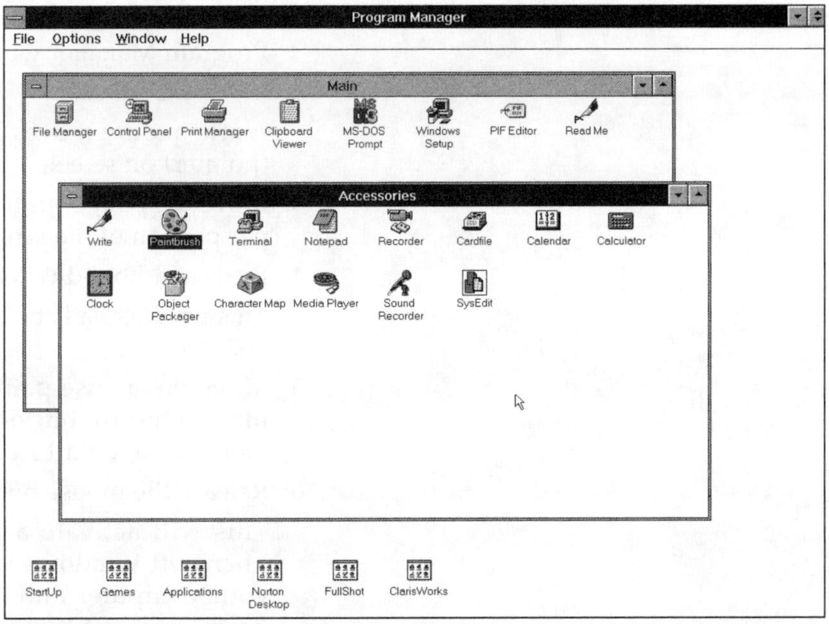

FIGURE D-1
The Windows opening screen.

The Mouse

The one piece of hardware most closely associated with Microsoft Windows is the mouse. While a mouse is not required to operate Windows, almost everyone who uses Windows uses a mouse. The reason is simple—mouse controls are available for virtually all Microsoft Windows activities. Therefore, it is a good idea to learn to use a mouse before you attempt to do many other tasks. Fortunately, learning to use a mouse is very simple.

On virtually every screen within Windows there is an arrow (or some other specialized symbol) known as the *mouse pointer,* or simply the *pointer.* Moving the mouse across a flat surface moves the pointer on the screen. The process for issuing a command or starting a program is to move the pointer onto the desired selection, then press the left mouse button two times in rapid succession. This is known as *double-clicking.* Sometimes you need to click the mouse button only one time. This process is known as *point and click.* That's it. Developing the hand-eye coordination to use the mouse may take a bit of practice, but that is all there is to controlling the computer with a mouse.

Guided Practice

1. Turn on your computer.

   Check with your instructor for any specific requirements for the model of computer you are using. You should notice the opening screen. This screen may differ depending on how your computer and Microsoft Windows are set up. Ask your instructor for help if you do not see the Program Manager window on your screen.

2. Move the mouse.

   As the mouse moves on the table, so does the small arrow (pointer) on screen.

3. Move the pointer until it points to the word Help in the upper portion of the screen.

4. Press and hold down the mouse button.

   This produces a list of Help menu options, shown in Figure D-2.

5. Move the mouse pointer down the screen without releasing the mouse button. This is called dragging. Drag the mouse down until About Program Manager is highlighted.

6. Release the mouse button.

   This will activate a message explaining the version of Microsoft Windows you are using and information about your computer and the product license. This appendix used Microsoft Windows version 3.1; if you have another version, some of the procedures may differ slightly. See Figure D-3.

7. The About Microsoft Windows message is contained within a window (hence the name *Windows*). Move the pointer onto the small box in the upper left corner of this message screen or window. This is called the Control Menu box. Click the mouse button, drag to Close, then release the mouse button.

   Selecting Close closes this window.

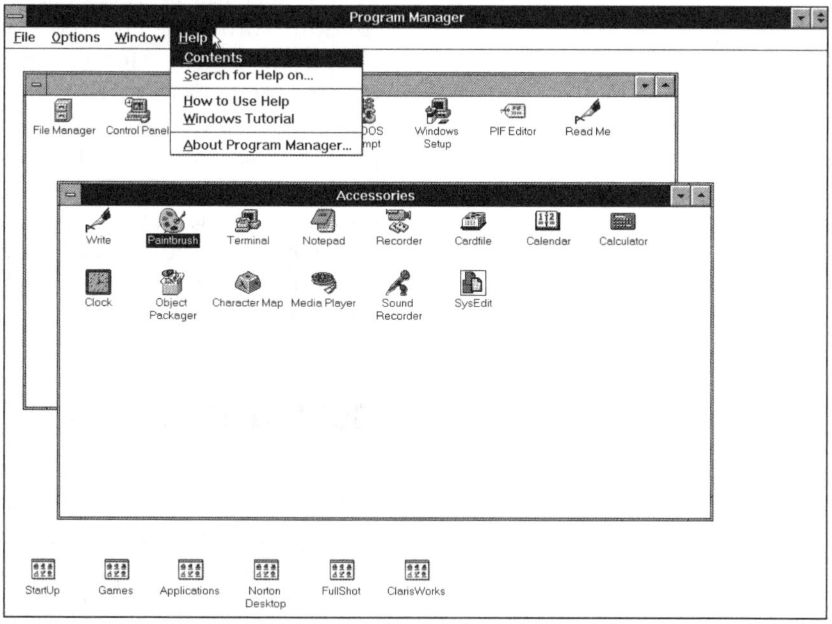

FIGURE D-2
The Help menu.

FIGURE D-3
The About Program Manager window.

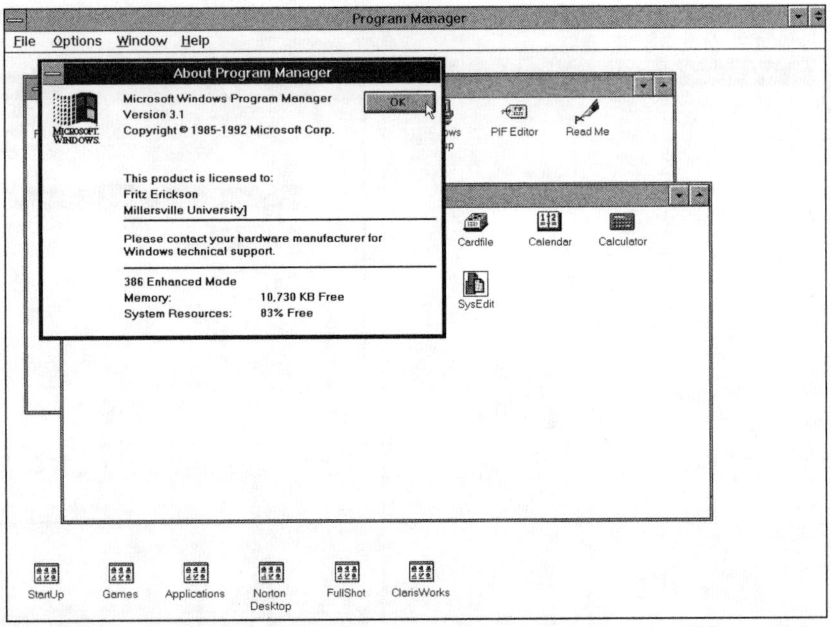

WINDOWS

When you start Microsoft Windows, a very special program goes into effect. This program is called the Program Manager. As with all programs within Microsoft Windows, the Program Manager resides on a screen called the Windows *desktop.* The Microsoft Windows desktop is like your own desktop, but instead of holding pads of paper, pencil holders, and piles of paper, the Windows desktop holds windows.

All Microsoft Windows activities occur within a window. If you want to run a program, that program runs in a window. If you want to create a word processing document, that document is created in a window. If you want to group programs together, that group is a window. So the most important part of learning how to use Microsoft Windows is learning how to control each window.

Window Components

Every window is designed to contain the same basic components. This standardization helps make learning to use and control Microsoft Windows very easy. Once you learn the parts of one window, you will be able to use any window in any program. The following is a list of the major window components; see Figure D-4.

Control Menu box Every window has a Control Menu box that, when selected, allows you access to several window-controlling commands. One of these commands is Close. Selecting this option closes the window.

FIGURE D-4
Window components.

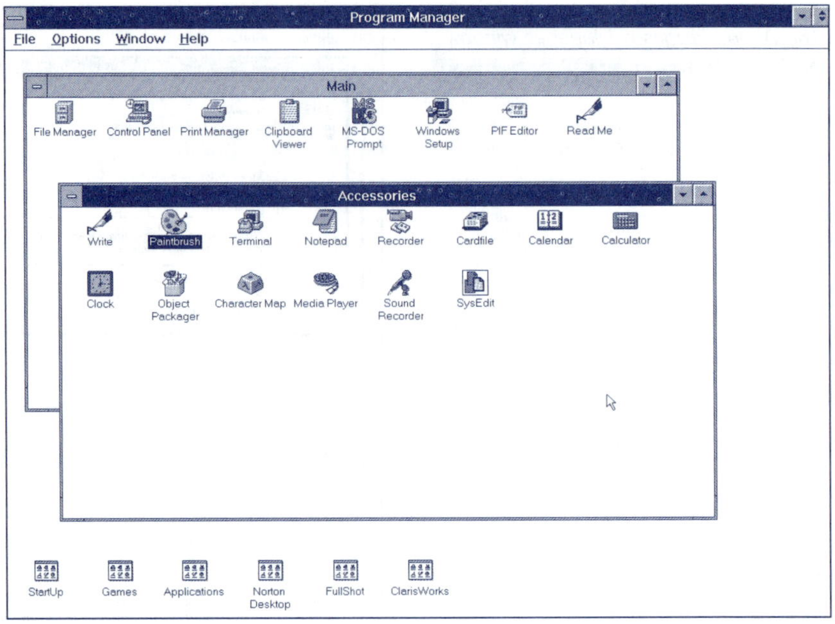

Title Bar and Title The Title Bar appears across the top of every window. Inside the Title Bar is the window Title. Typically, the Title Bar has a different color or shade when that window is active.

Minimize and Maximize buttons Every window can be reduced to an icon by clicking on the Minimize button. (An icon is a graphic representation, or picture, of a program or a group of programs.) The Maximize button enlarges a window to fill the entire desktop.

Menu Bar Below the Title Bar is the Menu Bar. This component contains all menus associated with the window. The contents of the Menu Bar differ slightly according to which program is running in the window. For example, the menus in the Menu Bar are somewhat different for the ClarisWorks window than for the Microsoft Word window.

Scroll Bars Scroll Bars are often available to allow you to access different areas within a window. Often a window displays only a portion of what is available in that window. The Scroll Bars allow you to view all icons contained within a window.

Window border Every window is surrounded by a border. This is important because it not only identifies the boundaries of the window, but it serves as a tool for changing the size and shape of a window. By pointing at any border and clicking the mouse button, the pointer changes to a bi-directional arrow. Dragging this arrow changes the size of the window. Clicking on the corners allows you to change both the height and width of a window.

Window Types

There are three different types of windows available on the desktop—application windows, document windows, and group windows. Application windows contain programs running under Microsoft Windows. Document windows do not appear on the desktop, but as a window within an application window. When you create a word processing document within a word processing application, that document is created as a document window. Finally, there are group windows. Group windows are organizational tools that contain icons (pictures that represent other potential windows). A group window may contain several program icons. When you select one of these icons, a program window appears.

The Program Manager

The Program Manager is the most important window of all. This application is designed to manage all other windows. It is through the Program Manager that you actually control most of the activities within Microsoft Windows. The Program Manager is really an access and organization tool.

The Program manager is an access tool because you must use the Program Manager to access application windows. For the most part, when you install a program within Microsoft Windows, it resides within the Program Manager. The Program Manager is also an organizational tool because it controls group windows. Group windows are also available only within the Program Manager.

Most operations accomplished through Microsoft Windows begin and end with the Program Manager. In fact, windows that are open in the Program Manager stay open only within the Program Manager and cannot be placed directly on the desktop. For all practical purposes, it is the Program Manager that you use to control Microsoft Windows.

UNDERSTANDING AND SELECTING ICONS

When you start Microsoft Windows, the two features that stand out most are windows and icons. Windows and icons are closely related. In fact, an icon is nothing more than a small picture representing a window. Double-clicking on an icon opens a window. When you close a window, it becomes an icon.

There is one notable exception to the relationship of windows and icons—icons that represent programs not specifically written to work with Microsoft Windows do *not* open a window. Instead, these icons automatically launch the program as if you were directly in DOS and outside of Microsoft Windows. The reason is simple. Not all programs written to run on IBM and IBM compatible computers were designed to work directly with Windows. Nevertheless, many Microsoft Windows users still like to use these programs.

Microsoft Windows accommodates these programs by allowing icons to represent non-Windows programs (usually called DOS programs). When you finish using a DOS program, Microsoft Windows returns and the DOS program returns as an icon.

Icon Types

There are two types of icons available in Microsoft Windows. First, there are the program icons. These represent programs that either run directly under Microsoft Windows or that represent DOS programs. Double-clicking on any of these icons launches the program. The second type are group icons. Group icons represent windows whose sole purpose is to organize program icons. Double-clicking on a group icon opens a group window. Inside the group window are program icons. For example, you might have a group icon called Communications. Double-clicking on this icon will produce a window filled with all of the program icons that you use for communications software. If you have more than one word processor, you might choose to have a group called word processing. Groups keep related programs in the same window.

PUTTING WINDOWS AND ICONS TO WORK

One powerful feature of Microsoft Windows is its ability to display more than one window at a time. For example, clicking on a program icon in the Program Manager launches that program as a window (assuming it is a Windows application). You can return to the Program Manager without exiting the program and click on a second icon to open a second application. Both programs can run concurrently either on the desktop or within the Program Manager.

Though several windows may be open at any one time, only one window may be active. To activate an open window, move the pointer anywhere in the window and click the mouse button. Normally, the Title Bar of the active window appears in a different color than all other windows on the desktop.

There can be one problem with having multiple windows open, especially within the Program Manager. Since windows can share the same space, it is possible that one window will sit wholly on top of another. In other words, one window is hidden by another. If this happens, you need to adjust the size of the top window or move the top window, making the other window accessible.

Moving Windows

The window Title Bar is very useful because it not only contains the name of the window but also serves as a tool for moving windows.

By clicking, holding, and dragging the Title Bar, you can move a window to any location you want—even on top of other windows.

Adjusting Windows

With group windows, it is common for only some of the icons contained within the window to appear. With document windows, there may be much more than can appear in the window. That is, what you see through a window is often only a small portion of the entire window. There are three primary ways to see additional information. First, you can expand the size of the window by clicking and dragging any of the window borders. Second, you can click on the Maximize button. This causes the window to expand to fill the desktop. Finally, you can use the Scroll Bars to move the contents within the window. Arrows at either end of the Scroll Bar move the window screen up, down, left, or right.

Scroll Bars are only available if there is more information within the window than appears on screen. For example, with group windows, the Scroll Bars appear only if there are more icons present than can appear in the window. This occurs if there are too many icons to display in the window, or if the window is too small to display all the icons. If all icons appear within the window, the Scroll Bars do not. If there are no icons below the window, but there are some to the left or right, only the horizontal Scroll Bars appear.

Moving Icons

Not only can you move windows to new locations within the Program Manager or desktop, you can also move icons within a window. Clicking, holding, and dragging an icon is all that is needed to move an icon. In the Program Manager, you can also drag icons from one window to another. This allows you to create a new group window, then move related icons from any other window to the new group window.

Guided Practice

1. In most cases, starting Microsoft Windows automatically launches the Program Manager. Click on the Maximize box in the upper left corner.

   The Program Manager window expands to fill the entire desktop. See Figure D-5. If the Program Manager window is already expanded, clicking on this button reduces the size of this window.

2. Assuming you have a Games group icon, double-click on this icon.

   This opens another window containing game icons, as shown in Figure D-6.

FIGURE D-5
The Program Manager Window.

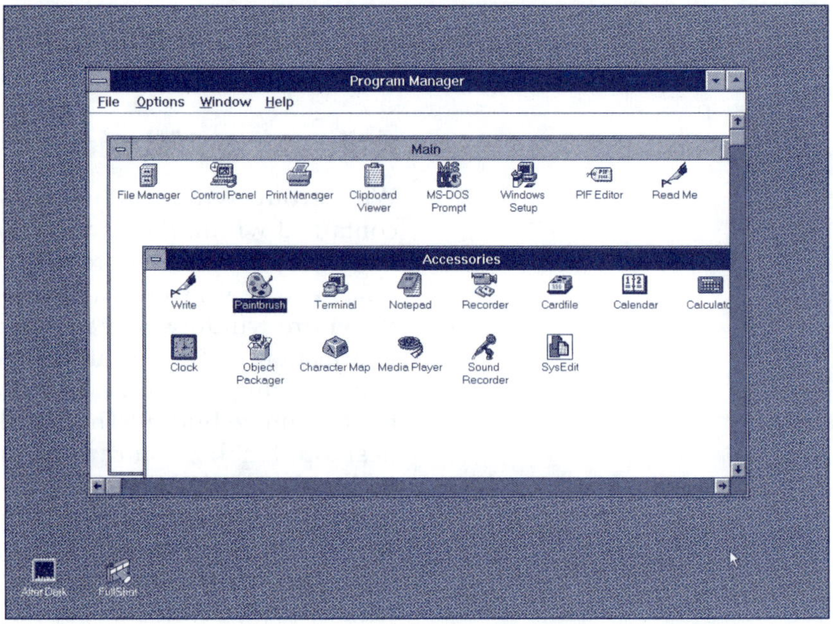

3. Locate the Applications group icon and double-click on it. This opens the Applications window. See Figure D-7.
4. Using the window borders, adjust the size of each open window so no windows overlap, as in Figure D-8.
5. Click and hold on the Solitaire icon in the Games window.
6. Drag this icon into the Accessories window and release the mouse button.

FIGURE D-6
The opened Games window.

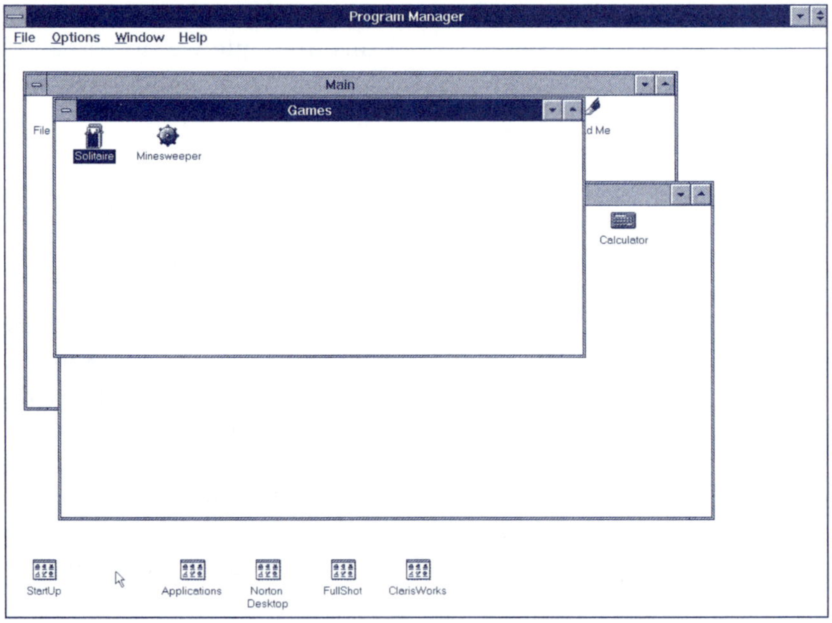

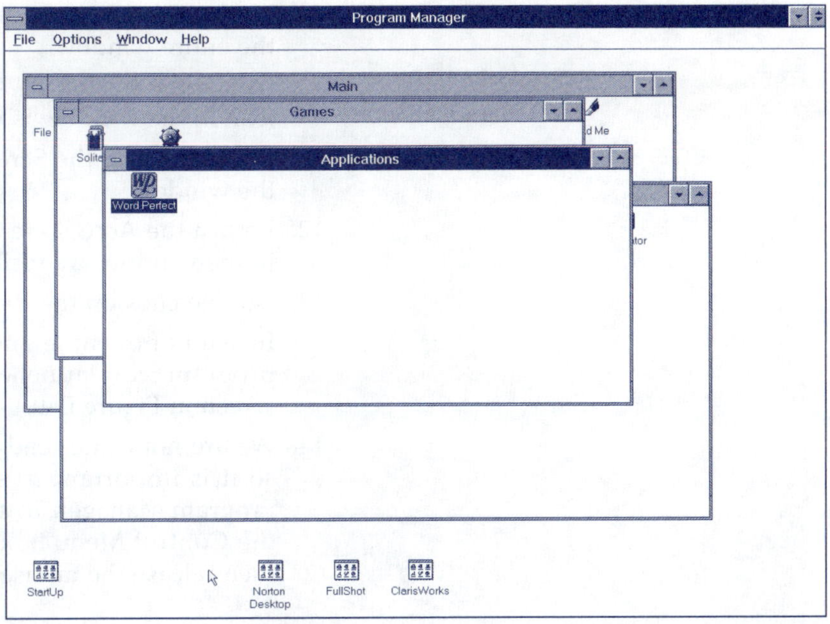

FIGURE D-7
The opened Applications window.

The icon moves from one window to another.

7. Drag the Solitaire icon back to the Games window.
8. Activate the Games window, then click on the Control Menu box and select the Close option.

   This closes this window and the Games icon appears.
9. Click on and hold the Title Bar of the Accessories window, and drag this window to a new location within the Program Manager.

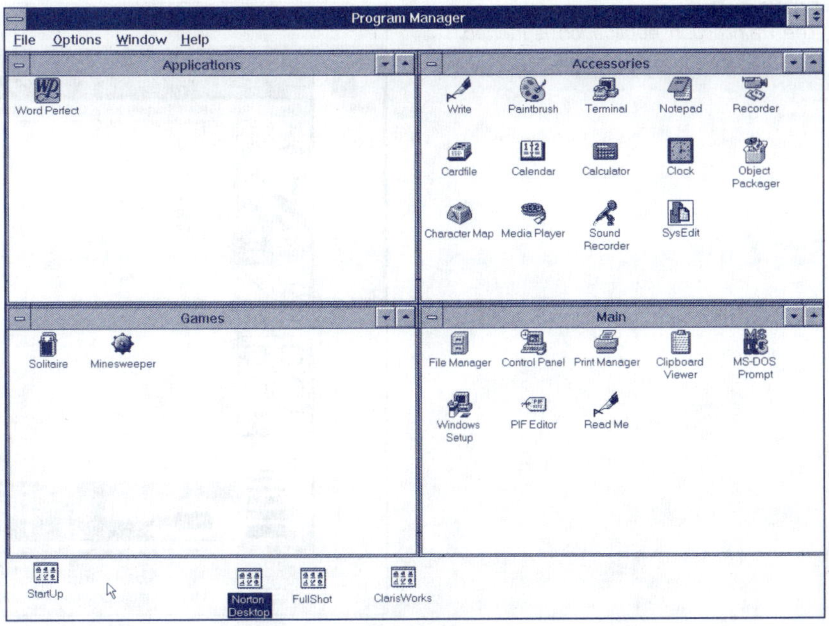

FIGURE D-8
The Applications, Games, Accessories, and Main windows sized to fit without overlapping.

Notice that clicking on and dragging the Title Bar moves the entire window.

10. Adjust the size of the Accessories window so that only one icon in the window is visible.
11. Practice using the Scroll Bars to view different portions of the window.
12. Return the Accessories window to a size at which all icons in the window are visible.
13. Double-click on the Paintbrush icon.

    Instead of opening another window, double-clicking on a program icon launches the program. Notice the opening screen in Figure D-9.
14. We are not quite ready to start working with Paintbrush, so it is important to exit the program and return to the Program Manager. To do this, move the mouse and click on the Control Menu box and select Close (See Figure D-10), then release the mouse button.

USING MENUS

Microsoft Windows provides several menus and menu options for additional control. While it is beyond the scope of this chapter to discuss every option, a few options are especially important.

The common term for a menu in Microsoft Windows is *pull-down menu*. Pull-down menus provide several important options for almost every program. In fact, the pull-down menu option in Microsoft Windows is much the same for all programs—word

FIGURE D-9
The Paintbrush application launched.

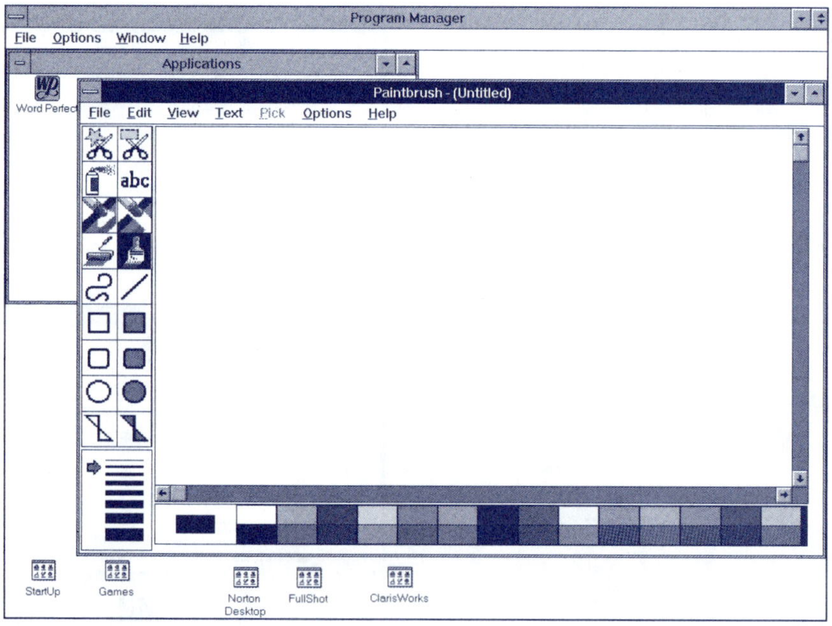

FIGURE D-10
Closing Paintbrush.

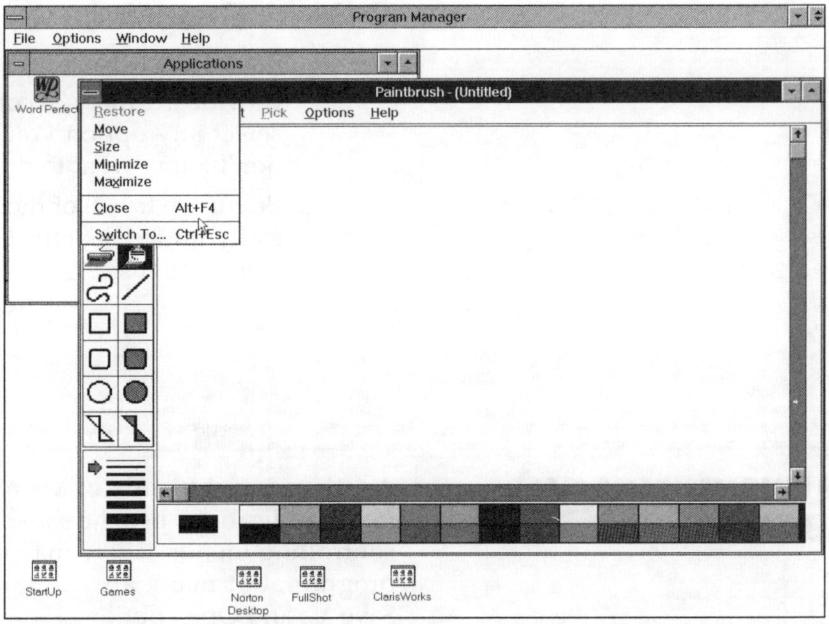

processors, databases, spreadsheets, and all other software that runs under Microsoft Windows. This is one reason why programs controlled by Microsoft Windows are easy to learn and use. After learning to use pull-down menus for one program, many of the commands are the same for every other program. For example, selecting Save is much the same for all Microsoft Windows-based programs.

Below the Program Manager Title Bar is a list of available pull-down menus—the Menu Bar. Listed are the File, Options, Window, and Help menus. In addition, to the left of the Title Bar is the Control Menu box. The Control Menu box contains several options, including Restore, Move, Size, Minimize, Maximize, Close, and Switch To. These options allow you to control much of a window. For example, selecting Minimize from the Control Menu box has the same effect as clicking on the Minimize button.

Selecting a menu option begins by activating the pull-down menu. All you need do is place the pointer on the desired menu name and click the mouse button. A list of all available options appears. Darker items are available for selection. Lighter, or shadowed, options are not currently available and cannot be selected. To select an available option, move the pointer onto the desired option and click the mouse button. You may also click and hold on a menu title and drag to highlight a desired option. With this method, releasing the mouse button executes the highlighted menu selection.

Some options produce secondary menus. That is, placing the pointer on these options causes another menu to appear. Select items from a secondary pull-down menu by dragging the pointer down the secondary menu onto the desired option, then releasing the mouse button.

Guided Practice

1. Time to explore! The menus in the Program Manager provide a variety of controlling features. Don't be afraid to select any option you want. If you get to a window and don't know what to do, try selecting Cancel.
2. Be sure to try all of the options in the Window menu. Especially notice the effects of the Cascade, Tile, and Arrange Icons options.

USING DIALOG BOXES

Another useful feature of Microsoft Windows is the way in which most applications use the same basic design for accessing data and controlling menus. There may be some variation from program to program, but many are the same. Most programs have the Save, Save as, and Open options.

Another standard feature is the use of special screens or windows to help control the software. These special screens or windows are known as *dialog boxes,* because through them, users converse directly with the software. As with other features, the design and use of dialog boxes is standard from program to program.

A very important dialog box handles the saving and retrieving of files from disks. For example, after launching a word processing program and creating a new document, it is important to save the document to disk. Selecting Save As from the File menu produces the Save As dialog box.

Dialog boxes that manage the saving and retrieving of files always have three important features—drive, directory, and file name. First, every time you save a file, you must specify the location of the file. This is done by selecting the desired drive letter. Second, directory allows you to specify a directory from the group of directories found on the disk. Most users do not create multiple directories for their floppy disks. However, there are almost always multiple directories for the hard drive. If you are saving on the hard drive, you must specify the desired directory. Finally, the file name. You specify the exact name of the file. You are limited to eight characters and a three character extension.

Loading or retrieving a file brings up a very similar dialog box. Again, you must specify drive, directory, and file name. Underneath the File Name box is a file list of all available files from the selected drive and directory. If one of these is the desired file, all you need do is click once on the file name, then click on OK.

Dialog boxes almost always have two buttons—OK and Cancel. Cancel is available in most dialog boxes as a means of leaving the dialog box without invoking any of the available selections. If you accidentally select a menu that produces a dialog box, use the Cancel button. Clicking on OK accepts and executes all settings within the dialog box. It is not enough to click on an item or insert information into a dialog box. You must click on OK (or press the Enter key) to complete the process. In many cases, double-clicking on a dialog box selection has the same effect as clicking once on the selection then clicking on OK. This is provided as a shortcut, and the decision is up to you—double-click or click and then OK.

Guided Practice

The only way to practice using dialog boxes is to use a program such as ClarisWorks, Microsoft Word, or another to explore dialog box functions. Launch any application available to you and experiment. Don't forget the close option in the Control Menu box and dialog boxes' Cancel button.

HELP AND THE WINDOWS TUTORIAL

Some of the most useful features of Microsoft Windows appear as options in the Help menu. Help allows you to obtain information about Microsoft Windows on the screen. Help is so popular that many programs have the same basic Help process.

When you select the Help menu, five options appear—Contents, Search for Help on.., How to Use Help, Windows Tutorial, and About Program Manager. Contents and Search for Help on.. allow you to locate specific Help topics. When you select Contents, a table of Help contents appears. You can select any topic from the contents and receive instruction. If you are not sure which area within the contents is appropriate for your problem or concern, you can always use the Search for Help on. With this option, you can type in a topic name, and Microsoft Windows will help you locate information about the topic within the Help feature.

The easiest way to learn to use Help is through the How to Use Help option in the Help menu. This option takes you step-by-step through the Help process.

Another very useful feature of the Help menu is the Windows Tutorial. Selecting this option produces an on-line tutorial to guide you through the basic steps of using Microsoft Windows. If you are having any trouble controlling your computer with Microsoft Windows, use the Windows Tutorial option. This will provide you with direct instruction.

Guided Practice

1. From the Program Manager window, select the Help menu.

   This menu contains the five options shown in Figure D-11.

FIGURE D-11
The Program Manager Help menu.

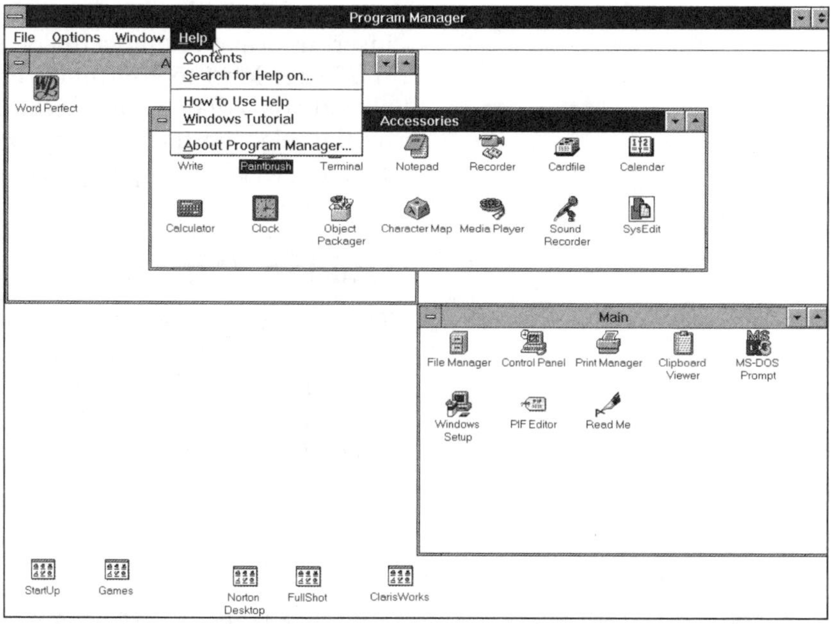

2. Select the Contents option from the Help menu.

   This produces a window containing Contents of Program Manager Help, as shown in Figure D-12.

3. Within the Help window, select Window Menu Commands.

   This produces an explanation of all options within the Window menu, as in Figure D-13.

4. Click on the Search button.

FIGURE D-12
Program Manager Help Contents.

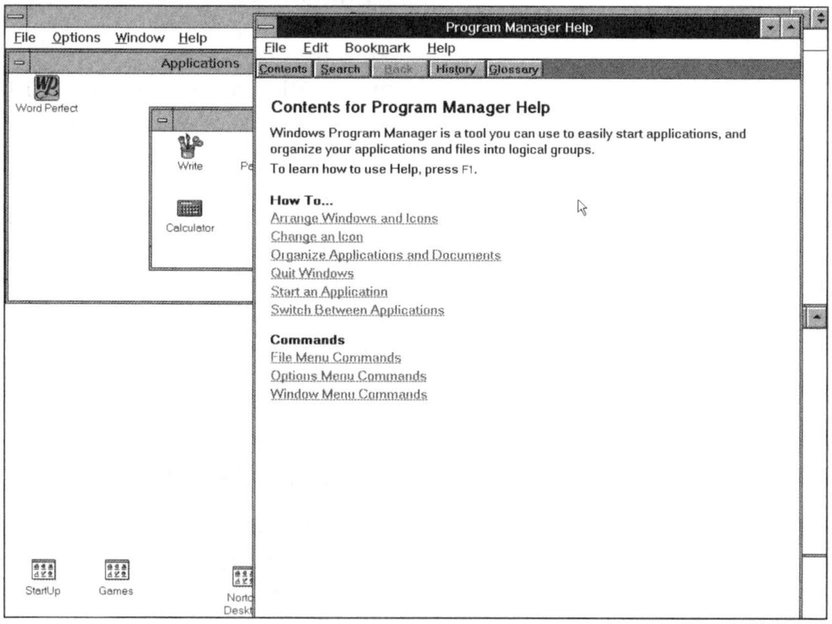

FIGURE D-13
Information on window menu commands.

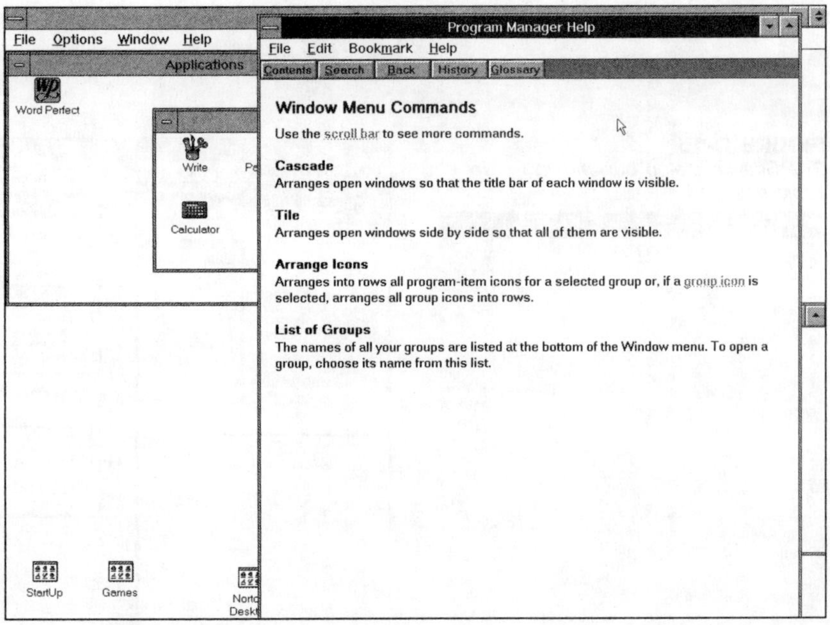

The Search dialog box will require you to type in the subject for which to search. See Figure D-14.

5. Type "icons."

   The list of topics changes.

6. Click on the Go To button.

   An explanation of icons appears in the Help window as in Figure D-15.

FIGURE D-14
The Search Dialog box.

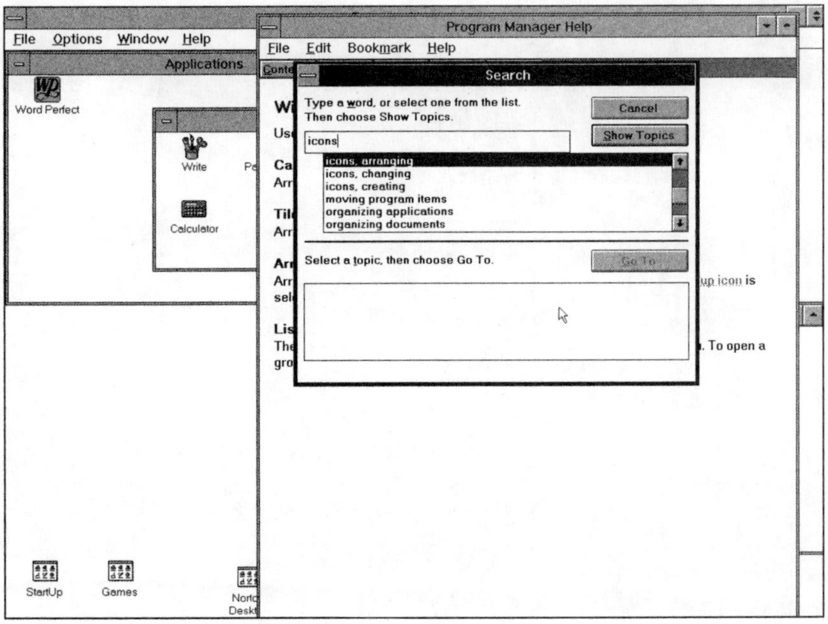

7. Select Exit from the File menu of the Program Manager Help window. This closes the Help feature.

FIGURE D-15
The Search dialog box with a Go To topic selected.

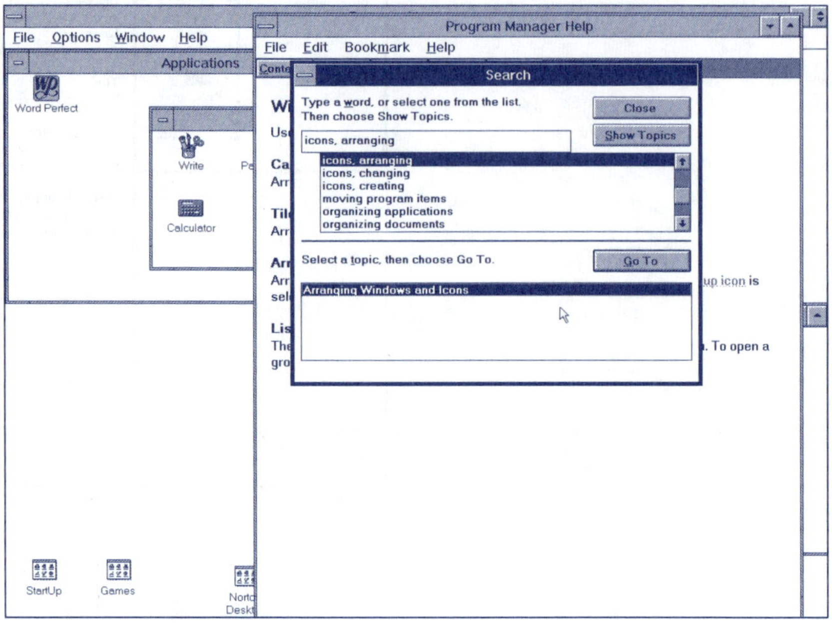

Glossary

+ symbol (spreadsheet) a plus sign delimits the contents to follow to a formula, not a label. Labels and formulas begin with a character. A plus sign indicates that a formula follows.

@ symbol (spreadsheet) an at sign indicates that the contents to follow are part of a function, not labels. A function begins with a character. To avoid having the spreadsheet identify it as a label, an @ sign is used to signify that a function follows.

absolute reference (spreadsheet) when copying a cell containing a formula designated as an absolute reference, the calculation will not change to fit a new address.

abstract condensed presentations of articles or books. Usually, abstracts present a fact-oriented summary.

alphanumeric data all characters that are available from the keyboard, including all letters, numbers, and special keyboard symbols. This data is treated as non-numeric, so even numbers cannot be manipulated mathematically.

analog an analog signal is a continuous information flow similar to sound waves. Computers convert digital information to an analog format to send information via modem. Information is converted from analog back to digital by the receiving computer.

Apple II a family of computers made by Apple Computer, Inc. Apple II computers are often used in schools.

applications generator a program generator that specifies program operations without the user having to write program code.

applications software programs people use to have their computer perform tasks such as word processing, telecommunications, playing games, or calculating numerical data.

architecture the design of electronic pathways available on different types of computers. For the IBM and compatible family of computers, there are the Industry Standard Architecture (ISA), Micro Channel Architecture (MCA), and Extended Industry Standard Architecture (EISA).

artificial intelligence the ability of machines to think, respond, and adapt to situations using processes similar to those of human intelligence.

assembly language a programming language that relies on a series of abbreviations and uses alphabetical characters and numerical information.

asynchronous for modems, a data pattern sending one byte at a time. Asynchronous communications require a start bit and a stop bit.

authoring system a program generator similar to applications generators. Authoring systems create programs from a graphical- or menu-oriented interface. Authoring systems are popular for creating educational or instructional software.

auxiliary memory another term for secondary memory. *See* secondary memory

BASIC *B*eginners *A*ll-purpose *S*ymbolic *I*nstructional *C*ode. A general high-level language used for a variety of applications.

batch processing a processing mode in which all commands execute without interaction of the user.

baud a unit of measure of data transmission speed for asynchronous communication.

bibliographic citation information necessary to locate a particular book or article in a library. It may provide some information about the contents of the book or article.

binary a numbering system for computers consisting of two symbols, zero (0) and one (1).

bit an electronic impulse represented by either a zero (0) or a one (1). Bit is a shortened term for *bi*nary digi*t*.

bit-mapped pictures generated as a set pattern of pixels.

block text in a document selected for change. Blocked text may be moved, deleted, edited, printed, or altered in a number of different ways.

boldface boldfaced text appears darker and thicker than normal text. Text is boldfaced to call attention to the word or text.

bulletin board application software that permits people with similar interests to share information and software, or to solve common problems via telecommunications.

bus network a network with all computers connected by a single line. Information transmits directly from one computer to another.

button used with a graphical user interface, a button is a method of selecting an item, typically by using a mouse.

byte a fixed series of bits. Each byte refers to a character, a space, or one piece of data.

C a structured programming language popular with many commercial application developers.

CAD Computer Aided Design software can generate two- and three-dimensional graphics from data. Complex schematics are frequently designed with CAD applications software.

CAM Computer Aided Manufacturing software can be used to develop complex solutions to manufacturing problems. Graphic displays of manufacturing procedures can be analyzed with this type of graphics software.

camera-ready printed output of such high quality that it is ready for production. A photograph is taken of the printed page to produce printing plates.

card a screen display used in hypertext. A series of cards in hypertext is called a *stack*.

CD-ROM Compact *D*isk-*R*ead *O*nly *M*emory is an optical disk used for data storage. CD-ROM is extremely fast and can store very large amounts of information.

cell a specified location in a spreadsheet at the intersection of a row and a column.

cell cursor identifies the cell in which information will be entered.

center refers to centering text between the margins. Centered text is placed in the middle of margins, not the middle of the page.

chip several miniaturized transistor circuits etched on a piece of silicon. A single chip replaces thousands of transistors and increases the speed and reliability of a computer.

clock speed a system clock controls the rate of information flow to and from the CPU. Generally, the higher the clock speed, the faster information can be processed by the computer.

COBOL Common *B*usiness *O*riented *L*anguage is the dominant language for creating business applications.

code a set of instructions, or commands, understood by the computer.

Color Graphics Array (CGA) a graphics adapter that displays 640 x 200 pixels, with two colors. With four colors, it is 300 x 200 pixels.

column (spreadsheet) a group of vertically contiguous cells. Columns can extend far below the bottom edge of the screen.

command-driven software that uses commands embedded in the document to control output.

compiler converts all commands written in a high-level language at one time. It is a permanent conversion to machine language.

CompuServe a telecommunications information service offering information to both individual and business users.

computer a programmable machine that receives, stores, processes data, and outputs information.

computer crime using computers to commit crime. Computer crimes range from stealing by computer in the banking business to stealing information from businesses, schools, and government agencies.

conventional memory the main memory of the computer system. For MS-DOS and PC-DOS operated computers, there is a 640K limitation.

core memory small, doughnut-shaped ring magnets, or cores, used for internal memory in second-generation computers. Core memory was faster and more reliable than earlier mechanical drums.

CPU the *C*entral *P*rocessing *U*nit (CPU) does the actual processing of data in the computer. The CPU receives input, processes data, and sends output.

credit report a computer database that generates reports containing information about an individual's credit. These profiles are frequently shared among several databases.

cursor typically, a flashing symbol displayed on a monitor, indicating the location of the next action to take place.

data a set of unprocessed or raw information placed into a computer.

database software designed to store, sort, locate, and recall specific types of data. Data may be stored and sorted in a variety of different formats, then retrieved to present the data in a desired format.

data format the format of data in a cell can be changed to reflect the type of data entered. Formats may be set to reflect currency, percentages, number of decimal places, and locations of commas.

data-generated graphics graphics generated from data sets. For example, pie charts, bar graphs, and line charts are generated from data.

data set a file of raw information or data. The file may be a word processing file, spreadsheet file, database file, or any other type of file.

data size the number of characters typically specified in database software.

data types (database) the most common data types include alphanumeric data, numeric data, logical data, and date.

date field (database) a term for a location for entering a date. Some spreadsheets and word processors also allow for special date fields.

debug to find and correct program code errors.

delete a command to remove or erase.

desktop publishing applications software designed to integrate text input on a word processor and graphics made in a graphics program. With desktop publishing, documents have many of the same characteristics as high-quality typeset publications.

deviant text a desktop publishing and word processing term for text that appears at a different alignment from the rest of the text.

device-generated graphics graphics created using special hardware and software. For example, a graphic image created with a scanner.

digital electronic impulses that either are on or off. Digital information is represented with the binary numbering system. All information used by the computer is in the form of bits or digital information.

disk drive a device used to read and write information to a floppy disk or a hard disk.

diskette/disk a magnetic media used to store information processed by a computer. Disks must be formatted to the requirements of the specific family of computers before use as secondary memory or auxiliary storage.

display adapters a computer interface that allows a computer to generate and display graphic images.

distributed processing a linkage of several independent computers into a network. The network allows data and information sharing, but leaves most computer operations independent of other computer operations.

DJNService the *D*ow *J*ones *N*ews *S*ervice offers a financial data bank to its subscribers. DJNS information includes Wall Street Journal highlights, weekly economic surveys, and other business services.

documentation instructions on how to operate a program.

DOS *D*isk *O*perating *S*ystem. A set of commands that controls the input and output of information into the computer. MS-DOS and PC-DOS are common Disk Operating Systems for the IBM and IBM-compatible computers.

DOS Shells DOS shells are enhancements to MS-DOS and PC-DOS designed to make controlling DOS simple and easy.

dots per inch (dpi) dots per inch determine resolution. The higher the dpi, the greater the resolution.

double-sided text printed on both sides of the paper.

downloading downloading is the process of accessing and copying information of shareware from a bulletin board to an individual computer.

draw-type graphics graphic design software that creates object-oriented graphics. Object-oriented graphics integrate several distinct objects. For example, a triangle and a rectangle may be placed together to represent a house.

drop caps an enlarged first letter of a paragraph. The drop cap is placed down and into the rest of the paragraph.

drop shadow darker, offset lines that create the illusion of depth. Drop shadows give a three dimensional appearance to a box or rectangle.

duplex a setting used in sending information over telephone lines. There are two duplex settings—full and half. Half duplex is data sent in one direction at a time. Full duplex sends and receives information at the same time.

editor permits the changing of text. Almost all word processors allow for changing text in an editing mode.

electronic bulletin board special telecommunications software allowing access to a host computer, this is typically used to share information and for electronic mail.

electronic mail (E-mail) a popular method of distributing digitized information among individuals or members of a large organization.

encyclopedia base a large collection of highly detailed and specific information. These are collections of other databases, so they can become very large.

Enhanced Color Graphics (EGA) a graphics adapter that displays 640 x 350 pixels with 16 colors.

expanded memory memory that exists above the 640K limit for conventional memory. Expanded memory is supported by some software.

extended memory memory that exists above the 640K limit for conventional memory. Again, only certain software supports extended memory.

facing pages a design layout in which the design of even-numbered pages mirrors the design of odd-numbered pages.

facsimile (fax) a device that reads information on a page and sends that information over telephone lines to another facsimile machine.

field individual locations for data in each record of the data base. Fields make up the primary control of a data base.

field name in database software, a field name specifies a field. All database fields must be named.

file the collection of related data or information. When storing a document on a disk, a computer stores a text file. Input files place data into the computer, output files store information for later use.

file server the host or controlling computer on a network.

file transfer sending entire data sets and computer programs from one computer to another via telecommunications.

film recorder software that takes the equivalent of a photograph of a screen to produce color slides or prints of computer generated graphics.

finder the controlling program for the operating system on the Macintosh family of computers. Finder controls the input and output of information.

flat-file a flat-file database allows for only one file to be accessed and used at any one time. This is different than relational data bases, which allow for multiple files to interact and cross-reference.

flowchart a symbolic outline of a program. A flowchart is made up of symbols, including ovals, rectangles, diamonds, rhombi and circles.

font the design of text or characters. The terms *font* and *typeface* are often used interchangeably.

footer a few words placed at the bottom of every page to organize groups of similar pages. Usually, footers identify groups of pages, such as chapters of a book or sections of a document.

format (word processing) how text is to appear on paper. Text may be justified, centered, single-spaced, double-spaced, or appear in several other formats.

formula (spreadsheet) special types of values directing the mathematical manipulation of values in other cells. Formulas may be created to perform many different types of mathematical functions.

FORTRAN *FOR*mula *TRAN*slator is a programming language used for applications in mathematics, engineering, and science. FORTRAN works well with mathematical formulas.

free-form database database that allows for paragraph text entry and retrieval.

function (spreadsheet) a standard mathematical formula, which can designate a range of cells and perform a mathematical operation. Functions include the common activities of adding, multiplying, subtracting, and several other routine operations.

games applications software used in play that can challenge one intellectually and enhance manual dexterity.

generation the succeeding versions of computer hardware characterized by major developments in electronic engineering and applications.

graphical interface sometimes called a display adapter or graphics adapter, it generates images.

graphics applications software designed to create visual displays of data. Business graphics, such as pie charts or bar graphs, are included in several types of applications software. Graphics software permits the creation of complex graphic designs. Also, term that refers to pictures used and generated by computers. Graphics include visual displays of data, as well as pictures used in computer games.

graphics adapter computer devices necessary to generate graphics. Graphic adapters determine if a display is to be two-color or full-color.

graphics interface *see* graphics adapter.

graphics software software to take data generated from outside sources and allow users to create an assortment of graphics.

graphics tablet used with a stylus, a graphics tablet passes information into a computer. Some graphics software use special graphics tablets containing symbols frequently used in drafting.

graphing graphic capabilities used to depict data. Standard graphs include bar graphs, line graphs, and pie charts. More sophisticated spreadsheets offer more complex graphing capabilities.

hard copy information or data printed on paper.

hard return pressing the return or enter key enters a hard return. In word processing, hard returns are used to indicate the end of a paragraph.

hardware the physical devices that make up a computer system. Usually, hardware is classed into three groups—input devices, output devices, and the CPU.

header a few words placed at the top of every page to organize groups of similar pages. Usually, headers identify groups of pages, such as chapters of a book or sections of a document.

Helvetica a popular sans serif typeface or font.

Hercules Graphics a graphics adapter that displays 750 x 348 pixels in a monochrome display.

hierarchical database a type of database that organizes data top-down.

high-level language a programming language that takes on a command structure that is easy to learn and use. Commands used in high-level languages are similar to the human language.

host the computer that maintains all files and programs used by computers connected on a network.

HyperCard a type of hypertext used on Macintosh computers.

hypermedia a combination of video, music, sound effects, voice, and animated graphics in hypertext creates hypermedia. Hypermedia is a multisensory information delivery system.

hypertext a program generator that creates a set of logically organized screen displays. Each screen display may be thought of as a card. A series of screen displays, or cards, is a *stack.*

hyphenation many word processors automatically hyphenate words; however, they do not always do so correctly.

IBM *I*nternational *B*usiness *M*achines. IBM is the manufacturer of a very popular family of microcomputers and also of mainframe computers. Computers that function in many of the same ways as an IBM are referred to as IBM clones or IBM compatibles.

IBM compatible computers that use the MS-DOS operating system.

imported graphics graphics created on applications software, such as a graphics design program, used by desktop publishing software.

imported text information created on one applications software that is used by another application.

indent an entire paragraph moved in from the left or right margins.

index (database) for a database, a temporary sorting or organizing of data. Indexing is temporary, so a database may create multiple sorting patterns. For a word processor, identifying important words so they may be automatically placed in an index and keyed to the proper page number.

information data processed by the computer is presented in the form of information.

information management database software used to manage information. Information may be stored, manipulated, sorted, recalled, and presented in a variety of formats.

ink-jet printer a type of printer frequently used to print documents in several colors. Color ink cartridges spray paper with several different ink colors.

input data entered into the computer for processing. Also, devices used to enter data into a computer.

input devices the parts of a computer system used to pass data into the computer. Input devices typically enter or read information into the computer in a format the computer understands.

insert text entered into the document at the location of the cursor. Inserting text does not affect text placed before the cursor.

integrated circuits found in computers from 1964 until about 1970, entire electric circuits were imprinted on a small card or chip.

interactive video interactive video uses a 12-inch disk to store digitized video displays. Interactive video provides for storage and retrieval of sound, text, and graphic images.

interpreter a program that interprets and translates high-level commands into machine language one command at a time.

justify usually refers to making a margin end in a straight line. Documents may be justified on the right, left, or both margins. Some word processors refer to centered text as *center-justified.*

kerning control of the amount of space that appears between certain letters. Space between letters may be increased or decreased.

keyword used to search a database for specific text.

kilobyte a unit of measure representing 1,024 bytes.

label (spreadsheet) any character entered from the keyboard to describe the numeric content of other cells. Labels describe numbers.

landscape landscape orientation turns the paper so that the long edges of the paper are at the top and bottom and the short edges are on the sides.

languages variants of English used to communicate with computers. Computers translate the language into a binary code understood by computers. There are several types of programming languages.

laser printer a high-quality, high resolution printer. Laser printers operate on many of the same principles as a copy machine.

leading a desktop publishing and word processing term that indicates the space between lines of type.

letter space determines the standard amount of space between letters in a single word.

line art a graphic that does not use halftones and can be accurately reproduced on most types of printers.

Linkway a type of hypertext used on IBM and IBM compatible computers.

Local Area Network (LAN) computers in close physical proximity connected by a network. Usually, computers in a LAN are in the same building or are within a short distance of each other.

logical data a database term that indicates one of two states—true or false.

LOGO a programming language developed by Seymour Papert to teach both the concepts of programming and problem solving.

machine language the native language of a computer, made up of a series of bits for each character.

Macintosh a major family of microcomputers developed and produced by Apple Computer, Inc.

macro stored keystrokes in a special memory. The entire set of keystrokes needn't be re-entered; simply recall the macro to enter the repeated keystrokes.

magnetic tape an input medium found in second-generation computers developed by Eckert and Mauchly. Magnetic tape made data entry 50 times faster than punched cards.

mainframe very large, fast computers that can be used by several people at the same time. Mainframe computers are often used by governmental agencies, very large companies, and universities.

margins the amount of space from each edge of the paper to the information display. This includes top, bottom, right, and left margins.

megabyte a unit of measure representing 1,024,000 (1000 X 1024) bytes of information.

megahertz the unit of measure for clock speed. A hertz is a unit of frequency equalling one cycle per second. One megahertz equals one million cycles per second.

memory *see* Random Access Memory *and* Read-Only Memory

memory cell the intersection of sectors and tracks on a disk. Depending on the disk and the disk drive, different amounts of information may be stored in a memory cell.

microcomputer a small computer system typically used by one person at a time.

microprocessor a chip consisting of the condensed circuitry of many circuit boards. The equivalent of several circuit boards are etched onto a single piece of silicon.

minicomputer computers that are larger, faster, and have more storage devices than microcomputers. Minicomputers typically accommodate multiple users.

modem (*MO*dulator-*DEM*odulator) a communication peripheral permitting computers to exchange information over telephone lines. Data transmission rates for modems are measured in baud rates.

monitor A screen that displays information sent from the CPU. Monitors are also referred to as Visual Display Units (VDU) and Cathode Ray Tubes (CRT).

MS-DOS *M*icro*S*oft *D*isk *O*perating *S*ystem. One of the common operating systems for the IBM and IBM compatible family of computers.

multimedia an integration of video, animation, and sound into presentation graphics. Multimedia software frequently employs video disks.

multitasking a term indicating that more than one piece of software is in operation at the same time.

natural language a high-level programming language which closely resembles human language and thought processes. Most natural languages are in the developmental stages.

network two or more computers physically connected. All connected computers share information and use the same software.

network database a database type that enables multiple terminal access to the same data on a network.

networking several computers (workstations) connected to a single computer (host or file server), which enables all workstations to have access to the same programs and data.

numeric data data which can be manipulated mathematically—numbers.

object-oriented graphics images created using a series of mathematical formulas.

official airline guide part of a telecommunications information service through which people can examine airline schedules, request information for specific flights, reserve seats, and select airline carriers.

operating systems commands that control the flow of information to and from memory, peripherals, and auxiliary storage devices.

optical storage a rapidly developing data storage device using laser light to read and write information.

orientation the direction that information appears. Portrait orientation has the narrow sides of the page at the top and the bottom. Landscape orientation has the narrow sides of the page at the right and left of the page.

orphan a single line of a paragraph that appears alone at the end of a page.

output data processed by the computer is presented in the form of information as output. Also, output devices. Output devices receive and display information coming from a computer.

packed switching packing computer information into leased computer lines.

page design a set of commands to control the layout of a page. These controls include such features as page size, orientation, and margins.

page layout the page design. It includes margins, headers, footers, orientation, and several other page design characteristics.

page makeup a type of simple desktop publishing software.

page numbering automatically placing page numbers in several locations on a page.

page size the size of the paper. Page sizes include letter size, legal size, tabloid, and several other sizes of paper.

paint-type graphics software that generates a graphic as a set of pixels. Each dot is an integral component of the entire graphic image.

parity a method of verifying data transmission with telecommunication software.

Pascal a programming language for a variety of applications. Pascal provides easy techniques for developing structured programming and works well with graphics.

PC-DOS IBM's disk operating system that is functionally equivalent to MS-DOS.

peripheral devices a variety of items added onto the CPU. Peripheral devices include a monitor, keyboard, printer, and several other types of devices added onto a computer.

pixel the dots on the screen. The more pixels, the greater the resolution of a computer monitor.

plotter a printing device designed to produce line drawings. Plotters are most frequently used with systems that produce architectural drawings or other types of line art. Plotters use ink pens to create lines, moving both the pen and the paper. By using pens with different color inks, color graphics may be printed.

point size the size of text. Points are units of measure, 72 per inch. Point size varies from very small, 2 point, to very large, 128 points or larger.

portrait portrait orientation turns the paper so the short edges of the paper are at the top and bottom, and the long edges of the paper are on the sides.

presentation graphics a combination of text and graphics in individual displays used to produce a presentation sequence. Presentation graphics permit several visual effects.

primary memory primary memory consists of two basic types of memory—RAM and ROM. RAM is *R*andom *A*ccess *M*emory. ROM is *R*ead *O*nly *M*emory.

print default the pre-programmed settings the software prints from. Default print settings usually determine top, bottom, left, and right margins, type size and style, locations of page breaks, standard headers, and page numbering procedures. Default settings may be changed if desired.

printer output devices to create hard copies of information sent from the computer. There are several distinct types of printers, ranging from relatively inexpensive dot matrix printers to very costly laser printers.

print format output design controls such as margins, headers, footers, page numbers, page length, fonts, and other design features.

printout once text has been printed on paper, it is frequently referred to as a printout or hard copy.

procedure a method of breaking a program into several parts.

Prodigy a telecommunications partnership between IBM and Sears. Prodigy is a family-oriented service designed for young children as well as adults.

program the set of instructions used by the computer. The program tells the computer what type of data it will receive, how to act on the data, and what to do with the information.

program generator a type of software that builds much of the detail of programming into a few simple steps. Program generators are known for their simple command structure.

programmable a machine that can receive data and be instructed to act on a set of data is programmable.

programming creating or writing instructions in a language a computer can understand.

proportional spacing a type of letter spacing where different characters occupy different amounts of space. For example, an I uses less space than a W.

protected software software constructed to inhibit piracy or electronic counterfeiting. Software publishers develop elaborate techniques to protect their software from being illegally copied and distributed.

protocol rules governing the transfer of files over telephone lines require establishing file transfer protocol. Both sending and receiving computers must use the same protocol; several are available.

query a procedure for locating specified data within a database.

RAM *R*andom *A*ccess *M*emory is where the computer stores data entered into the computer. Programs or software are also stored in RAM, permitting the computer to process data.

recalculate in spreadsheets, mathematical computation. Manual recalculation occurs only after issuing a specific command. Automatic recalculation occurs after entering new numerical data. Natural recalculation checks each formula to determine if it needs information in another formula before continuing.

record (database) a set of fields. That is, records contain the related information established by fields.

relational database permits changes made to a record in one file to automatically change a record in another file.

relative reference (spreadsheet) when copying a cell containing a formula designated as a relative reference, the calculation changes to fit a new address.

report formatted output of a database.

report generator controls the display of information. It is used to format the type of display desired.

resolution the sharpness and clarity of the display, commonly measured in pixels.

reversed type type that appears as white on black instead of black on white. Sometimes referred to as *inverse type.*

robotics the use of computerized robots to perform routine, repetitive, dangerous, or boring tasks.

ROM *R*ead *O*nly *M*emory. Permits the computer to read or retrieve sets of instructions. The computer cannot write information to ROM.

row (spreadsheet) horizontally contiguous cells.

ruling lines lines above or below text used to separate the words from the rest of the text. Ruling lines may also be used to separate multiple columns.

sans serif type without the small line or extension at the ends or tips of each letter or character.

save the process or command for storing information to a disk.

scaling a graphics term indicating the scale of a graphic relative to the graphic size.

scanner a machine that reads or scans an image of text or graphics and sends it to the computer. Scanners convert an image, such as a photograph, to a standard digital format, then pass this information into the computer for editing.

search to quickly locate and access data or information.

secondary memory a type of memory that is external to the CPU. One of the most common types of secondary memory is the disk drive. Also referred to as *auxiliary storage.*

sectors a formatting division on a disk. *Tracks* are concentric circular areas on a disk, and sectors are similar to slices cut into a piece of pie. Memory cells are the intersection of sectors and tracks.

serif the small line or extension at the ends or tips of each letter or character.

simulation applications software designed to approximate "real life" situations. Users can make a variety of decisions and see the consequences of their decisions.

single relation a database term, indicating data entry and retrieval is linked to only one file.

sizing a graphic term indicating the relative size of a graphic.

soft return (word processing) when text passes the right margin of a document, the word processor issues a soft return to flow text to the next line. Also known as *word wrap.*

software the set of instructions, or program, that determines how the computer is to operate.

sort (database) similar to indexing, sorting is usually a permanent change in the record order and record number.

sorting (spreadsheet) a rearranging of data. Data entered in rows and columns can be sorted alphabetically or numerically. In addition, data can be sorted in ascending or descending order.

spacing the leading between lines of text or paragraphs of text. Editing a document frequently involves changing the spacing of the text. Text may be changed from single-space to double- or triple-spacing. Spacing of entire documents may be changed, or single or multiple paragraphs within the document may be altered.

spell check programs designed to check the spelling in a document. These are provided with many word processing programs. The spelling of each word is checked but the program cannot check context.

spreadsheet applications software designed to manipulate and control numerical data. Strengths of spreadsheet software include developing budgets and asking "What if" questions.

stack a series of screen displays, or cards, used in hypertext.

start bit with modems, a bit that indicates the beginning of a byte of data.

statistical software applications software designed to do complex statistical analysis of large amounts of data. This software is frequently used by universities, research bureaus, school districts, corporations, and by individuals with research projects.

stop bit with modems, a bit that indicates the end of a byte of data.

structure (database) the structure of the field organization. Structure indicates how fields display and store data for each record.

structured programming a programming standard or technique that makes it easier to develop software and for others to make modifications.

structured query language (database) a standardized format for locating and retrieving data.

style the appearance of a document or the contents of the document.

supercomputers the most powerful computers. Supercomputers can process data at hundreds of millions of instructions per second (MIPS).

suppress to not print. Headers, footers, and page numbers may be suppressed on a desired page. That is, they will not print on the designated page.

synchronous a data transmission pattern sending information in a long string of bits. Synchronous communications do not use start and stop bits.

system bus an electrical pathway for transporting information or data from one location to another.

system software programs with the sets of commands allowing the computer to communicate with other parts of the computer system.

tab a specified number of blank spaces at the desired location. Tabs only affect text on the line where they are entered.

table of contents automatic compilation of a table of contents can be accomplished with some sophisticated word processors or desktop publishing software.

tag a list of type attributes for text paragraphs. The list of attributes is given a name, or a tag. Rather than setting paragraph attributes for each similar paragraph, the paragraph is assigned a tag.

tape drive a device used to store and retrieve information on a magnetic media. Computer tapes are very similar to the types of tapes used in VCRs. Data must be read sequentially.

tax preparation applications software allowing individuals to prepare their own income tax forms. Specialized software permits certain tax preparers to submit tax forms electronically.

telecommunications communication between computers using modems, telecommunications software, and telephone lines. Telecommunications software allows computers to share information through telephone lines and requires the use of a modem to transfer data or files.

Telenet a packed switching service providing access to national databases such as The Source and CompuServe.

template a worksheet constructed without data and used to standardize data entry format.

terminal emulation a software option permitting a personal computer to perform in the same fashion as a directly-connected workstation.

text any set of letters, spaces, or words. For the most part, word processors specialize in dealing with text.

text attributes the major types of text attributes include typeface, typestyle, and point size.

text wrap a desktop publishing and word processing term that indicates that text moves automatically down to the next line after reaching a margin setting.

thesaurus a thesaurus provides a set of synonyms for selected words in a document. Many sophisticated word processors provide a thesaurus with the word processing program.

The Source an information service available to computers via modem. The Source provides information in a variety of areas, including portfolio management and financial market analysis.

TIFF (Tag Image File Format) a special type of bit-mapped format for storing graphic files in less space.

Times Roman a popular serif typeface or font.

tracks concentric circular areas around a disk. Memory cells are the intersection of sectors and tracks.

transistor an electronic device consisting of a semiconductor with at least three electrodes. Transistors were developed at Bell Laboratories in 1947, but did not replace vacuum tubes in computers until 1959.

Tymnet a packed switching service providing access to national databases and Wide Area Networks. Tymnet is very similar to Telenet.

type attributes the style of type, including bold, underline, strike-through, superscript, subscript, italic, and so on.

typeface a style of print, or font, describing the overall appearance of text.

typesetting (desktop publishing) fine control of text, graphics, and the overall design of a document.

type size the size of type as measured in points.

typestyle the appearance of a typeface, including boldfaced, italic, double-strike, underline, and others.

typographical a desktop publishing and word processing term that indicates the overall appearance of text on a page.

underline placing a line under text. It is possible to underline blank spaces created by tabs or the space bar.

user-generated graphics graphics created with special draw and paint type software.

utility graphics software providing specific limited graphic capabilities. For example, some software will create calendars, signs, awards, and certificates.

utility software software designed to provide secure and easy access to information and provide more control than the operating system alone.

value (spreadsheet) numbers entered in a spreadsheet. Values may be mathematically manipulated.

Video Graphics Array (VGA) a graphics adapter that displays 640 x 480 pixels in 16 colors. With 256 colors, the display is 320 x 200 pixels.

virtual reality a type of hardware and software that immerses the user in a multisensory interface with the computer.

virus a destructive computer program placed on a disk or other storage device designed to destroy program information or data.

weather forecasting applications software allowing professional and amateur meteorologists to store large amounts of weather information and make predictions based on data.

What if? by combining numerical data and mathematical formulas, spreadsheets allow users to ask What if questions. A numerical value in one cell will be automatically recalculated by a formula, thus allowing the user to ask, What if the numerical value increases or decreases?

Wide Area Network (WAN) computers connected to each other, but separated by several miles.

widow a single line of a paragraph at the top of a page.

word processing applications software designed to manipulate and control text. Entering, editing, and changing a document are strengths of word processing.

word wrap with continuous text, a word processor automatically wraps text to the next line when text exceeds the right margin.

workstation a computer physically linked to a host computer. Users at workstations begin working by addressing the host computer.

WYSIWYG *What You See Is What You Get.* Software that shows the user his or her document onscreen exactly as it will print.

XMODEM, YMODEM, ZMODEM file transfer protocols for telecommunications software.

Index